ACUA
Underwater Archaeology Proceedings 2015

Edited by Marco Meniketti

An Advisory Council on Underwater Archaeology Publication

© 2015 Advisory Council on Underwater Archaeology

Library of Congress Control Number: 2015951165

Made possible in part through the support of
the Society for Historical Archaeology.

Cover Image: Postcard published by Central News Co., Tacoma Wash.
Postmarked 1913 (from Seattle)

Contents

Foreword vi

Maritime Archaeology in Albania: Connecting the Dots Along
an Overlooked Coastline 11
    Loren Clark

Recreating Holocene Wetlands: New Paleogeographic Models in
the Humber Estuary 21
    Eric A. Rodriguez

Underwater Survey of the Historical Anchorage for Portsmouth, Dominica 33
    Raymond Hayes
    Dennis Knepper
    Bill Utley
    James Smailes
    Greg German
    François van der Hoeven

The Meaning of the Offshore: The Role of Islands in the
Maritime Cultural Landscape of Peru 43
    Vicente Cortez
    Carlos Ausejo

Gulf of Mexico Shipwreck Corrosion, Hydrocarbon Exposure,
Microbiology, and Archaeology (GOM-SCHEMA) Project:
Studying the Effects of a Major Oil Spill on Submerged Cultural Resources 51
    Melanie Damour
    Robert Church
    Daniel Warren
    Christopher Horrell
    Leila Hamdan

Reconstructing the Forward Crew Compartment of the H.L.
Hunley Submarine 63
    Benjamin Rennison
    Michael Scafuri
    Maria Jacobsen

Oil and Shipwrecks: An Overview of the Sites Selected for the
Gulf of Mexico Shipwreck Corrosion, Hydrocarbon Exposure,
Microbiology, and Archaeology (GOM-SCHEMA) Project 73
    Daniel J. Warren
    Robert A. Church
    Robert F. Westrick

The Search for the Lost French Fleet of 1565: Results of the 2014 Survey 81
    Chuck Meide

The Shelburne Shipyard Steamboat Graveyard: Four Early
Nineteenth-Century Steamboats from Lake Champlain 91
    CAROLYN KENNEDY

"Railroaded" - The Wreck of the Schooner Plymouth 99
    DAVID VANZANDT
    JAMES PASKERT
    KEVIN MAGEE

"Reaching Across the Pond: The Archaeological Investigation,
Stabilization, and Management of the HMS Fowey Shipwreck in
Biscayne National Park." 109
    JOSHUA MARANO

"Old Al's Going to Get It," At Least For A While: Recent
Riverine Archaeology in Arkansas" 119
    LESLIE C. STEWART-ABERNATHY

A Canoe on a Sand Bar: The Guth Canoe in Northeast Arkansas 125
    JEFFREY M. MITCHEM

A Comparative Study on the Speed of Dutch and British Ships, 1750–1830...131
    PATRICIA SCHWINDINGER

Into the Blue: Underwater Archaeology in California State Parks 139
    TRICIA DODDS
    DENISE JAFFKE

A Job Market and Benchmarking Survey of Maritime Archaeology ...145
    LYNN B. HARRIS
    JENNIFER F. MCKINNON

Foreword

Maritime Archaeology in Seattle 2015

The venue for the 48th annual conference offered an exciting blend of the historical and the current, a fusion of past development and innovative technology, making it a fitting location for archaeologists to gather. Seattle began with a sawmill 150 years ago and has grown through shipping, immigration, and tech related industries. Various attractions within easy reach of the conference hotel included Pike's Market, underground Seattle, and the Space Needle, not to mention coffee shops too numerous to count. Seattle is one of the great gateways to the Pacific despite its inland location. The official city flag pays tribute to Chief Sealth, while the stylized waves on the flag and even the city's major league baseball team the Mariners, pay homage to Seattle's heritage as a seaport.

As the Conference on Historical and Underwater Archaeology closes in on its 50th anniversary, the meeting in Seattle made evident that Maritime Archaeology has progressed from an interesting sideline supported by a dedicated and passionate few, to a dynamic and mature discipline in its own right that intersects with terrestrial-based archaeology in intriguing and often innovative ways. The conference in Seattle provided a vibrant site for scientific papers addressing topics and issues that spanned the globe and reached beyond particularistic studies into scholarly arenas not commonly associated with maritime studies. Conference attendees were treated to a wide range of research agendas. From the documentation of traditional and indigenous watercraft to the application of cutting-edge technologies allowing shipwreck research at depths that could only be fantasized about a decade ago, Maritime Archaeology has, in the words of last year's editors, "transcended frontiers." One could not escape the ubiquitous applications of technology, whether probing the seabed 4000 feet down or sonar-imaging of lost ships. Underwater archaeology has always been tech-heavy and in the midst of our embracing the latest tech innovations it remains vital that we not lose sight of the principal goal of archaeology—to make sense of the human experience and reconstructing the human past. Some of this breadth is represented by the scholarly contributions contained in this volume. The contributions to the 2015 proceedings include traditional approaches to shipwrecks, and geophysical investigations of paleo-maritime landscapes, as well as iconographic, ethnographic, and computer modeling as diverse means of reconstructing the maritime and cultural landscape.

Perhaps more significant than the scope of maritime papers at Seattle are the statistics concerning participation. Maritime papers represented one third of all presentations, which underscores not only the health of maritime archaeology generally, but also highlights the contribution to historic and prehistoric studies being made within the field. Overall the conference hosted 358 papers and 24 symposia. Of these, 120 were maritime related papers. Nine maritime oriented symposia came close to forty percent of the total. Five posters and one maritime workshop rounded out the participation. In addition there were a record number of entries in the ACUA photo contest. Organizers of the Conference and the ACUA can take pride in their accomplishment.

The 2015 Seattle conference maintained the trend articulated by the editors of the previous year's proceedings, and one which many support, that the boundaries of terrestrial and underwater archaeology are blurring and that conference organizers should continue to encourage research that makes connections across the discipline while avoiding segmentation or compartmentalization. There is much to be learned from one another. It should be noted that the increasing use of the label Maritime Archaeology, rather than Underwater Archaeology, is a significant shift in conceptualizing the field. The maritime paradigm encompasses shipwrecks, of course, but also indigenous lifeways, maritime cultures and landscapes, networks of trade, and much more. As was clear from the many papers at the conference, Maritime Archaeology reflects a welcome focus on integrated and interdisciplinary research.

These Proceedings reflect the changing character of Maritime and Nautical Archaeology. As ACUA Proceedings Editor I have had the distinct pleasure of assembling an eclectic cross section of papers that encompass the breadth and inclusive nature of Maritime Archaeology.

It has been my privilege to work with the talented and professional crew at the PAST Foundation and I would like to acknowledge the hard work of the 2015 Organizing Committee whose efforts were justly rewarded with a successful conference.

Presenters at future conferences are warmly encouraged to contribute their papers for consideration to be published in the proceedings. While the Proceedings will always represent only a fraction of presentations, it is critical for the sustained growth of the field that we share our research with our colleagues.

Marco Meniketti Ph.D., RPA

Department of Anthropology
San Jose State University

ACUA
Underwater Archaeology
Proceedings
2015

Maritime Archaeology in Albania: Connecting the Dots Along an Overlooked Coastline

Loren Clark

Albania sits in an area of the world renowned for its ancient civilizations, yet very little research has been done to learn about the significance of the coastline and the submerged cultural resources hidden by its waters. Thanks to government agencies supporting research in many different fields targeting the coast and in the offshore regions, more datasets are becoming available. By combining these datasets, it is possible to create a foundation that documents how Albania's coastline has changed since the Neolithic and what implications that has for the potential for submerged archaeological sites.

Introduction

The Mediterranean Sea and its coastline has long attracted historians, antiquarians, and archaeologists due to the depth of human occupation and cultural development that is centered in the diverse countries that make up its border. While there are many areas that have seen extensive research and international attention, many Mediterranean coastlines have been only partially or poorly studied. The coastline and continental shelf of Albania is one of these less studied areas. Terrestrial archaeological investigations have provided valuable datasets for many of the major inland cultural sites that provide insight into Albanian connections to other regions within the Balkan Peninsula as well as the rest of the Mediterranean. However, while it is important to note that Albania has not been entirely overlooked, archaeologically speaking, there is a significant gap in the research in relation to its coastal regions. Submerged archaeological material along the Albanian coast and on the continental shelf of the Adriatic has the potential to significantly add to the wider archaeological record and deserves further investigation.

Albania lies between Greece and Montenegro along the Eastern Adriatic coast and has a rich history of occupation since the Paleolithic. It controls over 300km of diverse coastline, characterized by small coves and steep cliffs in the South and large bays and long, open coastal plains in the central and northern areas (Figure 1). This project specifically sought to focus on a small portion of Albania's past relating to maritime cultural influence along the coastal waterways and the adjacent Adriatic Sea. In raising awareness and creating a baseline of research on Albania's coast, it was the aim of this study to provide a foundation that will support and encourage future research.

Conceptual Framework

When investigating the potential for submerged cultural sites along any given coastline, one perspective from a single discipline rarely gives the whole picture. Even with a multidisciplinary approach, details that are crucial to locating and identifying cultural resources can be lost. However, when investigating dynamic coastlines, like the ones present in Albania, the more datasets that can be incorporated, the more likely that research can be conducted in an accurate and efficient manner. The most

FIGURE 1. A VARIED COASTLINE. (A) FOOTHILLS LEADING TO THE BEACH IN THE VILLAGE OF RRJOLL IN NORTHERN ALBANIA. (B) PLAIN NEXT TO THE SITE OF APOLLONIA LEADING TO THE COAST IN CENTRAL ALBANIA. (C) MOUNTAINS AND CLIFFS ALONG THE KARABURUN PENINSULA IN SOUTHERN ALBANIA. (D) VIVARI CHANNEL LEADING TOWARD THE LARGER CORFU CHANNEL NEAR THE SITE OF BUTRINT IN THE FAR SOUTHERN SECTION OF COASTAL ALBANIA. (PHOTOS BY AUTHOR, JULY 2014)

abundant research for this study came from past and current archaeological and historical investigations, both terrestrial and maritime. It also centered heavily around sea-level change and geological research within the Eastern Adriatic.

This project has sought to combine some of the known datasets from these different disciplines and present them within the context of cultural resource management in Albania. In doing so, the intent was to provide insight into some of the major factors that affect the overall potential for submerged cultural material along the entirety of the Albanian coastline. This intentionally deviates from the usual course of archaeological investigation in order to take a broader view. Placing this coastline in the larger cultural contexts of the Adriatic and Mediterranean during the time periods presented is fundamental to enhancing the understanding of submerged cultural material in the study area. The site specific studies that are usually associated with archaeological methodologies have incredible merit and provides enormous amounts of information on technological, cultural, architectural, and social constructs for a specific area or region. However, it is equally important to consider the entire coastline and the cultural variants through time that can be observed from an expanded perspective rather than focus on a single community setting. A comprehensive chronological assessment relating to submerged sites in Albania was beyond the scope of this initial study. As such, the focus period of this study encompasses the Neolithic through the beginning of the Roman occupation of the Balkans (approx. 7000-250BC). This is by no means a short time frame, but it is important to note that the potential for submerged cultural resources is not limited to the parameters presented in this study.

Methodology

The majority of the research done for this study was desk-based. Some work was completed in the field re-analyzing recently collected datasets as well as taking advantage of the resources available only within Albania, but due to time and funding constraints, most of the research dealt with understanding what has been done and what could be done in future projects in Albania. When completing this research, it was important to split the lines of inquiry into two distinct sections. The first section was centered on archaeological and cultural reports, ancient texts, and personal testimonies. The second section focused on quantifying coastal change in Albania. This section required looking into the physical sciences surrounding coastal morphology. The lack of specific coastal change studies for Albania make quantifying these changes a challenge. As this section of the study is also large and complex, it became necessary to determine the specific factors involved and which are relevant to maritime archaeology. These factors include relative sea-level change, tectonics, sedimentation, and erosion along the Albanian coast as well as some of the smaller processes associated with each. It is important to note that this is not a study solely focused on the physical dynamics of the coast. While only the most relevant processes were addressed, it is likely that some of the more intricate details of each discipline mentioned above were not fully incorporated. However, the further research into all areas involved in this study will only aid in informing future archaeological investigation.

Although there are still some datasets that may be available within and outside of Albania that were unable to be consulted during this project, some larger datasets were provided. One of those datasets consisted of multibeam swath bathymetry collected from 2007-2012, along the southern third of the country by RPM Nautical Foundation. This dataset was useful in looking at the topography of the Adriatic shelf on the Albanian coast. ArcGIS was used to combine this dataset with some of the locational data from government and local records of archaeological sites. For the more archaeologically centered sections of this study, it became abundantly clear that to understand the potential for archaeological sites underwater, it would be necessary to collect a baseline knowledge of the coastline of Albania throughout the time periods relevant for this project. The research done within Albania was also supplemented by drawing on archaeological publications in Greece, Montenegro, and Croatia, which border Albania's coast to the North and South. First-hand observation was also conducted over a two week period in July of 2014 to gain a better perspective on the diverse nature of Albania's coastline. The first part of the fieldwork was spent in the capital of Tirana meeting with the Albanian National Coastal Agency and conducting archival research. The rest of the time in Albania was spent traveling from the far northern coastal regions down to the southernmost section near Lake Butrint. As well as providing a personal perspective of the Albanian coastline, this time spent along the coast also allowed for the opportunity to speak with locals about their coastline and cultural heritage.

The Albanian Coast from the Neolithic through the Roman Occupation

The Neolithic

Seafaring in the Neolithic was a common practice within the Mediterranean world. The Albanian coast offers natural harbors and protected bays where seafaring would have been a natural skill to exploit as well as an abundance of marine resources that could have easily facilitated maritime connections. There is no concrete evidence regarding Neolithic coastal settlements in Albania outside of some isolated caves near major lakes and lagoons. This is not unexpected as the physical changes that have impacted the coastline over the past 10,000 years are significant and present certain challenges when dealing with some of the oldest sites.

The Neolithic period in Albania and the Balkans is roughly dated from 7000 BC – 5500 BC and shows elements of a transition from a hunter gatherer type of community structure to a more agricultural one. Most of the Neolithic references that exist in Albania are from cave sites up in the mountains near Korce and in the inland plains. Lafe and Galaty (2009:107) note that "few of these sites are located in western Albania and none are found directly along the Adriatic coast, which appears to have been only sparsely populated in Neolithic times." Some sites have been located near Lake Maliq and Lake Prespa that date to the Neolithic as well as others in the inland plains. The archaeological site at Konispol cave in southern Albania is shown to have connections with the Straight of Corfu and Ionian Sea through the Pavel River, but it is much too far inland to be associated with coastal resources and no marine organisms were noted in the report (Schuldenrein 1998). According to research done by Aleks Trushaj and Ermal Sina (2014), Neolithic caves are found extensively along the coastline of the Karaburun Peninsula and in the region of Vlore, however, no other evidence for these sites could be found and the report provided no evidence of further documentation. Additionally, these cave sites would be located on a very steep portion of the coastline; to properly utilize marine resources, Neolithic peoples would have had to travel for miles to get to a more accessible section of the coastline. The presence of seafaring in the surrounding areas in the Paleolithic suggests that areas in Albania could have supported communities in coastal regions that made short journeys in and on floating vessels (Ferentinos 2012).

The Bronze Age

The Bronze Age occupations of Albania's coast are documented by a much more complex, and better informed, set of studies and archaeological finds. The Bronze Age in Albania is shown to begin c.4000 BC and lasted tentatively until 1200BC. It is during this time that settlement is noted along some of the rivers that flow down from the more occupied inner mountains. Certain settlement areas along the river Mat specifically show a link to wider contact in the Mediterranean with material showing up from trade with the Mycenaean cultures. Outside of the Korce basin in southern Albania, these materials would have been traded by sea and along inland waterways (Lafe and Galaty 2009). The trade network to get up the coast of Albania is hard to track as the Mycenaeans seem to have had an interest in metal resources from this region as opposed to the desire to set up colonies (Galaty 2005). The same studies note that Southern Albania also had many more connections to the trade going on in Greece and Italy. The networks of islands and peninsulas that make up the north-western corner of Greece would have provided a somewhat safer method of transporting materials by sea as opposed to the much longer voyages that would take place in later eras as connectivity in the Mediterranean grew. Customs such as burial practices also link the southern portion of Albania that would later be referred to as the Greek poleis of Epirus to some of the Greek customs of cist tombs, tholoi tombs, and tumuli (Papadopoulos 1987). These customs have been shown to have reached all the way into central Albania during the Late Bronze Age, though the more northern examples of tumuli in Albania have also been linked to the later Illyrian styles of burial (Galaty 2005; Wilkes 1992). Even with the increased amount of study done that relates to Bronze Age sites in Albania, the focus falls mostly, again, on the inland and riverine sites.

The Iron Age and the Early Illyrians

The Iron Age, roughly dated to 1100 BC-150 AD in Albania, overlaps with different cultural times in Greece and in the northern Balkans with the expansion and formation of empires. This time period built upon the maritime trade that was begun in the Late Bronze Age. Larger and more complex settlements started appearing along the coastal margin to take advantage of this trade. The "Illyrian" tribes that populated much of northern Albania also used this time to expand and set up more solid towns and villages along the coast. The trade patterns that encourage movement toward the coast during the early Iron Age also attracted Greek colonization and the building of some of the cities that are still seen in modern Albania. While it is noted that the tribes that were documented by Galaty (2005) in the highlands of northern Albania were not overly affected by the influx of trade networks like the coastal margin experienced, the rest of the Albanian lands were brought into a much larger Mediterranean world through trade and association with two major colonizing forces, the Greeks and the Illyrians. The transition between the Bronze and Iron Ages also begins to reflect the issues with dealing with culture from a linear perspective. The inland geography of Albania provides distinct natural boundaries for the transport of ideas and goods and some sited have been noted to belong to a specific culture and lay outside of the general date range with which it is generally associated. These time periods become increasingly complex as connectivity over land or sea facilitates the transport of ideas, technologies and political agendas.

The Illyrian tribes occupied the northern stretch of the Adriatic coastline stretching down into and encompassing some of the tribes in northern and central Albania. The 2nd century AD Roman author Appian relates that the name was more of a reference to a large but diverse grouping of people that inhabited the areas currently referred to as the Balkans and parts of the Adriatic coast (Wilkes 1992). The Illyrian cities were characterized by larger fortifications with stone walls that encircled large hilltops, which provided some of the oldest hill forts described in Albania dating in the Iron Age. The site of Gaitan, near Shkodra in northern Albania is an excellent example of this type of construction and occupation near the Albanian coastal region (Pollo and Puto 1981). The Illyrians were allegedly known as pirates and raiders by ancient writers, especially by Polybius, who wrote in favor of Roman expansion and covered the Illyrian Wars. The Illyrian state was organized into 'federative states' in the 7th and 6th centuries BC, but due to the large geographic area and major inequalities in social and economic development, two different Illyrian 'states' were developed. The combination of the northern tribes was referred to as the Kingdom of the Illyrians, while the southern tribes that were in and around the Greek state of Epirus went by the Koinon (community) of the Molossians, and both were federative in nature (Pollo and Puto 1981). This new political era led to wars with the Macedonians as well as some smaller conflicts with the colonizing Greeks. The formation of these states also added a certain amount of security to the Illyrians and Greeks alike as the organized armies helped discourage and block the Macedonian armies from gaining control of the coastal regions of Albania.

Greek and Roman Colonization of Albania

The Greek expansion beyond the northern areas of Epirus (modern southern and central Albania) with the founding of cities like Epidamnos, Apollonia, Orikum, Lissos and Buthrotos (Butrint) solidified connectivity of those new colonies with the rest of mainland Greece (Figure 2). This is evidenced by various Greek pottery styles being found at these sites from around the Aegean. These sites were chosen, in contrast to the evidence from earlier periods, for their proximity to the coast and presence within the growing trade networks in the Adriatic. Natural harbors along the Albanian coastline made the geography ideal for any colonization attempts. The cities that did not fall on natural curves of the coastline that were protected from the seasonal northern and southern winds were placed along major coastal rivers that provided a protected harbor inland of the sea. Specifically, the colonies at Epidamnos and Apollonia, which were founded by the Greeks in the 7th and 6th centuries BC, were some of the first colonies to encroach on the lands of Illyrian tribes. Wilkes (1992) notes that it was seafaring that initiated contact between the Illyrians and the Greek colonists, but the evidence that suggests immediate contact with Illyrian tribes settled in the area directly conflicts with this claim. Because the Illyrian peoples were skilled seafarers, there is no doubt that connections of a maritime nature were made with these coastal cities. The relations with the Illyrian tribes of Taulantians and Abantians were essential in the success and survival of these two cities (Pollo and Puto 1981). During this intense and influential period of growth in the Greek coastal colonies, the economic state of these cities increased dramatically and large amounts of goods were being traded through to the rest of the Adriatic. The coins of Epidamnos and Skhodra in the northern coast even depicted maritime scenes and boats and reflected the importance of the sea in these coastal towns.

Not many regions of the Mediterranean were able to resist Roman occupation for very long, and the Eastern Adriatic coasts were no exception. After enduring crafted attacks from Illyrian privateers and pirates along the northern Adriatic coasts, the Romans entered into more formalized engagements with the Illyrian navy. What is now the Croatian and Montenegrin coast and some of the more rocky areas of the Albanian coastline proved to be ideal for piratical activity and at certain times there were no organized political structures to keep them in

FIGURE 2. MAP OF ANCIENT EPIRUS AND ILLYRIA (UPPER LEFT SECTION) AS WELL AS OTHER GREEK POLEIS. (AVAILABLE AT HTTP://WWW.ANTIQUAPRINTGALLERY.COM/ANCIENT-GREECE-EPIRUS-EUBOEA-AETOLIA-THESSALIA-MACEDONIA-SDUK-1848-OLD-MAP-165951-P.ASP)

check. Due to this issue with Illyrian 'piracy' as well as Rome's early desire for eastward expansion, the so-called Illyrian wars were fought from 229-168 BC. Polybius in particular notes the Illyrian Wars as a significant event for Roman expansion by saying "this is a matter not to be lightly passed over, but deserving the serious attention of those who wish to gain a true view of the purpose of this work and of the formation and growth of the Roman dominion"(Polybius 2.2.2). The victory of Rome in those conflicts with the Illyrian tribes marked the first battle fought across the Adriatic, which is most likely why Polybius treated it with such high regard as a military victory. Once the Romans had a foothold on the eastern shore of the Adriatic, their quest to unite the boundaries of the Mediterranean progressed at a rapid pace.

Physical Coastline Changes

As was noted in the beginning of this study, much more than the archaeological and cultural background of Albania is needed to properly investigate the potential and state of submerged sites in and along Albania's coastline. Like the accessibility and abundance of archaeological information within Albania, the geological and oceanographic datasets for this country desperately need to be expanded. Fortunately, some key studies have been done on a larger regional framework that can be used to gain an overall picture of what coastal changes have happened in Albania through time.

Sea Level Changes and Tectonics

Sea-level change as defined by Lambeck and Purcell (2005) and Lambeck et al.(2004) is the measured difference in relative vertical movement between the land and sea surfaces in a given area. The most widely accepted sea-level models for the Mediterranean come from these studies and cover the time period from 12 – 2kya. The problems with these general models have already been discussed, but in the absence of more specific local and regional data, these models can give an acceptable idea as to coastal changes within Albania. As seen in Figure 3)], the model shows sea levels along the Eastern Adriatic coasts gradually rising represented by the values -125-130m at 20kya, -50-55m at 12kya, -4-6m at 6kya, and

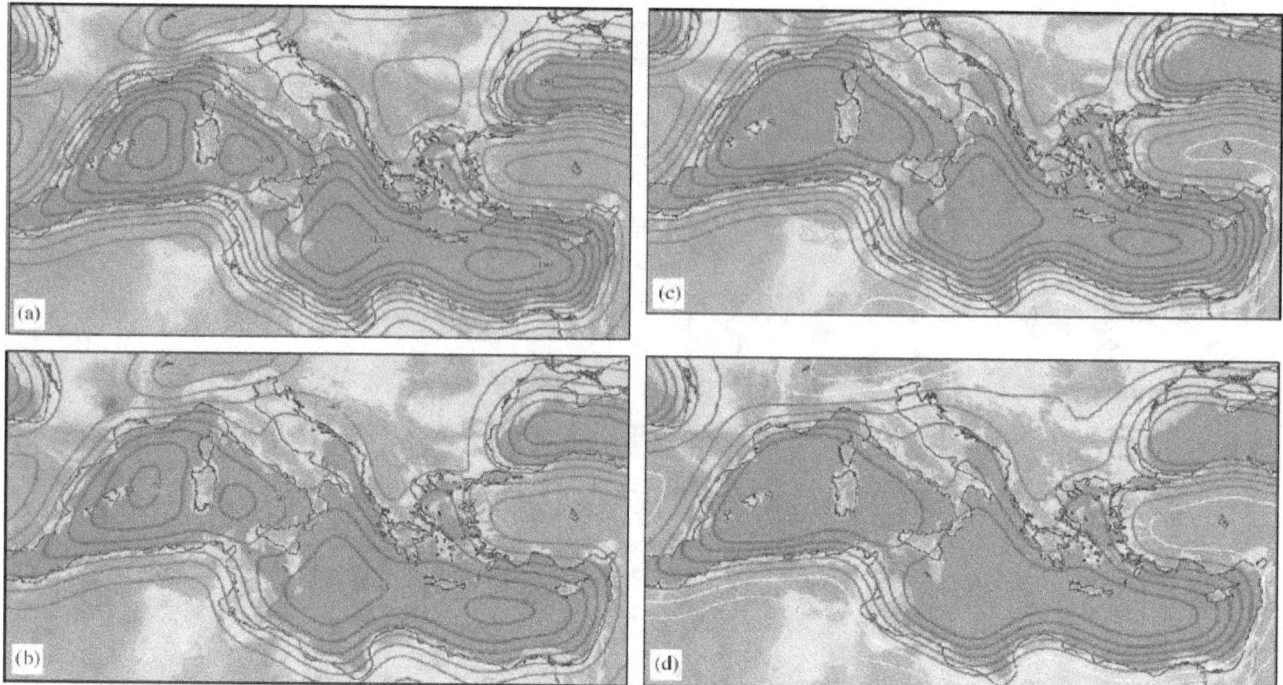

FIGURE 3. PREDICTED RELATIVE SEA LEVELS AND SHORELINES ACROSS THE MEDITERRANEAN REGION AT FOUR EPOCHS: (A) 20 KA, (B) 12 KA, (C) 6 KA, (D) 2 KA. THE PALEOSHORELINE POSITIONS ARE DEFINED BY THE GREEN–BLUE TRANSITION. FOR 20 AND 12 KA BP, THE CONTOUR INTERVALS ARE 5M. FOR 6 AND 2 KA BP, THE RED CONTOURS DENOTE NEGATIVE VALUES, THE ORANGE CONTOURS DENOTE POSITIVE VALUES, AND THE YELLOW CONTOUR CORRESPONDS TO ZERO CHANGE. THE CONTOUR INTERVALS ARE 1M AT 6 KA AND 0.25M AT 2 KA. THE PREDICTIONS ARE BASED ON THE NOMINAL MODEL PARAMETERS (E2, NE-2, NA-2), (LAMBECK AND PURCELL 2005)

-3-4m at 2kya (Lambeck et al. 2004; Lambeck and Purcell 2005).

Albania sits in one of the most tectonically active regions of the Mediterranean. Fortunately, since the opening of the borders after communism, several studies have been done that map out tectonic evolution and patterns within the country (Aliaj et al. 2000; Muco et al. 2002; Nieuwland et al. 2001). Albania, specifically, is made up of numerous tectonic plates that interact with each other with varying consequences for the landscape associated with them. From the Pliocene-Quaternary period through to the Pleistocene, the whole of Albania and the Adriatic experienced a gradual uplift with isolated areas of subsidence. Often, changes related to tectonics can be seen more easily along the coast where the land-sea relationship plays a large role in the social dynamics and maritime cultural activities. Within Albania specifically, the Bay of Vlore exhibits continuing tectonic activity where the marked subsidence of the microplate that encompasses the bay has been seen in both an ancient and modern context. While this is a small area in relation to the overall coastline, the Vlore region shows just how varied the tectonic trends can be on a regional level.

Sedimentation and Erosion

Sea-level change and tectonics are not the only factors to contribute to a changing coastline. The processes surrounding sedimentation, erosion, and overall fluvial transport near rivers and lagoons in Albania play a vital role in determining the morphology of Albania's current coast. Bruckner notes that "the deltas of the Mediterranean have witnessed the most extensive coastal changes in history" and that they hold a great wealth of information about past erosion and environmental issues (Bruckner et al. 2005). Albania has a complex network of rivers and streams that are heavily affected by seasonal shifts and climatic variations as they run west toward the Adriatic Sea. When approached from a broad time frame, such as the one used in this study, the vast amount of sediment that has been transported by these rivers becomes apparent. For example, what was once an active river harbor for the larger hilltop town of Apollonia now sits approximately 10km inland with no river access and only a distant view of the Adriatic to the West. The harbor of the ancient city sat adjacent to the ancient course of the Aoos River (modern Vjosa) and just south of the ancient Apsos River (modern Seman).

Though the ancient harbor was not on the sea itself, it only included a short traverse across a lagoon and a short run up the river to transport goods. The drastic changes in the courses of these two rivers has been extensively documented by Fouache et al. (2001, 2010), who believe that these changes played a large role in the westward migration of the current plain. After the rivers changed course, the pattern of fluvial deposition and allowed for the transition to alluvial plain and finally into the modern environmental situation. In this case, much of where evidence of maritime activity might have been found in a riverine or lagoon context would then become a part of a terrestrial investigation.

Erosion is also a major factor when considering the location and context of submerged archaeological features. Anthropogenic activity, such as farming and waterway manipulation, in both an ancient and modern context have been seen to cause significant changes to the local and regional landscapes through increased erosion. In Albania, the site of Butrint, in the far southern region, is a distinct example of anthropogenic activity having long term environmental effects.. Butrint sits on a small spit of land that juts into the Vivari Channel that separates Lake Butrint from the Corfu Channel near the Greek border. This site has had varied occupation and use as a strategic port and trading outlet since the Late Bronze Age all the way through the Ottoman Empire. The area to the South of Lake Butrint is called the Vrina plain and the northern section of the lake is bordered by the Vurgu plain. Archaeological evidence suggests that the Vrina plain has progressed significantly toward the lake since Roman occupation of the site (Martin 2004). The modification of the northern river channels in the 20th century greatly affected the amount of fresh water that was supplied to the lake. This in turn increased the salinity of the lake due to the fact that the Vivari channel was the largest source of water flow remaining in the area (Ariztegui et al. 2010). The human diversion of the river channel for irrigation and agricultural benefits only hastened the migration of the Vrina plain toward the lake and the ancient site (Figure 4). This type of significant erosion can greatly change the appearance of the landscape and make what was once a large

FIGURE 4. MULTIBEAM IMAGE OF THE CONFLUENCE OF THE VIVARI CHANNEL AND THE VRINA PLAIN NEAR LAKE BUTRINT. THE RED AND YELLOW COLORS SHOW THE EXCESSIVE AMOUNTS OF SEDIMENT ENTERING THE STRAIT OF CORFU FROM THE PROGRESSION OF THE VRINA PLAIN. (COURTESY OF RPM NAUTICAL FOUNDATION)

and accessible channel into a much smaller connective waterway. Many of the structures associated with the settlements at Butrint dealt with the channel and the progression of the Vrina plain into the channel could have potentially covered many of the port structures on both sides of the channel.

Conclusion

When conducting research into archaeological finds and geological and oceanographic trends in Albania, the overwhelming theme that presented itself was the intense need for further research into this area. This area cannot depend on the general research done that presents models for the Mediterranean as a whole. No local regional area should rely on such overarching datasets, but Albania in particular presents too many variables to fit into a larger framework for geological and cultural themes. When investigating records of Neolithic, Bronze Age, and Iron Age sites specifically, it was noted that the scarcity of records for these sites is most likely not due to the lack of occupation or exploitation of these coastlines, but reflected more the absence of study and knowledge on the specific coastal zones for these time periods. It is by combining these datasets and knowledge bases that archaeologists can get a much clearer picture of not only where to look for sites, but how the context of those sites may have changed.

Coastal research is by no means limited to the field of maritime archaeology and any sites found along the coastline of Albania during any time period could add to the depth of knowledge that places Albania within the framework of maritime connections for the wider Mediterranean. It is the aim of this research to provide a foundation, upon which future archaeological and geological investigations and build. The Albanian coast has been, thus far, generally overlooked in archaeological research. That is changing in Albania, and this country, that has been isolated and overlooked, can finally prove how much it can contribute to the understanding of maritime culture in the Adriatic.

Acknowledgments

I would like to thank the faculty of the Centre for Maritime Archaeology at the University of Southampton. Specifically, my advisor Fraser Sturt, as well as professors Jon Adams, Lucy Blue, and Julian Whitewright who were instrumental in supporting this work. I also owe a debt of gratitude to the Albanian National Coastal Agency and their director Auron Tare, who worked closely with me during my time in Albania and provided aid for the in-field portions of this research. Further, I wish to thank the members of RPM Nautical Foundation who graciously allowed me access to their data and research vessel.

References

ALIAJ, S., BALDASSARRE, G. AND SHKUPI, D.
    2001 Quaternary subsidence zones in Albania: some case studies. *Bulletin of Engineering Geology and the Environment* 59(4):13-318.

ARIZTEGUI, D., ANSELMETTI, F., ROBBIANI, J., BERNASCONI, S., BRATI, E., GILLI, A. AND LEHMANN, M.
    2010 Natural and human-induced environmental change in southern Albania for the last 300 years - Constraints from the Lake Butrint sedimentary record. *Global and Planetary Change* (71):83-192.

BRUCKNER, H., VOTT, A., SCHRIEVER, A. AND HANDL, M.
    2005 Holocene delta progradation in the eastern Mediterranean--case studies in their historical context. *Mediterranee. Revue geographique des pays mediterraneens (Journal of Mediterranean Geography)* (104):95-106.

FERENTINOS, G., GKIONI, M., GERAGA, M. AND PAPATHEODOROU, G.
    2012 Early seafaring activity in the southern Ionian Islands, Mediterranean Sea. *Journal of Archaeological Science* 39(7):2167--2176.

FOUACHE, E., VELLA, C., DIMO, L., GRUDA, G., MUGNIER, J., DENEFLE, M., MONNIER, O., HOTYAT, M. AND HUTH, E.
    2010 Shoreline reconstruction since the Middle Holocene in the vicinity of the ancient city of Apollonia (Albania, Seman and Vjosa deltas). *Quaternary International* 216(1):118-128.

FOUACHE, E., GRUDA, G., MUCAJ, S. AND NIKOLLI, P.
    2001 Recent geomorphological evolution of the deltas of the rivers Seman and Vjosa, Albania. *Earth Surface Processes and Landforms* 26(7):793-802.

GALATY, M.
    2007 "There are Prehistoric Cities up There": The Bronze and Iron Ages in Northern Albania. In Between the Aegean and Baltic Seas: Prehistory Across Borders, I. Galanaki, H. Tomas, Y. Galanakis and R. Laffineur, editors, 1st ed. Belgium: KLIEMO, pp.133-139.

LAFE, O. AND GALATY, M.
    2009 Albanian Coastal Settlement from Prehistory to the Iron Age. In A Connecting Sea: Maritime Interaction in Adriatic Prehistory, S. Forenbaher, editor, 1st ed. Oxford: BAR International Series 2037. Archaeopress, pp.105-111.

LAMBECK, K. AND PURCELL, A.
    2005 Sea-level change in the Mediterranean Sea since the LGM: model predictions for tectonically stable areas. *Quaternary Science Reviews* 24(18):1969-1988.

LAMBECK, K., ANTONIOLI, F., PURCELL, A. AND SILENZI, S.
    2004 Sea-level change along the Italian coast for the past 10,000 yr. *Quaternary Science Reviews* 23(14): 1567-1598.

MARTIN, S.
    2004 The topography of Butrint. In Byzantine Butrint: Excavations and Surveys 1994–99, Hodges, R., Bowden, W., Lako, K. editors. Oxbow Books, Oxford, pp. 76–103.

Muco, B., Vaccari, F., Panza, G. and Kuka, N.
    2002 Seismic zonation in Albania using a deterministic approach. Tectonophysics 344(3):277-288.

Nieuwland, D., Oudmayer, B. and Valbona, U.
    2001 The tectonic development of Albania: explanation and prediction of structural styles. Marine and Petroleum Geology 18(1):161-177.

Papadopoulos, T.
    1987 Tombs and Burial Customs in Late Bronze Age Epirus. Aegeum 1: 1137–142

Pollo, S. and Puto, A.
    1981 The history of Albania. 1st ed. London: Routledge & Kegan Paul.

Polybius
    1979 . The Histories. 1st ed. Harvard University. Press Cambridge, MA [u.a.].

Schuldenrein, J.
    1998 Konispol Cave, southern Albania, and correlations with other Aegean caves occupied in the Late Quaternary. Geoarchaeology 13(5): 501-526.

Wilkes, J.
    1992 The Illyrians. 1st ed. Blackwell.Cambridge, MA, USA

· · · · · · · · · · · · · · · ·

Loren Clark
Centre for Maritime Archaeology
University of Southampton, UK
6312 N 300 E
West Lafayette, IN, USA 47906

Recreating Holocene Wetlands: New Paleogeographic Models in the Humber Estuary

Eric A. Rodriguez

The recent application of palaeogeographic modelling on prehistoric wetland environments has provided the opportunity to observe how the dynamic nature of these environs influenced the phenomenology and settlement patterns of wetland societies. Focusing on two areas from northern England's Humber Estuary, this paper describes the interaction between the recreated palaeolandscapes of Roos Carr and Ferriby and the past settlement patterns from the Late Neolithic to the Early Bronze Age given the rapid sea-level rise of these periods. This study is not solely situated on describing reconstructive modelling techniques, but rather, investigating the role of dynamic maritime landscapes in crafting Holocene wetland phenomenologies.

Introduction

In 1913 Clement Reid published his quintessential work on the submerged forests of Britain. Unknown to him at the time, his research would eventually open an inquiry into dynamic landscapes that would incorporate recent technologies and serve as the principle investigation into the impacts of shifting environments on the phenomenologies of past peoples. True to Reid's examinations, this paper approaches the study of inter-related spatial and temporal patterns of environmental change and human activity during the Late Neolithic and Early Bronze Age (4000 BC—1500 BC) of the Humber Estuary. Building upon recent developments in landscape archaeology over the past two decades, this study focuses on wetlands, a particular feature of the British terrain. Comprising almost 20% of English landmasses, wetlands encompass a wide variety of features including raised bogs, fens, mires, estuarine saltmarshes, etc. In the past, scholars have treated these landscapes as social and physical boundaries rather than as part of the everyday experience of prehistories communities. However, recent literature has approached landscapes in this more social context, most notably, the works of Bell (2000), Coles (1998), Rippon (1997) and Van Der Noort (2002, 2004, 2006, 2011). Additionally, investigations into prehistoric environments have benefited from the incorporation of palaeo-environmental studies and paleogeographical reconstructions. These approaches convey the formation processes and evolution of past landscapes as they housed human activity (Berg 2013; Sturt 2013; Westley 2013; Chapman and Gearey 2014). It is through paleo-surface modelling that this paper approaches the two case studies of the Humber Wetlands, Ferriby and the southern Holderness. Relying on datasets from previous surveys, quantitative methods such as geospatial analysis and paleo-surface creation will reconstruct the evolution of past wetland environments and the role of the landscape in crafting the experiences, activities, and perceptions of prehistoric communities. From the quantitative and theoretical approaches employed in this paper, wetlands can be approached not simply as a singular spatial feature, but rather as a culmination of a range of cognitive landscapes that are constantly redefined by the dynamic environments and the human responses they evoke. The study of wetlands presents a unique opportunity for landscape archaeology to observe the interactions of multiple 'scapes' and their role in crafting the everyday experiences of prehistoric communities.

Previous Studies in North Sea Paleogeographies

Reid's work with submerged forests and peat development first prompted a discussion of the dynamic landscapes of northern Britain and their potential to contribute to the understanding of past human activities. This dialogue was carried out over decades by researchers such as Godwin (1933), Clarke (1936), and Coles (1998), demonstrating the capacity of submerged deposits to contribute to the prehistoric and palaeo-environmental narratives of the British Isles. Their endeavors redefined submerged landscapes as active environments significant to the archaeological record. With the turn of the millennium, new technologies provided the means to visualize, predict, and observe paleolandscapes through computational methods. One project that incorporated these approaches was the Land-Ocean Evolution Perspective Study (LOEPS). From this endeavor, researchers led by Shennan created a database of Holocene sedimentary sequences, paleo-graphic models, tidal changes, and

Holocene vegetative models for the North Sea regions including the Humber Estuary.

While early approaches to paleo-surface modelling were content with adjusting sea-levels to mimic glaciation, Lambeck et al. (2010) and Shennan (2000a) emphasized boundaries and considerations for the creation and application of relative sea-level (RSL) over long periods of time. This topic requires a complex understanding and consideration of:

> *"(1) changes in ocean volume, (2) radial displacement of the land surface by changing load, (3) changes in the gravitational potential as a result of the deformation of the planet and redistribution of mass across its surface, (4) changes in the shape of ocean basins and, (5) the redistribution of water within these basins" (Sturt 2013 citing Lambeck 2010).*

Recent attempts by Sturt (2013) and Berg (2013) and Westley (2014) have incorporated these considerations in their paleogeographies employing RSL data from recent glacial isostatic adjustment (GIA) models produced by Bradley (2011). Additionally, Sturt's work emphasizes the need for developing future palaeogeographic models "on a more human scale" (Sturt 2013: 3964), incorporating 500-year intervals rather than 1000-year models that have been produced in the past (Shennan 2000; Metcalfe 2000). Through a digital medium, archaeologists hold "The potential for reconstructing past landscapes ... [by] stripping back the temporal layers to provide a basis for quantifiable analysis" (Chapman 2006: 21). As much of archaeology is drawn to a study of dramatic events played on macro temporal and spatial scales. This paper sets out to observe less-dramatic changes that still influenced a perception of maritime space.

The Humber Wetlands

Located on the eastern coast of Northern England, the River Humber lies 120 km long, 14 km at its widest. The river itself is part of a larger network of inland waterways comprising the Humber Estuary, responsible for draining one-fifth of England (Van Der Noort 2004:1). The estuary's current landscape reflects a flat and near-featureless agriculturally-designated terrain—the result of several large-scale drainage projects, embankments, and canalization that rapidly transformed the Humber during the 17th Century. However, his area once offered a complex delta system that actively engaged its residents and invited them to utilize its marine resources. This interaction with the Humber Wetlands extends back as far as 11,400 BC (Sheldrick et al 1997).

Archaeological evidence has yielded lakeside settlements from the Southern Holderness, several vessels and trackways from Brigg and North Ferriby, and a plethora of wooden and flint deposits scattered throughout the region conveying the presence and intensity of human activity in the region. While previous endeavors such as the Humber Wetlands Project and the Land-Ocean Interaction Study (LOIS) have addressed the region's archaeological potential and described the geologic history, a study of the human response to the dynamic maritime space has not been properly approached in the Humber Estuary. For this paper to undertake this examination, two case studies were determined based on their archaeological and paleo-environmental sources described in the following sections and outlined in Figure 1.

Ferriby

The greater Ferriby area extends from the East Riding of Yorkshire into North Lincolnshire and spanning the Humber's drown river valley. Ferriby's place in archaeology was solidified with the findings of early Bronze Age Boats in North Ferriby. Discovered by Ted and Edward Wright from 1937 to 1963, these vessels are the oldest recorded sewn-plank boats in Britain. These vessels have been used to assess larger exchange and trade networks in northern England later stretching to continental Europe. Supplementing these finds, additional features including a paddle, Neolithic spikes, flint assemblages and Early Bronze Age trackways contribute to the significance of this area in prehistoric Britain.

While paleo-surface creation has been applied over Ferriby in the past (Metcalfe 2000), recent methodological considerations and wider datasets allow for a more detailed understanding of these features as part of the phenomenology of the prehistoric landscape, as habitation continued through the prehistoric and into the modern age. While similar regions such as the Hull Valley boast a larger geologic and archaeological dataset, Ferriby was selected as a case study due to evidence of continued occupation and its archaeological significance in British prehistory.

The Southern Holderness

Located in the valleys of the East Riding of Yorkshire, the alluvial lowlands of southern Holderness present one

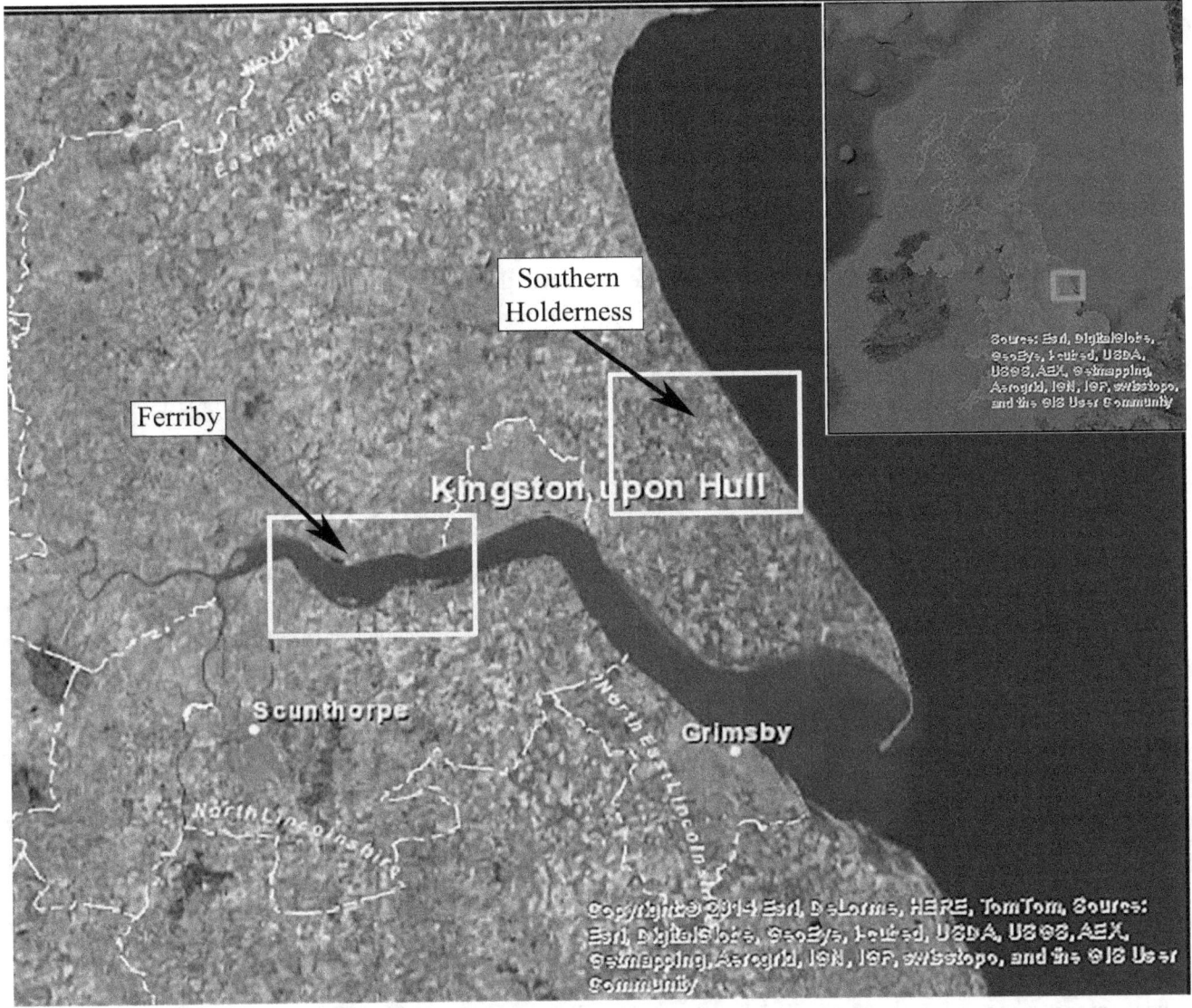

FIGURE 1. THE GENERAL TOPOGRAPHY OF THE HUMBER ESTUARY WITH THE BOUNDARIES OF THE FERRIBY AND SOUTHERN HOLDERNESS CASE STUDIES.

of the most dynamic landscapes of the British countryside. Comprised of low-lying hills and deposits of gravel and sand left from the late glacial period, the area separates the North Sea from the Humber Basin. Despite its proximity to the North Sea, the Holderness drains into the Humber Estuary and Hull Valley. The current landscape of the southern Holderness still bears the scars from its time under glacial ice exhibiting features such as drumlin mounds, hummocky terrains, ridges, and kettle holes.

Favored as areas of habitation by late Mesolithic and early Neolithic peoples, the southern Holderness credits this trait to the presence of meres, post-glacial lakes that once dominated the region. These meres have supplied a number of finds to the archaeological record. Previous fieldwalking surveys yielded an array of prehistoric finds such as worked bones and antlers from sites like Brandensbruton, Hornsea, and Star Carr. The study of the post-glacial features reveals the intimate relationship between waterbodies and human activity (Clark and Godwin 1956). As one of the first areas of the Humber to be dramatically transformed by large efforts of deforestation and habitation occurring around 4000 BC, the southern Holderness presents the largest timeframe in which to study human-environment interactions in the Humber Estuary. Additionally, the southern Holderness offers the opportunity to study the creation and evolution of ritual landscapes in the Humber Wetlands as votive deposits have been recovered from Roos Carr. Despite dating to a later period, earlier evidence suggests the Humber Wetlands maintained this tradition since the Bronze Age as decorative jadite axes have been found in other areas of the Humber Estuary, including the Haxey Carrs in the Humberhead Levels (Van De Noort 2004).

While the region holds a sizeable amount of evidence for Mesolithic-early Neolithic activity, the evidence for late Neolithic—Early Bronze Age activity is limited. Whether this phenomenon is due to the previous archaeological efforts of the region or simply that little activity existed during this time remains to be investigated. While the extent of the southern Holderness stretches from Alderborough to Spurn Point, the focus of this study's paleo-environmental modelling will focus on the Halsham, Roos Carr, and Keyingham areas, collectively referred to as southern Holderness for the purposes of this paper. The lack of human evidence for this time period and the disrupted habitation of the area provides a stark contrast to the Ferriby tradition. Additionally, employing palaeo-environmental modelling on the southern Holderness presents the opportunity to gauge both the physical and cognitive creation of a ritual areas and the role inaccessibly may serve in their development.

Reconstructing Cultural Wetlands: Theory and Method

The induction of wetlands into the larger discussion of landscapes is a delicate task. With a variety of features and lack of a cohesive definition, it would not be beneficial to treat wetland archaeology as a separate entity or grant it a unique branch of landscape. The concept of wetlands must be treated as a fluctuating and variable environment, whose general characteristics and role in shaping human activity must be approached from the specific contexts of the individual communities and their archaeological record (Bradley 2000). Within this framework, the Humber wetlands must be integrated into the general landscape of the Humber Estuary through reconstructive techniques.

The methodology employed to reconstruct the paleogeography of the Humber Estuary is detailed in the following subsections. While this general approach has been applied in Northwest Europe and in the East Anglian Fenlands (Sturt 2009, 2013; Westley 2013), there are significant differences that address the specific nature of this paper's data sources. The methodology can be broken down into three tiers: determining the study boundaries; reconstructing the Holocene landscapes; and spatial analysis of Late Neolithic-LBA settlements.

Determining the Study Areas

For the selected case studies of Ferriby and the southern Holderness, two central points were established for each area: the excavated boatyard at Ferriby serves as the central point for the area, while the general location of Halsham was chosen for the southern area. 100 km2 square buffers were established surrounding these points while Topographic and bathymetric datasets acquired from the UK Environmental Agency determined the final extents for each case study.

Reconstruction of the Holocene Paleo-surfaces

The borehole datasets was provided by the Onshore GeoIndex Viewer of the British Geologic Survey. Of the 423 that were available, only 290 were chosen for inclusion in the study due to their low penetration depths, non-confidential status, and the quality of core assessment. The boreholes were then plotted and rasterized through the inverse distance weighting technique to create an isopach of the pre-quaternary sedimentology. The individual isopachs were then subtracted from the combined digital elevation models for each case study resulting in the creation of pre-Holocene paleo-surfaces. These surfaces were then built up using the depths of radiocarbon-dated peat samples acquired from the Humber Wetlands Project and LOEPS datasets. The difference between the individual peat sample depths and the elevations of the pre-Holocene paleo-landscapes was then added to the latter to reflect the surface during the time frame of the dated peat sample. Unfortunately, despite the large number of peat samples, dates for the Bronze Age (2500 BC—1500 BC) of the southern Holderness and the 3000 BC date of Ferriby were not available for this study.

Once the Holocene surfaces were created, the next step was to correlate the depths of the peat samples to the RSL values extracted from Bradley's GIA model at the corresponding 500-year intervals. The values of the RSL were extracted at the sample locations and used as a corrected depth for the peat, adjusting the overall elevations for each surface. These values serve as an additional limitation on the margin of error.

With the paleo-surfaces complete, elevation classes were determined to reflect areas that were completely submerged, exposed to tidal fluctuations, areas prone to inundation, and standing water. These classifications were based on the previous paleogeographical efforts (Dinnin 1995; Lillie 1998; Metcalfe 2000). For this, four classifications were determined, the "open water' classification distinguishes areas of the landscape that were likely areas of primary flow from the mouth of the estuary. "Subtidal" plains characterize areas that were previously in the inter-tidal zone and have since been submerged from the onset of the late-Neolithic. The 'intertidal-eutrophic wetlands' classification was determined from the creation of a mean high water spring tide (MHWST), which lies above the subtidal plains and within the 2.69 m tidal range recorded in previous paleo-tidal studies (Shennan 2000:313). Dry areas lying above the tidal range are referred to as "salt marshes".

Geospatial Analysis of Late Neolithic-LBA settlements

Archaeological data was provided from a number of institutions including the historic environmental records of North Lincolnshire and Yorkshire, Wessex Archaeology, and the volumes of the Humber Wetlands Project. Once plotted, the land-classifications values from each paleo-surface were extracted from the site locations. The values for each site were then compared to one another highlighting the shifting land classifications of the prehistoric sites. Table 2 presents a selection of the results.

Results

Figures 2 and 3 present the Late-Neolithic—Early Bronze Age paleogeographies for Ferriby and the Southern Holderness regions. While visual inspection of the produced paleo-surfaces may not properly reflect the changing wetland terrain, rates of inundation, sedimentation, and wetland formation are presented in Table 1. These rates as they pertain to each case study are presented below.

A selection of results of the settlement analysis are provided in Table 2 for both case studies. Despite the inability to model the southern Holderness during the Early Bronze Age, the values for known Bronze Age sites were still extracted in order to determine whether these sites were available to Neolithic inhabitants or employed as an alternative to sea-level encroachment.

Paleogeography of Ferriby

For the Ferriby area, sea-levels rose 3.80m from 4000 BC—1500 BC. As salt marshes in the area decrease at a rate of 0.31 km2/500yr, the inundation of the Humber basin is largely to blame for this occurrence as the rising RSL of the Holocene exposed formerly dry salt marshes to the large tidal ranges that typically characterize the Humber. As these areas are increasingly exposed to the

			Ferriby	
Year (BC)	Open Water	Subtidal Plains	Intertidal Eutrophic Wetlands	Salt Marshes
1500	0.258	22.915	14.076	73.513
2000	0.587	22.209	14.099	73.732
2500	7.442	15.339	14.101	73.745
3000	X	X	X	X
3500	13.885	8.869	14.108	73.765
4000	0.000	20.577	14.971	75.079
			Southern Holderness	
Year (BC)	Open Water	Subtidal Plains	Intertidal Eutrophic Wetlands	Salt Marshes
1500	X	X	X	X
2000	X	X	X	X
2500	X	X	X	X
3000	10.104	14.414	7.278	15.152
3500	14.584	14.584	4.82	17.349
4000	10.087	14.39	0	24.668

Table 1: Classification areas (km^2) for each case study and 500-year interval.

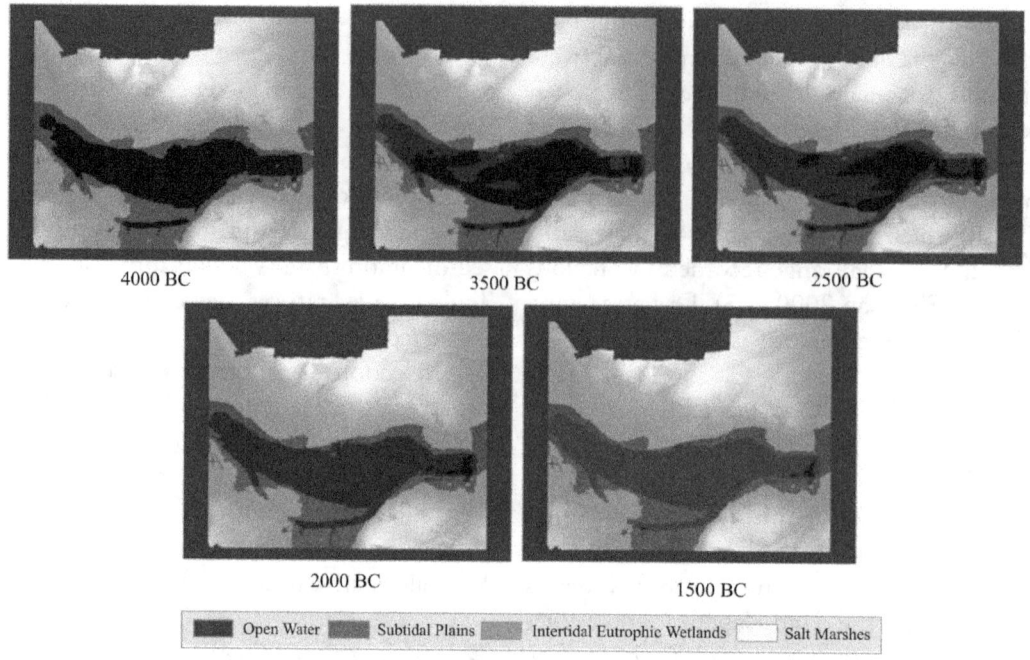

FIGURE 2. PALEOGEOGRAPHY OF FERRIBY FROM 4000 BC—1500 BC.

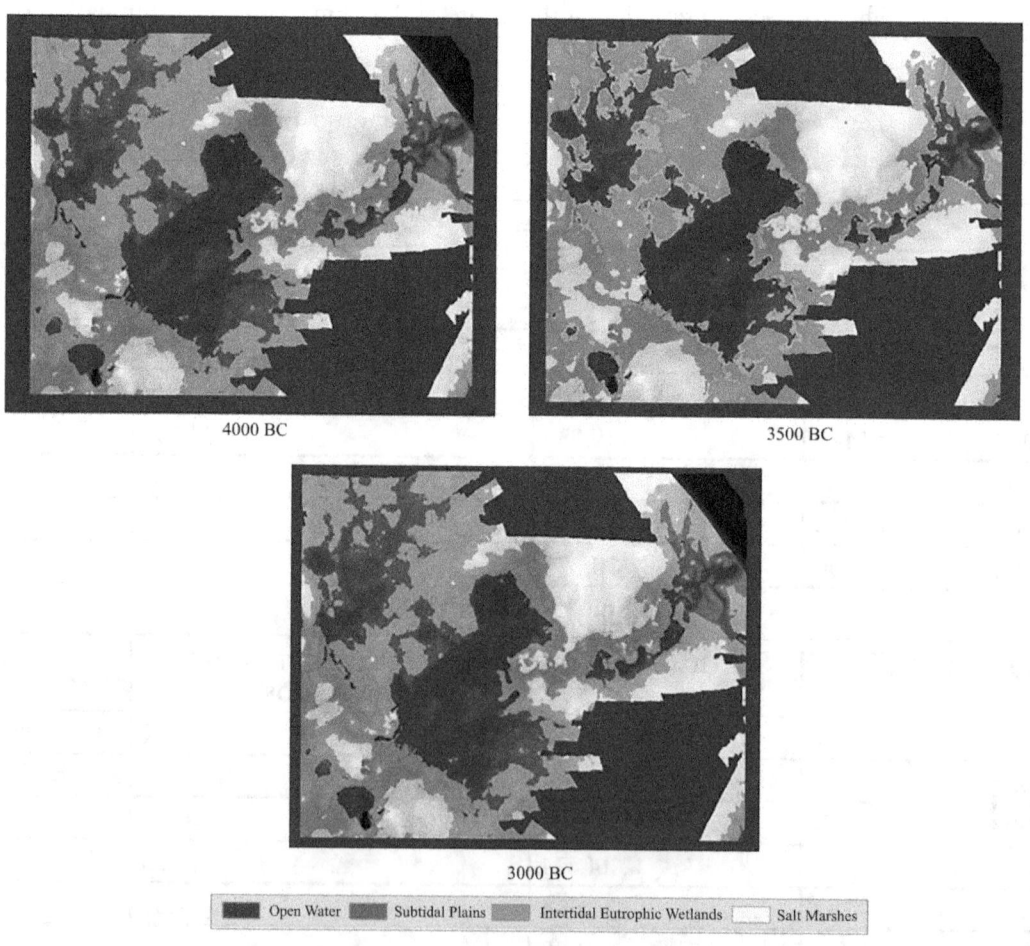

FIGURE 3. PALEOGEOGRAPHY OF THE SOUTHERN HOLDERNESS FROM 4000 BC—3000 BC.

Ferriby Sites	1500 BC	2000 BC	2500 BC	3000 BC	3500 BC	4000 BC
Melton-31	3	3	X	3	3	3
Melton-10	3	3	X	3	3	3
Melton-15	3	3	X	3	3	3
Melton-16	3	3	X	3	3	3
Melton-27	2	2	X	2	2	3
Melton-20	3	3	X	3	3	3
Melton-29	4	4	X	4	4	4
Melton-30	3	3	X	3	3	3
Melton-8	3	3	X	3	3	3
Melton-9	3	3	X	3	3	3
Site 6	4	4	X	4	4	3
Melton-5	2	2	X	2	2	1
Southern Holderness Sites						
Halsham-88	X	X	X	3	4	3
Halsham-65	X	X	X	4	4	4
Halsham-59	X	X	X	3	3	3
Halsham-39	X	X	X	3	4	3
Halsham-50	X	X	X	3	4	3
Halsham-55	X	X	X	3	4	3
Halsham-61	X	X	X	3	4	3
Halsham-100	X	X	X	4	4	4
Burstwick-19	X	X	X	3	4	3
Burstwick-7	X	X	X	3	3	3

Table 2. The extracted land classification values for a selection of sites Values for the reclassification are as follows: 1=Open Water, 2=Subtidal Plains, 3=Intertidal Eutrophic Wetlands, 4=Salt Marshes.

Humber's tidal zone, there is a potential for the formation and growth of eutrophic wetlands. While a decrease in dry areas could correlate to a growth in eutrophic wetlands, this is not the case in the Ferriby area. With inundation, the intertidal wetlands decreased at a rate of .179 km2/500yr. The natural topography of the areas is the main contributor to this rate as the shape of the natural watershed becomes stepper limiting wetland expansion in Ferriby. The inundation of the Humber also affected the subsurface levels. Rather than stripping the submerged sediment, the rapid rise in RSL carried additional sediment from the North Sea, which aggradated along the bottom of the Humber. This sediment, along with the tectonic rise of the British Isles created potential wetland areas. The rise in subtidal plains communicate this sedimentation process alongside the rate of intertidal wetlands claimed by inundation. Additional evidence for aggradation in the Ferriby area can be found in the open water classification. As this typology represents areas of possibly Mesolithic wetlands the decreasing rate of these areas show that sedimentation is occurring over the Humber, with the greatest change occurring from 2500 BC—1500 BC.

Sea-Level Encroachment in Ferriby

Settlement analysis of the Ferriby area revealed that none of the sites were lost to inundation throughout the Neolithic. Congruent with previous literature, the analysis presented Neolithic sites residing in the dry salt marshes. Which may indicate a lesser reliance on the Humber at Ferriby and the agricultural benefits were able to remain largely unaffected from the rapid inundation of Humber during this period. However, for the Bronze Age, many of these sites were located in the intertidal wetlands. This is not a result of continued occupation of Neolithic sites that were now inundated, as only 2 sites, Melton-5 and Melton-11 were continually inhabited. Only one site, Melton -20, was lost to inundation at this time. The data reveals that a majority (17 of the recorded 20) resided in wetlands. Only one flint deposit was located on the salt marshes, however, it was less than 200 m from the closet area of wetlands. Two sites resided in the subtidal range, most likely as a result of statistical errors in the interpolation methods. While the locations of these areas may not have been under threat of flooding the encroachment of the sea-water towards the areas of resident could reflect the phenomenology of these peoples as areas of known natural resources and proximities to potential ritual places could be increasing during this time. Additionally, the large number of abandoned Neolithic sites may indicate that the Bronze Age inhabitants shifted their subsistence strategies at this time. Another interpretation is that with the growing maritime networks at hubs such as the Ferriby boatyard, could expand the residence of these areas for their proximity to these marine highways. However, additional data is needed to justify these interpretations.

Paleogeography of the Southern Holderness

At the start of the late Neolithic, the southern Holderness is depicted as an archipelago defined by the presence of meres and heavily flooding. Within the limited 1000-year window of this case study, an issue with the radio-carbon dated samples. From the models the area depicts RSL fall, However, the RSL value from Bradley's model increase of 2.11 m for this time frame. These values may be in part due to the date range of the radiocarbon sample, 3990-3640|4230-3700 BCE. As it was the most proximal data to the 3500 BC interval, significant errors may have risen from its incorporation. While inaccurate, the results of this modelling express the importance of radiocarbon dates in this methodology. The values for the 3500 BC interval were not included in the calculations of inundation, sedimentation, and wetland expansion rates. Open water decreased from 9.516 km2 and subtidal plains accumulated 7.278 km2 reflecting a similar situation with Ferriby. Wetlands only slightly increased 0.024 km2 and salt marshes increased -0.017 km2. This phenomenon can be explained by the low-lying watershed and topography of the area as RSL could occupy larger portions of the terrain. While these values do not convey the same amount or significance when compared to the Ferriby results, they do hint at the potential of palaeogeographic modelling to contribute to the environmental and archaeological understanding of the southern Holderness once additional radiocarbon-samples and more detailed borehole records are acquired.

Sea-level Encroachment of the Southern Holderness

Of the 18 Neolithic sites in the area, 2 are located in the drylands and 7 reside in the wetlands. The remaining 9 are located in subtidal areas, most likely due to sampling errors as previously discussed. It is worth noting that of these 9, 6 of these are occupied in the Bronze Age, suggesting that these areas may have been opened later than 3000 BC. It is clear that available time frame of 4000 BC—3000 BC is not suitable for observing site occupation during the late-Neolithic and early Bronze Age. Conversely, the inundation of these sites may indicate that as the Southern Holderness was flooded, high sedimentation rates opened new wetlands for prehistoric peoples, allowing for additional industrial activities to be carried out on these newly deposited landscapes. Moreover, as previous surveys only broadly dated these sites, the paleogeographical models may be more specific than the findings and provide precise dates for these finds. While these paleo-surface reconstructions are strongly compatible with previous paleo-environmental studies of the area, the shifting settlement patterns in response to the growing wetlands cannot be accurately reconstructed. Additional surveys must be carried out before paleogeographical modelling can convey the prehistoric experiences of the southern Holderness.

Discussion

The results of this study alongside the previous studies carried out Humber present the opportunity to construct a narrative of the Humber evolution experience from 4000-1500 BC. Again, due to the shortcomings of the paleogeographies of the southern Holderness, the majority of these narratives are drawn from the findings of the Ferriby models.

4000 BC

Neolithic communities witnessed the inundation of the Ancholme Valley. Covering 0.23 km2 of the Ferriby area. Exposed wetland environments dominate the southwest portions of the River Humber at the mouth of the River Ancholme. The formation of these wetlands was likely understood to be a recent event as the RSL rise created noticeable changes in the landscape. As these large tracts expand outward to the Humber and Ancholme, the inhabitants of Ferriby and the Southern Holderness, both took advantage of the mineral-rich wetlands in these areas, and used these lands as seasonal hunting, gathering and fishing subsistence strategies.

3500 BC

Despite the RSL rise, The Ferriby wetlands diminish to 0.17 km2. The increased rate of inundation, salt marsh formation from sediment deposits, and the natural topography lead to a decrease of wetland expansion. With the inundation of the area, these diminishing wetlands are replaced by the formation of salt marshes by sediment and aeolian deposition. Despite the encroaching waters, many Neolithic communities did not consider it a significant threat and continued using the Humber riverbeds as hunting grounds.

3000 BC—2500 BC

The Ferriby area continues to experience flooding due to RSL rise. The wetlands, still constrained by the basal margins, further encroach on the salt marshes, but diminish to 0.13 km2. Despite the increasing proximity to the tidal range, Neolithic communities may have continually resided in this area for their increasing dependence on minerogenic wetlands.

2000 BC—1500 BC

The onset of the Early Bronze Age usheredin a change in settlement patterns for the Humber's inhabitants. Did the new proximity to the wetlands prompt Bronze Age inhabitants to utilize these areas for fish-traps and hunting? Or perhaps the start of larger trade networks prompted the Ferriby residents to reside in readily-accessible wetland areas. Whatever this influence, the Bronze Age sites left the dry areas of the Neolithic in favor of the wetlands. The high aggradation rates in Ferriby may have encouraged more intense fishing strategies as the increasing subtidal plains brought many of the fish closer to the wetland landscape making them easier to trap. At the close of the Early Bronze Age, the shift in settlements towards wetlands was a response to the inundation of the area.

Conclusion

This study approaches the landscapes of the Humber Estuary, not as a passive force, but rather as an active agent influencing the everyday experiences of the prehistoric residents, redefining the landscape from a natural to a cultural sense. As a result of this transformation, the phenomenologies, temporalities and cultural landscapes margins become intertwined with the natural history and evolution of the wetlands. As cognitive constructs, landscapes are still dynamic forces, as they are constantly altering and being altered by the perceptions of these areas. Illustrating the interconnectivity of cultural and natural wetlands during the Late-Neolithic and Early Bronze Age, this study has presented new paleogeographies of two areas of the Humber and the individual human responses to this environments based on geologic records, settlement locations and finds data taken from previous studies.

Approaching a quantitative study of cognitive phenomenon is a difficult task. Quite often, the results are only indicative, rather than definitive (Sturt 2006:130). However difficult the approach may be, modelling of cultural landscapes is a feasible task. Just as landscapes and culture are intertwined and cannot be separated, these forces are in a constant state of cyclical flux (Lefebve 2004:38-41). This relationship over time creating a dimension of social rhythms. These rhythms, grow more complex as the human responses to these environments are constantly being redefined. These temporalities forge a phenomenology that is just as variable as the wetlands in which they reside. However fluid these concepts are, it is essential to remember that culture and space cannot be separated: The history of the earth is the history of our own experiences, this notion is the root of cultural wetlands—the experiences of these landscapes craft our own interpretations and define the margins in which daily life operates. From the natural history and archaeological evidence of the Humber Estuary, wetlands provided a wide range of experiences that influenced human activities. As a chief component of the prehistoric past, palaeographical modelling provided the means to study the evolution of the wetland environment, thus, investigating the factors that influenced human activity. As it is possible to see the responses to these environmental changes it is possible to reconstruct the phenomenologies of past societies. For the Humber Estuary, the inundation of the area during the Holocene did not deter residents from this area, instead the changing environments were seen as a welcomed change made evident by the influx in river settlements alongside the Ferriby boatyard. For the prehistoric communities, the wetlands of the Humber Estuary were not simply the arenas in which they occupied, they were part of the lived spaces, crafting the experiences and becoming part of their identity.

Acknowledgments

I wish to thank the following institutions for providing the necessary data for this paper: the Historic Environmental Records of North Lincolnshire, the Humber Archaeology Partnership, the Historic Environmental Office of East Yorkshire, English Heritage, Wessex Archaeology, the Geomatics Group of the UK Environment Agency, and the British Geological Survey. Additionally I wish to thank Fraser Sturt and Tyra Stanten for their guidance and instruction throughout this paper. Lastly I wish to thank the University of Southampton and the Centre for Maritime Archaeology for their support and for supplying the licenses and software essential to this study.

References

BELL, M., A. CASELDINE, H. NEUMANN, B. TAYLOR, AND J. ALLEN
2000 Prehistoric intertidal archaeology in the Welsh Severn Estuary. 1st ed. York: Council for British Archaeology.

BRITISH GEOLOGIC SURVEY
2014 GeoIndex | map index to British Geological Survey (BGS) data. http://www.bgs.ac.uk/geoindex/. Accessed 17 Sep. 2014.

DINNIN, MARK AND M. LILLIE.
1995 The palaeoenvironmental survey of southern Holderness and evidence for sea-level change. In Wetland Heritage of Holderness Robert Van De Noort and Steven Ellis editors pp.87-120. University of Hull, Exeter UK.

CHAPMAN, H.
2006 Landscape archaeology and GIS. Tempus, Gloucestershire, UK.

COLES, B.
1998 Doggerland: a speculative survey. Paper Presented at the 64th Prehistoric Society Conference in Sheffield, UK.

GODWIN H. AND M. E. GOODWIN
1933 British Maglesmose Harpoon Sites. Antiquity. VII(25): pp. 36—48.

LEFEBVRE, HENRI
2004 Rhythmanalysis. Continuum, London, UK.

Lillie, M.
1999 The palaeoenvironmental survey of the Humber Estuary, incorporating an investigation of warp deposition in the southern part of the Vale of York. In Wetland Heritage of the Vale of York, An Archaeological Survey, Editors. The University of Hull, Exeter, UK.

METCALFE, S., S. ELLIS, B. HORTON, J., INNES, J. MCARTHUR, A. MITLEHNER, A. PARKES, J. PETHICK, J. REES, AND J. RIDGWAY
2000 The Holocene evolution of the Humber Estuary: reconstructing change in a dynamic environment. Geological Society, London, Special Publications, 166:1 pp.97—118.

REID, C.
1913 Submerged forests. University Press. Cambridge UK.

SHELDRICK, CHARLES, J. JOHN LOWE, AND MICHAEL J. REYNIER.
1997 Palaeolithic Barbed Point From Gransmoor, East Yorkshire, England.'. Proceedings of the Prehistoric Society 63 pp.359—370.

SHENNAN, I. AND J. ANDREWS, J
2000. An introduction to Holocene land-ocean interaction and environmental change around the western North Sea. Geological Society, London, Special Publications, 166:1, pp.1—7.

SHENNAN, I., K. LAMBECK, B. HORTON, J. INNES, J. LLOYD, J. MCARTHUR, AND M. RUTHERFORD
2000a Holocene isostasy and relative sea-level changes on the east coast of England. Geological Society, London, Special Publications, 166(1), pp.275—298.

SHENNAN, I., K. LAMBECK, R, FLATHER, B. HORTON, J. MCARTHUR, J. INNES, J. LLOYD, M. RUTHERFORD, AND R. WINGFIELD,
2000b Modelling western North Sea palaeogeographies and tidal changes during the Holocene.Geological Society, London, Special Publications, 166:1 pp.299—319.

STURT, F., D. GARROW AND S. BRADLEY
2013 New models of North West European Holocene Palaeogeography and Inundation. Journal of Archaeological Science, 40(11), pp.3963—3976.

STURT, F. F.
2006 Local knowledge is required: a rhythmanalytical approach to the late Mesolithic and early Neolithic of the East Anglian Fenland, UK". Journal of Maritime Archaeology, 1:2, pp. 119—139.

VAN DE NOORT, R.
2004 The Humber wetlands. Windgather Press, Cheshire, UK.

VAN DE NOORT, R. AND A. O'SULLIVAN,
2006 Rethinking wetland archaeology. Duckworth Publishing House, London, UK

Van De Noort, R.
2009 Exploring the ritual of travel in Prehistoric Europe: The Bronze Age sewn-plank boats in context. In Bronze Age Connections: Cultural Contact in Prehistoric Europe. Peter Clark, editor. pp.159-175. Oxford, UK.

Van de Noort, R.
2011 North Sea archaeologies. Oxford University Press, Oxford, UK.

Westley, K.
2013 "Taking the plunge: Investigating submerged prehistoric landscapes off the north coast of Ireland." Archaeology Ireland 27.4: 38—41.

. . . .

Eric A. Rodriguez, M.A
6 Circle Drive
Jacobus, PA 17407

Underwater Survey of the Historical Anchorage for Portsmouth, Dominica

Raymond Hayes
Dennis Knepper
Bill Utley

James Smailes
Greg German
François van der Hoeven

The town of Portsmouth, on the northwestern side of Dominica, is bordered by Prince Rupert's Bay. As a deepwater port off the Guadeloupe Passage, this coastline was preferred as a watering site by indigenous inhabitants, the Kalinago, and by sailing ships entering and leaving the Caribbean Sea. Dominica has been a British colonial outpost since 1763 and is strategically situated between two major French islands, Martinique and Guadeloupe. From its inception, Portsmouth was a planned community and exchange depot. Resources and troops for security of the area were stationed at Fort Shirley on the adjacent peninsula of Cabrits. During this survey, GPS-referenced circle searches of 15 m (49 ft) radius were scanned underwater for exposed artifacts within the area designated on historic charts. Artifacts were identified and photographed in situ, and their distribution was recorded to delineate the area. These data document European visits to Dominica and the development of today's town of Portsmouth. The Portsmouth anchorage is compared to other historical anchorages surveyed by Foundation STIMACUR.

Introduction

Study of the history of an island's coastal zone is not complete without consideration of the anchorage utilized by ships arriving there for offloading or loading of passengers, for transfer of their personal belongings and for delivery and pickup of assorted items of merchant and military cargo. From an archaeological perspective, the identification of submerged cultural remains lost or abandoned within an anchorage site represents the cumulative historical and cultural exchange occurring over centuries of time during the development of towns and fortifications on the island. Trade items found within an anchorage may have been discarded deliberately by ship passengers, crew or officers. Also, these objects may have fallen overboard accidentally during transfer from large ships to smaller shallow draft boats for shore or dock access. The time of loss may be difficult to determine, but the time range for production, the nationality of origin and the identity of the manufacturer are often identifiable from objects that are undisturbed and forgotten once abandoned.

Historical anchorage surveys offer unique glimpses of material culture that was transported to a harbor but lost or abandoned by ships at anchor. In our surveys, we begin by characterizing the site with remote sensing technology. Then we visually explore and map artifacts visible on the harbor bottom through transect-based diving. The study of the historic anchorage of Portsmouth, Dominica, was initiated in such a fashion. This was the second historical anchorage that we have surveyed on that island. Historical anchorage studies that have been conducted by Foundation STIMACUR are in St. Eustatius, Bonaire, Curaçao, St. Kitts, and Roseau, Dominica. In Bonaire, Curaçao and Roseau, shipwrecks have been found that have necessitated independent and focused analysis. For others, including the Portsmouth, Dominica survey, design of the survey has depended on the scope and complexity of the respective site.

Anchorage surveys by STIMACUR

In St. Eustatius, the STIMACUR survey consisted of a series of linear transects conducted by excavating along several transects of 400 m (1,312 ft.), 300 m (984 ft.) and 200 m (656 ft.) lengths and at regular 100 m (328 ft.) intervals. These transects were oriented perpendicular to the shore in physical relationship to a pier associated with the historical anchorage at the southern end of Orange Bay. Excavations were conducted at 40 sites and along these linear transects within the bay. Artifacts were recovered, identified and returned to the harbor bottom (Nagelkerken 2000).

In Roseau, Dominica, STIMACUR surveyed a circumscribed and limited area around the pilings of a newly constructed cruise ship pier. Bottom disturbance revealed dredged specimens that were cleaned, conserved labeled, catalogued, photographed and subsequently presented to the Dominica Historical Museum. Also found was the wreck of a wooden ship; the wreckage was surveyed, characterized and tentatively identified as

Yara, a British Royal Mail ship that was used as an inter-island mail carrier and that was lost during a storm in 1916 (Nagelkerken *et al.* 2003; Nagelkerken *et al.* 2006; Nagelkerken *et al.* 2007).

In St. Kitts, an anchorage for Sandy Point Town and its extensive system of coastal defenses associated with Brimstone Hill Fortress was surveyed. Because of the reef configuration, this anchorage lies well offshore and channels provide safe transport in small boats to several landings (Gill *et al.* 2014).

For the Bonaire historical anchorage survey, an extended linear baseline was set in 50-m increments, parallel to the shoreline in front of Fort Oranje at the edge of the forereef slope. The total length of the area surveyed was in excess of 750 m (2,461 ft.). The survey was made from the top of the sand flat at a depth of 10 m (33 ft.) to a depth of 35 m (115 ft.), where a horizontal shelf was located at the base of the forereef slope. The survey was conducted in proximity to the military fort and the site of the original town of Kralendijk. A cruise ship pier and a fishing pier were incorporated into the survey area. Remains were found of the wreck of *Sirene* (1831), a Dutch warship that was assigned to patrol the region, and that was lost during the Trinidad-Yucatan hurricane of 23 June 1831.

The work of STIMACUR in Curaçao addressed the underwater archaeological survey and excavation of two historic shipwrecks in St. Anna Bay, the narrow entryway to Willemstad harbor. The first wreck was that of *Alphen* (1778), a Dutch warship that exploded in the channel leading to the harbor proper (Nagelkerken 2009). The second wreck was that of SS *Mediator* (1884), a steamship from Liverpool, England, that sank after colliding with another ship while docked near the harbor entrance. (Nagelkerken, Knepper and Hayes 2014) Both of these wrecks required extensive excavation and recovery of submerged artifacts because of accumulated overburden and proximity to the extremely active, government-regulated shipping channel for tankers, cruise ships and commercial traders.

Historical ship anchorage for Prince Rupert's Bay

The island nation of Dominica constitutes the southernmost of the Leeward Islands in the Lesser Antilles group in the Eastern Caribbean. Prince Rupert's Bay borders the northwestern coast of Dominica (Figure 1). It is a long and wide embayment, well-sheltered and an excellent source of abundant fresh water. After a long trans-Atlantic voyage, merchant and naval sailing ships from Europe would traverse the channel between Guadeloupe and Dominica (Guadeloupe Passage) to enter the Caribbean Sea. They would anchor for several days at Prince Rupert's Bay to replenish potable water supplies, gather fruit and other local food and restock other supplies available from local traders. The concave

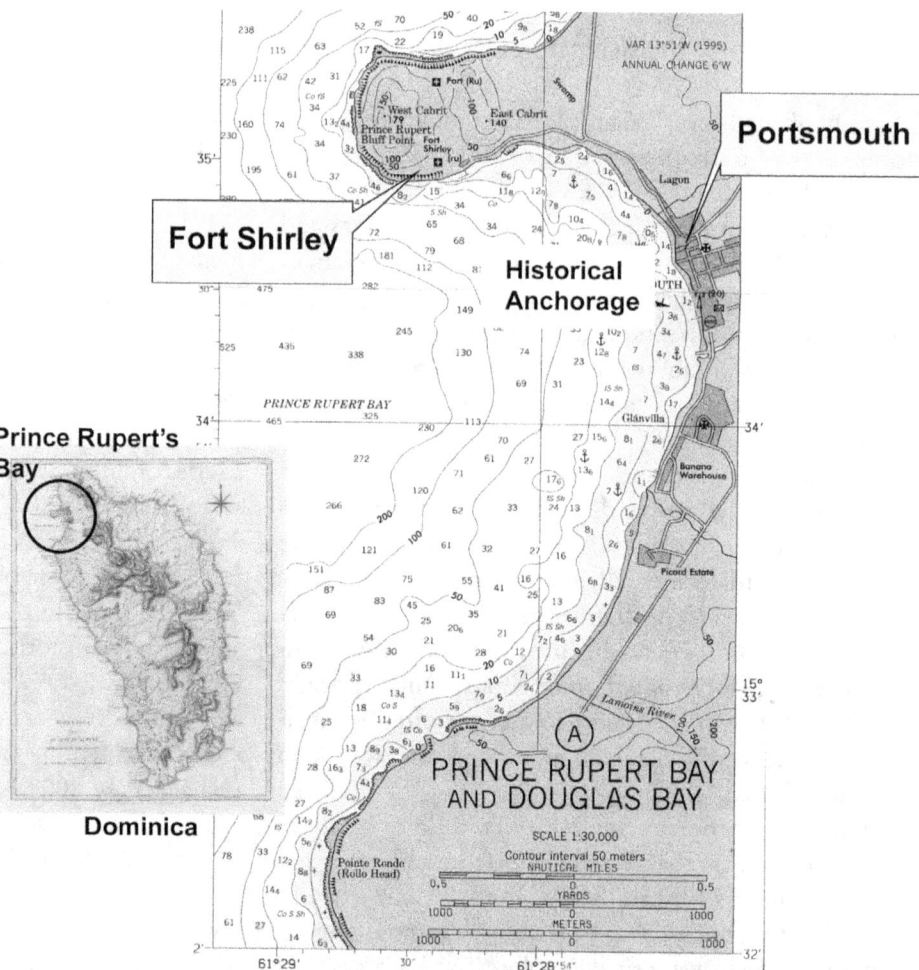

FIGURE 1. LOCATION OF THE TOWN OF PORTSMOUTH ON PRINCE RUPERT'S BAY IS SHOWN ON THIS NAVIGATION CHART OF DOMINICA. PREVAILING WINDS BLOW FROM EAST TO WEST. MAJOR LITTORAL CURRENT FLOW IS FROM NORTH TO SOUTH. (COMPOSITE BY AUTHORS).

shoreline represents the remnant of a partially collapsed volcanic cone resulting in a natural deep water harbor that slopes rapidly to great depths offshore.

Columbus first made landfall at Prince Rupert's Bay on his second voyage in 1493. In 1535, the Spanish Board of Trade in Seville designated the bay a point of replenishment for treasure fleets destined for Mexico and Cartagena (Honychurch 1995). The Spanish never settled Dominica, however, because of difficulties with the indigenous Caribs on the island. The presence of fresh water, wood, fruit and medicinal baths in Prince Rupert's Bay, however, contributed to its becoming a popular stopping point for sailing ships *en route* to and from the Atlantic Ocean, and a convenient site of coastal trading among the Leeward and Windward Islands of the Eastern Caribbean.

The inshore zone of the bay is expansive and free of submerged obstacles, providing suitable anchorage for deep draft ships. Although fringing coral reefs still line the shore, these reefs are submerged, erosional and patchy in configuration, and they do not pose any real threat to navigation. Depths of near shore anchorage sites allow holding without excessive scope of anchor lines and chains. According to the placement of anchor symbols on historic maps, these sites lie within 100 to 200 m (328 to 656 ft) of shore.

The island of Dominica traded hands between French and British until the Treaty of Paris in 1763, marking the end of the Seven Years' War (known in North America as the French and Indian War). A provision of that treaty ceded Dominica to Great Britain. The island has remained in English hands since that time. In 1765, the town of Portsmouth was designed as the colonial capital for the island. From its inception, the town was a planned community and exchange depot.

However, because of pestilence from swamps at the outlet of Indian River to the south and at the base of the Cabrits to the northwest, Portsmouth never truly developed into the anticipated major trading center and political capital. The capital of Dominica was established later at Roseau near the southern end of the island. By 1771, the fledgling town of Portsmouth had been deserted, although a small military post was established on the twin volcanic peaks of the Cabrits peninsula. That post eventually became Fort Shirley. This fort provided essential resources and troops for defense and security of the area (Honychurch 2011; Honychurch 2013). Fort Shirley is under active restoration as an archaeological preserve.

The goals for our study of the historical ship anchorage for Portsmouth were to conduct a systematic underwater archaeological survey, to collect information about utilization of the coastal zone by sailing ships, to promote an understanding of the island's history and culture, and to enhance awareness of the maritime heritage of this "nature island."

METHODS

The archaeological survey was a multi-stage process. It began with a remote sensing survey using side scan sonar technology and diver tows in shallow water. Our objective was to map bottom contours and to detect any submerged cultural resources observable on the sea floor. Side scan sonar was supplemented by a visual examination and photography of the bottom in selected areas. Finally, close inspection of the bottom was conducted by SCUBA divers using 15-m (49-ft.) radius circle searches around the anchor line of the dive boat and executed at selected points on a 50-m (164-ft.) grid.

The surface area of Prince Rupert's Bay is very large, measuring over three miles north to south and one mile east to west. To manage such an expansive scope, we split the bay into three sections north to south to plot short transects and maintain regular lane spacings of approximately 50 m (164 ft.). Survey coverage in the central and southern areas was less intensive than to the north. More effort was concentrated in the northern area since that was considered the most likely to have been the historical anchorage for the town of Portsmouth and the adjacent fort.

The anchor for the research/dive boat was set by GPS coordinates at intersections of the 50-m (164-ft.) grid over the anchorage area. Divers descended the anchor line, extended a fiberglass tape for 15 m (49 ft.) and swam a circular course. The two divers conducted a visual search around the anchor to encompass a circular zone of 30 m (98 ft.) diameter. Surface artifacts within that zone were identified, classified as historic or modern, and photographed or sketched to constitute the survey database. By design, no excavation or disturbance of the sea floor was conducted during our survey of Prince Rupert's Bay.

RESULTS

General description of the Portsmouth anchorage zone

Prince Rupert's Bay on the northwest coast of Dominica has provided suitable anchorage for sailing ships for many centuries. The bay opens to the Caribbean Sea on the western coast of the island. The bay is protected from direct exposure to the easterly trade winds by the high island profile, although winds freely course across the low-lying portions of the island between volcanic peaks. The Cabrits headland to the north also represents a geographic barrier to hold back the swell that comes through the Guadeloupe Passage and directly from the Atlantic Ocean.

The location of the town of Portsmouth at the northeast corner of the bay is within the most protected corner of the bay. The frontage of Fort Shirley on the Cabrits is also protected, but deep close to shore. Most wooden sailing ships would have anchored immediately off the coast because of the convenient proximity to town or access to Fort Shirley. One distinctive drawback of this anchorage site is that if the winds were to shift and enter the bay from the west, as will occasionally happen during the hurricane season, the bay would become a lee shore and egress would be very difficult. Ships would be trapped in the anchorage with no likelihood of a clear way out. Only preventive action from very good anchor equipment and anchoring remotely from shore would save a sailing ship from being pushed into shallow water or onto shore in such a situation.

Ocean-going sailing vessels, rigged with square sails on one or more masts and having less maneuverability in close quarters, would be prevented from anchoring very close to shore because of water depths, ship lengths and drafts in excess of 5 m (16 ft.). Depending on their sailing ability and size these ships would typically anchor in water between 10-50 m (33-164 ft.). Warships would almost always anchor in deeper water relatively far from shore. The area in front of the landing at Fort Shirley represents a deepwater anchorage.

The bottom of the bay has a well-delineated drop off. The shallow portion descends gradually from the shore to about 20 m (66 ft.). After that, a steep drop off begins. Ships would not normally anchor on a steep slope, because of poor holding power. The best holding would be in a horizontal or gently sloping reef, though the reef may make weighing anchor difficult. In our survey, two large navy anchors were found at depths of around 30 m (98 ft.), and several small anchors were found at shallower depths.

Bathymetry and Topography

The contour map that serves as the background for Figure 2 was generated from remote sensing data that covered the entire survey area. Within that area was a rectangular strip that was considered the closest and most probable site for access to the proposed town. These maps show the shallows near the shoreline to the right, from the shoreline to about a 7 m (23 ft.) depth; a relatively steep slope that included the remains of a reef wall; an erosional cut from the outflow of a river; and a deeper shelf, on the left side of the plot (down to more than 30 m or 98 ft.).

Distribution and Assessment of Submerged Cultural Resources

At each survey site, a 30-m (98-ft.) circular area of the bottom was examined for exposed artifacts. No excavation was conducted, so only artifacts that were visible to the dive team were recorded in this survey. A sketch was made in situ or a photograph of each artifact was entered

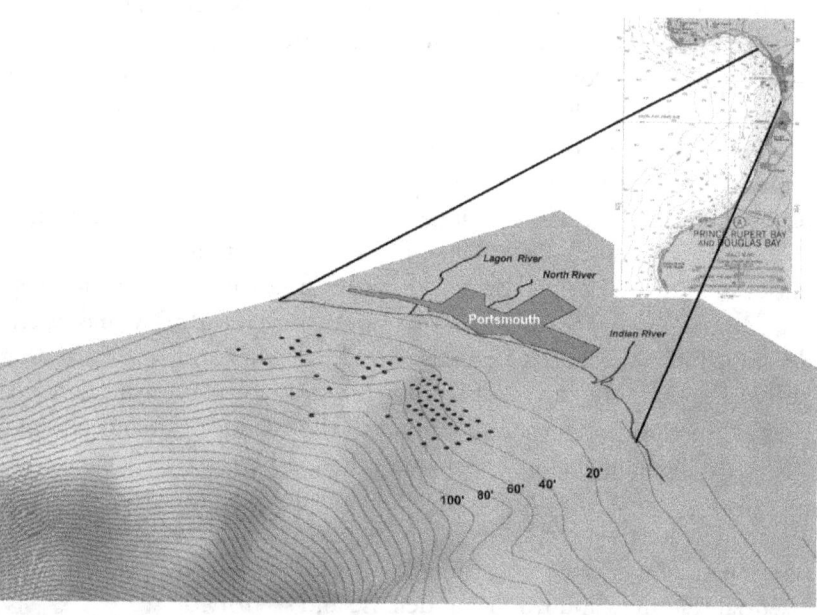

FIGURE 2. THIS CONTOUR MAP WAS PRODUCED FROM REMOTE SENSING DATA. IT SHOWS THE GRID POINTS FOR THE ANCHORING SURVEY WITHIN THE PORTSMOUTH ANCHORAGE. UNDERWATER CIRCLE SEARCHES OF 30 M (49 FT.) DIAMETER WERE CONDUCTED FROM THE ANCHOR OF THE RESEARCH BOAT. (DATA COMPOSITE BY AUTHORS).

into our computerized database following each dive. Age estimates of each artifact found were recorded, as was the composition of the seafloor at each site - either coral reef, sand flat, sea grass bed or mud. In addition, divers noted the water depth at the central anchor point and the slope of the survey area.

In total, 65 circle searches, representing an equal number of buddy team dives, were completed within the anchorage grid. Of those grid points surveyed, only 6 contained no observed artifacts. In 11 survey sites, historical artifacts were identified. Only modern cultural resources were found in 48 of the circle searches. Among modern debris were abandoned large items such as automobile parts and household appliances. Because of their size and distance from shore, local residents may have discarded some of these items underwater intentionally.

Historical artifacts were intermingled with modern artifacts and were most frequently sighted in coral reef and sandy bottom topographies. Because the anchorage in Prince Rupert's Bay has been in active use continually up to the present time, both historic and modern cultural resources overlap. Population growth and boating volumes for the town have increased over time, so modern artifacts predominate. However, the sparsely distributed historical artifacts were found at depths between 10 m (33 ft.) and 33 m (108 ft.). The geographic center of the historical artifact distribution corresponds to a water depth of 15 m (49 ft.) and is located 565 m (1,854 ft.) offshore. That center lies due west of the modern fisheries pier for merchant trading and local fishing in the modern town.

Minimal dimensions for this lozenge-shaped coastal anchorage zone, based upon results of this survey, are approximately 1,262 m (4,157 ft.) from north to south and 526 m (1,726 ft.) from east to west. In terms of total surface area, the ship anchorage for Portsmouth represents nearly seven hundred thousand square meters or more than seven million square feet. The distance from the shoreline to the closest location of historic artifacts in the southern portion of the zone is 482 m (1,582 ft.). The comparable distance from shore at the northern end of the anchorage is 312 m (1,024 ft.).

We assume that configuration of the coastal intertidal zone shifted over the past three centuries due to storm surge, sediment deposition or planned human restructuring of the coastline. Even so, the offset of the anchorage from shore protects ships at the site from random or unwanted access from land. Water depth is also sufficient to prevent accidental grounding of ships while at anchor.

This anchorage zone is very likely to be more extensive than our limited surveying procedure indicates. Delimitation of boundaries, should any exist, have not been determined. However, there is little doubt that our survey was conducted within the circumscribed area of presumptive anchorage, based upon depth, distance from shore and proximity to the town of Portsmouth. The anchorage that we describe would have sufficed for sailing ships seeking shelter in Prince Rupert's Bay or for transferring provisions to or from the business district of the town and its environs, throughout the historic period. This sailing ship anchorage would enable access to the shoreline, ranging from Fort Shirley and the Cabrits to the north around to the Indian River outflow to the south.

Local sailing ships, including sloops and schooners, would usually anchor close to shore in water between 5-10 m (16-33 ft.). This type of sailing ship can sail close to the wind and is more maneuverable than a square-rigger. If the wind turns to the west the smaller sailboats would have a good chance of leaving the bay safely.

The selection of a specific anchorarge by a sailing ship captain would depend upon local conditions of current, wind and surface action as the coastal zone was approached and when the ship's anchor was being deployed. Beyond the influence of those weather variables, the only other consideration for anchoring would be safety based upon the ship's proximity to neighboring ships already occupying the anchorage.

Artifact analysis

Several types of anchors, modern and historical, were discovered. Among the former were Danforth and Northill anchors, both lightweight anchors made of stainless steel. Among the historical anchors found in 15 m (49 ft.) of water were two small anchors that were carried often by merchant ships or by naval ships as accessory anchors (Figure 3). These historic anchors could not be identified by date or national origin, although both were used routinely throughout the 18th and 19th centuries. Two large Admiralty anchors were found at depths at 30 m (98 ft.). These were typical of the 18th and 19th centuries (Smith 1983; Rousmaniere 1989; Curryer 1999).

A number of historical bottles and bottle fragments were found, as illustrated in Figure 3. Several were dark olive green English wine bottles. These were typically free-blown and recognizable by their irregular outlines. They date from the latter 18th century into the 19th century, and show the typical sag at the base that results

FIGURE 3. THESE HISTORIC BOTTLES, GLASS SHERDS AND ANCHORS REPRESENT SOME OF THE SUBMERGED CULTURAL RESOURCES FOUND DURING THE SURVEY. THE BOTTLES DATE FROM THE LATE 18TH AND 19TH CENTURIES AND THE ANCHORS WERE FREQUENTLY USED BETWEEN THE 18TH AND 19TH CENTURIES. (PHOTOGRAPHS BY AUTHORS).

from setting the freshly blown bottle on a table where its weight caused it to settle and produce a basal bulge before cooling and hardening. Another bottle, shown in Figure 3, was blown into a Ricketts mold, and most probably dates between 1820 and 1840.

Figure 3 also includes a Dutch case bottle with squared sides that allowed tight packing in wooden cases. Though first manufactured in the late 18th century, this bottle may date to the early 19th century, based on both shape and condition. There were many other historic bottles found, both mold-blown and machine-made, representing a mixture of soda water, champagne and beer bottles. These historical artifacts of all types were most often found directly offshore from the town.

Dynamic Considerations of an Anchorage Zone

Prevailing winds blow from the east through a valley between the mountains and across Portsmouth to Prince Rupert's Bay. Littoral currents in Prince Rupert's Bay predominantly course north to south, with river outflows introducing localized and intermittent east to west flow following periods of heavy rain or tropical storms.

By applying known characteristics of historic sailing ships (Table 1), we calculated the area that would have been required for safe anchorage for each. Those ships included HMS *Royal William* 1719, man-o-war first rate; HMS Resolution 1650, man-o-war second rate; Bluenose 1921, schooner; *Cutty Sark* 1869, clipper; *Mayflower* 1615, galleon; *Bounty* 1787., frigate; *Tonnant* 1793, brigantine; and Beagle 1817, bark (Cucari 1976). On average, the area required for these ships at anchor would be 9,164 m2. The minimum depth for anchoring these sailing ships was 10 m (33 ft.), depending on the draft. These values correspond well to the distribution of historical artifacts in the Portsmouth anchorage that

Ship	r1	r2 (r1+10%)	A = πr1r2	Draft	Depth=2d
Man-o-war 1	69 m	76 m	16,466 m²	6 m	12 m
Man-o-war 2	59	65	12,042	6	12
Schooner	15	17	801	2	4
Clipper	86	95	25,654	6	12
Galleon	20	22	1,382	3	6
Frigate	55	61	10,535	6	12
Brigantine	32	35	3,517	5	10
Bark	29	32	2,914	4	8
Average	46 m	50 m	9,164 m²	5 m	10 m

TABLE 1. COMPUTATION OF THE ELLIPTICAL AREA (A) REQUIRED FOR ANCHORING SEVERAL HISTORIC SHIP TYPES. SAILING SHIP LENGTHS (R1) AND DRAFTS ARE AS REPORTED BY CUCARI (1976).

ranged between 12-20 m (39-66 ft.), assuming a modest rise in sea level during the past three centuries.

The schematics depicted in Figure 4 show the geometry of the surface area required for a ship at anchor. This area constitutes an ellipse, where r1 is the ship and surface length and r2 is the lateral drift of the ship because of current and wind. The area of the ellipse represents the product of the constant, pi (π), times r1 times r2 (van Dorn 1974; Maloney 1994).

Although efforts to overlay historical maps were inconsistent and inconclusive, we do know that Dominica lies in the middle of the "hurricane belt" and that several severe storms have devastated the island (Milas 1968; Chenoweth 2006). Many hurricanes made landfall in Portsmouth and across the bay during the 19th and 20th centuries as a matter of historical record. In fact, at least one major storm has struck the island of Dominica every decade since the early 18th century. Major hurricanes striking Dominica have been recorded and confirmed for the years of 1766, 1772, 1806, 1809, 1813, 1816, 1817, 1818, 1825, 1830 and 1834 (Chenoweth 2006). The earliest recorded hurricane to hit Dominica was that of 1567, when six Spanish ships were sunk off the north coast of the island. On 14 August 1788, an extremely powerful and destructive hurricane struck Dominica, killing 500 residents and causing widespread damage. Both the shoreline and the underwater topography of Prince Rupert's Bay would have been altered by that storm as well as by many other storms over centuries of exposure.

What are lacking from these records are detailed reports of specific damage to the coast, the littoral zone and shoreline ecosystems. Twentieth century storms, such as the Category 5 Hurricane David (1979) with 150 mph (240 km/hr) winds, were most devastating to the island (CARIBSAVE 2012). David was responsible for 42 deaths and damage to or destruction of over 75%

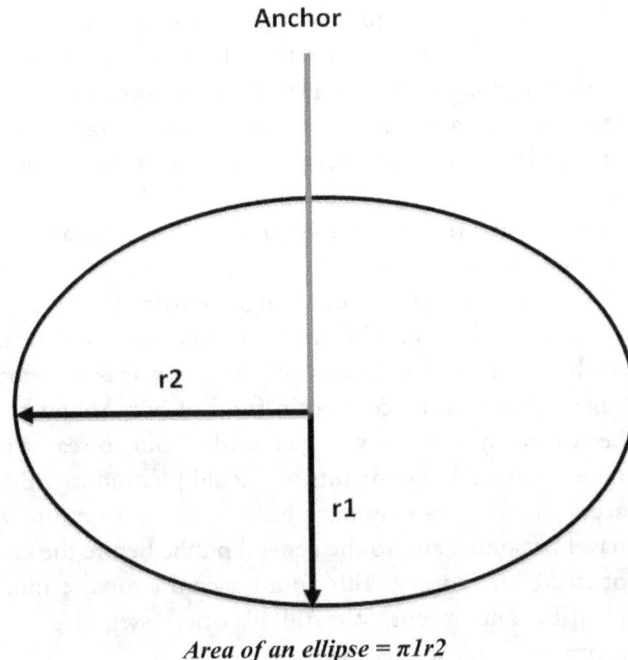

Area of an ellipse = π1r2

where r1 = minor axis and r2 = major axis
r1 is length of ship and surface rode;
r2 is lateral sway due to prevailing wind and current

FIGURE 4. PASSIVE MOVEMENTS OF A SAILING SHIP AT ANCHOR INCLUDE PITCHING (FORWARD AND BACKWARD), YAWING (SIDE-TO-SIDE OR LATERAL) AND SURGING (UP AND DOWN). THE RESULTANT ELLIPTICAL GEOMETRY DEFINES THE SPATIAL CLEARANCE REQUIRED FOR A SAFE OFFSHORE ANCHORAGE. (SCHEMATIC BY AUTHORS).

of homes across the island. Hurricane Hugo (1989) and Hurricane Omar (2008) were two powerful storms that severely damaged buildings and property on Dominica. Understandably, the documentation of human lives lost and property damage, such as homes and businesses, are detailed following a major tropical storm. However, alterations in shoreline configurations and damages to the coastal zone are not prioritized. Undoubtedly, anchorage sites all along the entire western side of Dominica were altered because of abrupt changes in depth, deposition of submerged obstacles from land sources and shoreline modifications during and immediately following these storms. Sea level rise, storm surges, erosion and ecosystem degradation are major influences on the shoreline and the littoral zone of the island (CARIBSAVE 2012) and would be expected to shift sea floor topography and subsequent change in the placement of safe anchorages for ships.

COMPARISON OF PORTSMOUTH AND ROSEAU ANCHORAGES OF DOMINICA

The anchorage in Roseau is very different in configuration from that in Portsmouth. The differences are evident from the surface areas of the two, the relationships to the local military base, the bathymetry and topography of the harbors, and the density and variety of surface artifacts identified from the sites.

The anchorage zone in Roseau and the town's military base at Fort Young, however, shares the westerly orientation with the Portsmouth anchorage. Island elevations protect both of these ship anchorages from the direct effect of the easterly trade winds. The Roseau anchorage zone, however, is very limited in area, is situated closer to the town's shoreline, and includes pilings and stanchions associated with a cruise ship pier and stone remnants of a pier that was destroyed in a storm at the turn of the 20th century. The presence of fairly extensive modern development is one of the major differences between the Roseau and Portsmouth anchorages.

The anchorage at Roseau harbor is not as deep or as rapidly sloping as the anchorage in Prince Rupert's Bay. The underwater topography at Roseau is a combination of rocky outcroppings, patch reefs and sand flats. Hence, remote sensing of the Roseau zone was not practical and SCUBA divers explored the area site by surface towing and underwater swimming transects. Submerged cultural resources were observed scattered widely across the sea floor. These artifacts were collected, identified, conserved, dried, photographed and recorded in a database for subsequent deposition and display at the Dominica Historical Museum on the waterfront in Roseau. That museum is a popular and frequent destination for visitors to the island and for groups of school children anxious to learn about their island history and cultural heritage.

Of significance, a wooden shipwreck was found within the Roseau anchorage. It was originally identified as an 18th century British warship because of its large size and copper sheathing. However, re-analysis of structural details indicates that this wreckage might fit that of a merchant ship. After reviewing a list of ships lost from the area, the wreckage was tentatively suggested to be that of *Yara*, a British Royal Mail carrier. *Yara* was built in 1872 and served as an intra-island postal delivery ship. That ship was normally docked at the stone pier whose remains were found nearby. The pier was destroyed in a tropical storm in 1916. The ship was lost during the same storm and was never found.

Artifacts from the Roseau anchorage site were more numerous, more varied and more recent than those from the Portsmouth site. This difference may be attributable to greater ship traffic to the capital town and commercial activity for a longer period of time. English ceramics were plentiful, along with mid-18th century bottles and ship repair components including rolled lead, brass spikes and lead weights. The absence of ceramics at Portsmouth may indicate that they were buried in sediment during storms. The dredging of the bottom during installation of the cruise ship pier in Roseau may have been responsible for exposing many of the lighter artifacts.

Because of the proximity of the anchorage in Roseau to shore and the shallowness of the water, it is also possible that artifacts recovered in front of Fort Young had been thrown into the water or washed out to sea from the shoreline. The remnants of the old pier indicate that access to the area may have been available to military/naval personnel and to the general public before the end of the 19th century. This could account for the more plentiful and recent, yet still historic, assemblages of submerged cultural resources.

CONCLUSIONS

Foundation STIMACUR has successfully completed or is surveying anchorages in several Caribbean islands including Curaçao (Nagelkerken *et al.* 2008; Nagelkerken 2009; Nagelkerken, Knepper and Hayes 2014), Bonaire

(Nagelkerken and Hayes 2002; Nagelkerken and Hayes 2008), St. Eustatius (Nagelkerken 2000) and St. Kitts (Gill et al. 2014). Based upon our experience in surveying historical anchorages, we suggest that the addition of data from historical anchorages to terrestrial and shipwreck archaeological surveys offers important supplementary information for historical interpretation. Therefore, we recommend that when coastal sites are positioned adjacent to a terrestrial or a submerged shipwreck study area, the anchorages for those sites be surveyed using appropriate design to complement and extend customary archaeological reports.

The historical anchorage for Portsmouth, Dominica, was selected for the most recent underwater archaeological survey by STIMACUR. Remote sensing data were used to determine the topographic and bathymetric characterizations of the sea floor and the selection of sites for exploratory dives. Using circle searches, submerged cultural resources were identified and documented within the anchorage zone in proximity to the town. Overlays of bathymetry, artifact distribution analysis, bottom ecology and relationships to the shoreline have confirmed the most likely location and extent of the town anchorage during historical times. Knowing the length and draft of sailing ships and applying basic principles of anchoring, requirements for the safe use of an historical anchorage have been determined. Underwater archaeological surveys of coastal areas benefit from descriptive data on historical anchorages that document cultural resources deliberately abandoned or accidentally lost by merchant and naval sailing ships.

References

CARIBSAVE REPORT
    2012   Caribsave climate change risk profile for Dominica. UK AID and Australian AID.

CHENOWETH, MICHAEL
    2006   A reassessment of historical Atlantic basin tropical cyclone activity, 1700-1855. Climactic Change, Springer, New York.

CUCARI, ATTILIO
    1976   Sailing Ships. Rand McNally and Co., Chicago, Illinois.

CURRYER, BETTY NELSON
    1999   Anchors: An Illustrated History. Naval Institute Press, Annapolis. Maryland.

GILL, CAMERON, RAYMOND HAYES, DENNIS KNEPPER, MONIQUE KLARENBEEK, BILL UTLEY AND FRANCOIS VAN DER HOEVEN
    2014   Preliminary Report of a Maritime Archaeological Survey at Sandy Point, St. Kitts, British West Indies., pp. 63-70. In Underwater Archaeology Proceedings 2014, Dagneau, C and K Gauvin, editors. Advisory Council on Underwater Archaeology.

HONYCHURCH, LENNOX
    1995   *The Dominica Story: a History of the Island.* Macmillan Education Ltd., London.

    2011   *The Archaeology of Dominica.* Island Heritage Initiatives, Ltd., Dominica.

    2013   *Dominica's Cabrits and Prince Rupert's Bay.* Island Heritage Initiatives, Ltd., Dominica.

MILAS, JOSE CARLOS
    1968   *Hurricanes of the Caribbean and adjacent regions, 1492-1800.* Acad. Arts Sci. Americas, Miami, Florida

NAGELKERKEN, WIL
    2000   *Ceramics of Orange Bay St. Eustatius Netherlands Antilles,* Foundation STIMANA No. 1, Curaçao.

    2009   De noodlottige geschiedenis van het Hollandse fregat *Alphen* geexplodeerd engezonken in 1778 in de haven van Curaçao. Foundation STIMACUR Number 3, Curaçao.

NAGELKERKEN, WIL AND RAYMOND HAYES
    2002   The historical anchorage of Kralendijk, Bonaire, Netherlands Antilles, including the wreckage of the Dutch brigantine Sirene (1831). Foundation STIMANA No. 2, Curaçao.

NAGELKERKEN, WIL, THEO VAN DER GIESSEN, RAYMOND HAYES AND DENNIS KNEPPER
    2003   *Preliminary survey of the historical anchorage of the harbor of Roseau, Dominica, including the finding of an early 19th century English warship wreck.* Foundation STIMANA report, Curaçao.

NAGELKERKEN, WIL, DENNIS KNEPPER AND RAYMOND HAYES
    2006   The historical anchorage of Roseau, Dominica, BWI. (Abstract) Proceedings 39th Conference SHA/ACUA, Sacramento, California.

NAGELKERKEN, WIL, RAYMOND HAYES, DENNIS KNEPPER AND LENNOX HONYCHURCH
    2007   *Re-analysis of submerged shipwreck remains within the historical anchorage site at Roseau, Dominica, BWI.* (Abstract) Proceedings 40th Conference SHA/ACUA, Williamsburg, Virginia.

NAGELKERKEN, WIL, THEO VAN DER GIESSEN, RAYMOND HAYES AND DENNIS KNEPPER
    2008   Development of maritime archaeological tourism using the wreck of the English SS *Mediator* in Curaçao, pp. 283-292. In *Underwater and Maritime Archaeology in Latin America and the Caribbean*. M.E. Leshikar-Denton and P.L. Erreguerena, editors. Left Coast Press, Walnut Creek, California.

NAGELKERKEN, WIL AND RAYMOND HAYES
    2008   The historical anchorage of Kralendijk, Bonaire, Netherlands Antilles, pp. 293-301. In *Underwater and Maritime Archaeology in Latin America and the Caribbean*. M.E. Leshikar-Denton and P.L. Erreguerena, editors, Left Coast Press, Walnut Creek, California.

NAGELKERKEN, WIL, DENNIS KNEPPER AND RAYMOND HAYES
    2014   Survey of the English Steamship *Mediator*: its history, voyages and wrecking in Curaçao (1884). Foundation STIMACUR Number 4, Curaçao.

ROUSMANIERE, JOHN
    1989   *The Annapolis Book of Seamanship* Simon and Schuster, New York, New York.

SMITH, ROBERT A.
    1983   *Anchors: Selection and Use.* 2nd edition, Robert A. Smith, Portland, Oregon.

VAN DORN, WILLIAM G.
    1974   *Oceanography and Seamanship.* Dodd, Mead and Co., New York, New York.

MALONEY, ELBERT
    1994   *Chapman's Piloting, Seamanship and Small Boat Handling,* 61st edition, Hearst Marine New York, New York.

• • • • • • • • • • • • • • • •

Dr. Raymond L. Hayes
1010 N. Noyes Dr.
Silver Spring, MD 20910, USA
Telephone: (301) 585-5892
E-mail address: hayes.ray@gmail.com

Dennis Knepper
7817 Accotink Place
Aleqandria, VA 22308, USA
Telephone: (703) 768-6005
E-mail address: dknepper@versar.com

Bill Utley
3905 Millstone Court
Monrovia MD 21770, USA
Telephone: (301) 865-5549
E-mail address: bufireinthehole4@gmail.com

James Smailes
144 North Carolina Avenue, SEE
Washington, DC 20007, USA
Telephone: (202) 543-4895
E-mail address: jasmailes@gmail.com

Greg German
12441 Donahoo Road
Kansas City, KS 66109, USA
Telephone: (913) 721-1515
E-mail address: ggerman9@aol.com

Dr. François van der Hoeven
San Sebastian B3
Curaçao
Telephone: 5999-864-8242
E-mail address: francoisvanderhoeven@gmail.com

The Meaning of the Offshore: The Role of Islands in the Maritime Cultural Landscape of Peru

Vicente Cortez
Carlos Ausejo

The authors present their research about the relationship between the islands and the Andean mainland over time, from prehispanic times to present day, emphasizing the island's role as sacred places, economic spaces, and harbors for oceanic crossroads. Using written sources such as ethno historic documents and travelogues, the authors compare historic views of the islands with archaeological evidence collected from the islands and representations of navigation and the sea from prehispanic coastal cultures. This approach includes a panoramic view of the role and value as cultural landscapes societies place on the islands located in the Peruvian offshore.

Introduction

The Peruvian coastline has over one hundred islands (Figure 1), with only about a dozen big enough to have settlements. The islands have a rocky surface and lack vegetation or fresh water sources, which explains why human occupation through time has been only temporary. The Humboldt Current, a large marine ecosystem that surrounds these islands, makes them the refuge of millions of birds whose excrements constitute the guano, a well-known plant fertilizer, that had an essential economic role in the 19th and 20th centuries. Peruvian islands were also a stopping point for travelers, pirates, and foreign armies in the region, who have left evidence of their presence.

We present our research about the relationship of the islands to the mainland in Peru, emphasizing the islands' change through time as well as their roles as sacred places, economic spaces, and harbors for oceanic crossroads. We present evidence from prehispanic times, and incorporate ethno historic documents as well as material culture collected during the guano extraction in the 19th century (Kubler 1948) and archaeological projects in the 20th and 21st centuries.

Prehispanic Times: Moche (A.D. 300–700)

The earliest and largest quantities of objects found on the islands belong to the Moche culture, which flourished in the northern coast of Peru between the 1st and 7th century AD. Most of the objects come from the Guañape and Macabí islands, located just in front of the Moche heartland. Other objects come from islands located out to sea (Lobos de Afuera and Lobos de Tierra Islands, ahead the coast of Lambayeque) or more than 600 kilometers away from the Moche area of influence, in the offshore of Ica region (Chincha islands). These objects and the placement of the islands signal the development of navigation techniques that might have been related to commercial routes or ceremonial purposes.

Most of the Moche objects depict prisoners; wooden stalks have also been recovered, as well as weaponry. Middle and Late Moche ceramics depict complex scenes in the islands (Hocquehghem 1981, Donnan & Mac Leland 1999) (Figure 2) and some of the elements depicted in the pottery are present in the archaeological record: square buildings or temples, textiles, fruits and seeds, weapons, and ceramics, to name a few (Kubler 1948).

We believe the Moche objects represented in their fine line drawings and the similar objects that have been found on Guañape and Macabí islands point to a belief system that considered islands a space where gods, ancestors, and men could communicate; it might be possible to think that sacrifices of prisoners and objects were done in the islands so prosperity would be assured for the living (Hocquehghem 1981). Some of the characters in these complex scenes appear in other mythical scenes, and they have been connected to actual burials excavated in the 1990s (for example the Priestess of Moro, or the Lord of Sipan).

Chimu and Chincha (A.D. 900–1438)

About three centuries after the Moche, Chimu society developed in roughly the same geographical area, expanding their territory further south. While Moche is frequently considered a state level society, Chimu is usually regarded as a more complex state that managed to defy the Inca rule. Chimu cultural material has also been found in the islands, mostly wooden staffs that represent libation scenes and a Peruvian dog called viringo (Kubler

FIGURE 1. MAP OF THE PERUVIAN SYSTEM OF GUANO ISLANDS, ISLETS, AND GUANO POINTS NATIONAL RESERVE, SHOWING THE PRINCIPAL ISLANDS MENTIONED IN THE ARTICLE (IMAGE COURTESY OF THE PERUVIAN NATIONAL PARK SYSTEM – SERNANP, 2011)

FIGURE 2. MOCHE ICONOGRAPHY DEPICTING THE CAPTURE OF PRISONERS, TRANSFER TO THE ISLANDS AND RITUAL PRESENTATION OF OFFERINGS TO SUPERNATURAL BEINGS (DONNAN & MCCLELLAND 1999, P. 183)

lands as ceremonial places connected with fertility and high-ranking burials.

Ichma and Inca (A.D. 1438–1532)

The Ichma culture had its center in Lima, the current Peruvian capital. Just in front of the Callao bay, San Lorenzo Island is one of the most salient features of the coastal landscape. Archaeological excavations conducted in 1907 and 2004 found evidence of an Ichma settlement, a port, and a cemetery in Caleta La Cruz, located on the southern tip of the island. The site also had evidence from other cultural groups (Chimu, Chincha, Chancay and Inca), which points to the continuous use of the islands during late prehispanic times (Hudtwalcker 2009, 2010; Hudtwalcker and Pinilla 2004, 2005).

The excavations uncovered several complex burials, among them females with textile implements. Some of the burials had unique signs of wealth, like a painted blanket from the Ichma period that depicts a dance possibly associated with ancestor worship and fertility rituals (Hudtwalcker 2011). Other objects found in the island include fish representations in metal and semiprecious stones; these underline the economic role of the islands. In addition, archaeological surveys have found seasonal camps and areas for marine food processing that were connected to the Ichma use of San Lorenzo (Hudtwalcker 2009; Hudtwalcker and Pinilla 2005).

The Spanish conquest of Peru in 1532 brought an interruption in the native cultural process of the Andean land were not the primary purpose of the chroniclers, they have created valuable sources for historic and archaeological research.

One of the first chronicles by Pedro Cieza de León (1553) describes the Ballestas islands, located in the southern coast of Peru, as places of worship. Pedro Pizarro (1571) mentions the hunt of sea lions, and Garcilaso de la Vega (1609) and Antonio de Herrera (1601) mention the use of guano as fertilizer.

Almost a century after the conquest, the Spanish launched an extirpation of idolatry campaign that also produced records of the islands' ceremonial role as sacred spaces. There are stories about ancestors transformed in islands (Avila 1608; Calancha 1631); souls of the departed being taken to the next world by sea lions, and "sacrifices" of silver sheets, chicha and food being made to ensure fertility (Arriaga 1621) – these sacrifices were connected to guano extraction and agricultural use in a ceremony called Akatay Mita, or "the return of the land", in honor to Guamancantac, the Guano Deity (Tello 1927, cited in Alayza y Paz Soldán 1951).

Colonial Times: Lord of the Guano (ca. 1550)

A coat of arms found in 1847 in the Chincha islands (Figure 3) offers a glimpse of how the islands were used during colonial times. It belongs to Don Pedro Guañeque, a "principal" of the valley in the 16th century (Cushman 2014). Although the coat of arms is done in European fashion, the elements inside are local references to the Chincha islands and valley, like the guanay

FIGURE 3. COAT OF ARMS OF DON PEDRO GUAÑEQUE, LORD OF CHINCHA ISLANDS (MID-16TH CENTURY), WITH REPRESENTATION OF SEABIRD, THE CHINCHA ISLANDS AND THE TYPICAL "U" SHAPE CORMORANT NEST (IMAGE COURTESY OF THE BRITISH MUSEUM)

or cormoran, a bird that is known for producing the best guano, and its typical u-shaped nest. This unique object is one of the first examples of the social recognition that native elites could achieve by serving the Colonial system as administrators; the multiple references to the Chincha islands possibly indicate they were included in their territories.

A Lost Connection (16th–19th Centuries)

After intensive extirpation of idolatry campaigns, many native beliefs disappeared from the colonial life in Peru, and with them were gone the spiritual connection to the islands and the knowledge about the fertilizing properties of guano. The islands became property of the Crown. The connection with islands and shoreline, formerly integrated to the societies from the coast and the highlands, lost strength during colonial times and was almost completely gone by the time Peru turned into a republic. The maritime cultural landscape was separated from the Andes and remained isolated, and only a few coastal villages kept using the islands as source for food and income.

Early Republic: The Times of the Guano (19th Century)

In the early 19th century, foreign researchers and travelers like Alexander von Humboldt helped "rediscover" the properties of guano. At the same time, the agricultural and industrial revolution was pushing the agricultural frontier and seeking ways to increase crop production. The young Peruvian republic, founded in 1821, received an important cash influx from the guano exports, creating a golden age that lasted until 1860.

The islands, as source of this sudden wealth, were seized by the Peruvian government and declared state property; European companies were contracted to extract and export the guano with little to no oversight from the government. As a result, guano deposits were depleted quickly – even with some of them being up to 30 meters deep (Figure 4).

Despite the role of guano exploitation in young Peruvian Republic economics, the islands did not play any other role in the Peruvian cultural landscape with regard to the rest of the mainland. Aside from the guano infrastructure, there was no other evidence of the presence of the government authority, not even lighthouses or navy control posts. As an example, we can tell an anecdote of Charles Darwin's visit to Peru in 1835: because the convulsed political situation of the country (coups d'état, ambiance of anarchy, gangs of thieves in the main roads), Darwin mentioned that the San Lorenzo Island was the only place to walk safely (Hudtwalcker 2009).

The islands were seen only as the location for economic activities and not as a fully integrated part of the territory, as evidenced by the covert slavery system used in them: people from China and Easter Island were forced to work on the island under indenture servitude, which was illegal in Peru at the time. There is historic

FIGURE 4. *"PILE OF GUANO", PICTURE OF THE EXTRACTION OF GUANO DEPOSITS BY CHINESE WORKERS, NORTH CHINCHA ISLANDS, 1865 (IMAGE COURTESY OF THE AMERICAN MUSEUM OF NATURAL HISTORY)*

and archaeological evidence that confirm these affirmations (Maude 1981).

Questioned Sovereignty

This situation of disconnection of the islands from the coastline and the monopoly of the riches generated from guano extraction prompted some foreign invasion attempts. In 1852, United States citizens occupied and attempted to extract guano from the Lobos islands, arguing they were inhabited. The Peruvian government and its diplomats used chronicles and historic and legal documents to settle the question in their favor. In 1864, Spanish war ships occupied the Chincha islands to reclaim them as war reparations for the Independence war. After 2 years of battle, the islands were abandoned and Spain recognized the Peruvian state as independent.

Foreigners on the Islands

Since the 18th century, because the weak presence of the Peruvian authorities, the islands were used as stops in the navigation routes that go near the Peruvian coast. Merchant and whaling ships enroute to the Eastern Pacific would stop there, sometimes with no permits, a situation that created a lot of paperwork for the government officials of that time and a valuable source of information for researchers. There are also shipwrecks around the islands that need to be scientifically explored so we can know more about the maritime history of Peru.

In the 1830s, San Lorenzo Island was used as sanitary station for quarantined travelers, some of whom were buried there in separate cemeteries to prevent the spread of disease. Later on, the island became a busy industrial enclave with a factory and a floating deck owned by Thaddeus Terry and later by Josiah Harris, both British nationals (Hudtwalcker and Cortez 2011).

During the war with Spain (1864–1866) and the War of the Pacific between Chile and Peru (1879–1883), the occupation forces buried their dead in the island. To this day, the cemeteries where some of these passing populations were laid to rest remain on the Peruvian islands as a testimony of the multiple nationalities that traveled our waters. Sailors, travelers, pirates, and soldiers remain there as silent witnesses of our history.

Recovery of the Islands (20th Century)

From the late 19th century until today, the islands have been the property of the Peruvian government. The Navy, the Ministry of Fishing, and the Ministry of Agriculture share the responsibilities of guarding and protecting the land, the surrounding sea, the fish, and the bird species that produce guano. Fishermen communities still use the islands in the traditional way under the regulations and supervision of government authorities. The Navy has a permanent base in San Lorenzo, while other islands were used as prisons until the 1980s.

Since the 1960s, the islands have started to acquire new meanings for Peruvian society. The presence of birds and sea lions has generated nature tourism in Lima and Ica, promoting non-intrusive tours that are increasingly popular. The Navy has sponsored a small number of archaeological projects in the San Lorenzo Island and is partnering with organizations like CPAMS (Peruvian Center of Maritime and Underwater Archaeology) to promote the study of their history and preservation.

Rebirth of the Islands (21st Century)

Despite these improvements, there are a number of challenges that remain, much like the challenges faced by other island and coastal environments. In 2009, the Peruvian Park Service – SERNANP created the National System of Guano Islands to protect the ecosystem, and the natural and cultural history of about 20 of the most representative islands of Peru.

The system promotes coordinated efforts, joining government officials, tourism companies, scientific communities, and local populations to study and protect the islands; a second goal is to maintain sustainability of the traditional activities developed in the islands. The islands' transformation from outliers to contributors in Peruvian society and history are creating opportunities and strengthening identity for the entire nation.

Final Ideas

The islands of the Peruvian offshore are plenty of significance, economic and natural as well as historical. They are part of the national territory and cultural landscape trough time: as important places of worship in the periphery of prehispanic societies' territory, or marginal places during colonial and early republican times, they now acquire new roles, economic, strategic and ecological in the border of the Peruvian territory.

Although the overexploitation and surface alteration two centuries ago, the islands of Peru are still key to understand the role of the cultural maritime landscape in the history of Peruvian societies.

Acknowledgements

The authors want to acknowledge all the colleagues and institutions that collaborated in their research. To the Peruvian National Park Service (SERNANP) for sharing information about the islands. To Juan A. Murro and Dr. Colin McEwan, from Dumbarton Oaks, who put us in touch with The British Museum. To Susan Haskell from the Peabody Harvard Museum and Dr. Jago Cooper and James Hamill from The British Museum, who bring us useful information about some of the specimens stored in their collections. To the San Lorenzo Archaeological Project, for sharing information and documentation about their research. To Dr. Fabio Amador from the OLAS Foundation, for make possible the participation in the SHA 2015 Conference in Seattle, Washington.

References

ALAYZA Y PAZ SOLDAN, LUIS
1951 *Las misteriosas islas del Perú* (The mysterious islands of Peru). Editorial Lumen S.A., Lima, Peru.

ARRIAGA, FRAY PABLO JOSÉ
1621 *Extirpación de la Idolatría del Perú (The extirpation of idolatry in Peru)*, n.p. Expanded and revised from 1968 edition. Biblioteca de Autores Españoles, Madrid, Spain.

ÁVILA, FRANCISCO DE
[1598] *Huarochirí: Manuscrito quechua del siglo XVII. Ritos y Tradiciones. Traducción del quechua por Gerald Taylor (Huarochiri: Quechua manuscript from the 17th century. Rites and traditions. Translation from the Quechua by Gerald Taylor)*, n.p. Expanded and revised from 2003 edition. Instituto Francés de Estudios Andinos, Lima, Peru.

CALANCHA, FRAY ANTONIO DE LA
1638 *Corónica Moralizadora del Orden de San Agustín en el Perú, con Sucesos Ejemplares Vistos en esta Monarquía (Moralizing Chronicle of the Saint Augustin Order in Peru, with extraordinary events seen in this Monarchy)*. Barcelona, Spain.

CIEZA DE LEON, PEDRO
1553 *Crónica del Perú. Primera Parte (Chronicle of Peru. First Part)*, n.p. Expanded and revised from 1986 edition. Pontificia Universidad Católica del Perú, Lima, Peru.

CUSHMAN, GREGORY T.
2014 *Guano and the Opening of the Pacific World*. Cambridge University, England.

DONNAN, CHRISTOPHER, AND DONNA MCCLELLAND
1999 *Moche Fineline Painting. Its Evolution and Its Artists*. UCLA Fowler Museum of Cultural History, Los Angeles, CA.

HOCQUENGHEM, ANNE–MARIE
1981 *Iconografía Mochica (Moche Iconography)*. Pontificia Universidad Católica del Perú, Lima, Peru.

HUDTWALCKER, JOSÉ ANTONIO
2009 Contexto histórico y evidencias de Darwin en la Isla San Lorenzo (Historical context and evidence of the presence of Charles Darwin in San Lorenzo Island), pp. 1–8. In *Boletín El Zarcillo*, Edición Especial, Año 2, Nº 2. Museo de Historia Natural Universidad Ricardo Palma, Lima, Peru.

2009 Ocupación prehispánica en la isla San Lorenzo: aportes del Proyecto Arqueológico Isla San Lorenzo (Prehispanic settlements in San Lorenzo Island: contributions of The San Lorenzo Island Archaeological Project), pp. 119-130. In *Arqueología y Sociedad*, Nº 20. Universidad Nacional Mayor de San Marcos, Lima, Peru.

2010 Investigaciones arqueológicas de Max Uhle en la isla San Lorenzo, Callao (1906–1907): un siglo después (Max Uhle's archaeological researches in San Lorenzo Island, Callao 1906–1907: a century on). In *Max Uhle (1856-1944). Evaluaciones de sus investigaciones y obras*. Peter Kaulicke, Manuela Fischer, Peter Masson, and Gregor Wolff, editors, pp. 295–312. Pontificia Universidad Católica del Perú. Lima, Peru.

2011 Chaupiñamca y el baile del Casayaco: alcances preliminares del estudio iconográfico del manto pintado encontrado por Max Uhle en la isla San Lorenzo (Chaupiñamca and the Casayaco dance: preliminary advances of the iconographic study on the painted clothing found by Max Uhle in San Lorenzo Island), pp. 93–132. In *Arqueología y Sociedad* Nº 23. Museo de Arqueología y Antropología de la Universidad Nacional Mayor de San Marcos, Lima, Peru.

HUDTWALCKER, JOSÉ ANTONIO, AND VICENTE CORTEZ
2011 El Dique Flotante Terry: Historia de un Naufragio (Terry's Floating Dock: story of a Shipwreck). In *Arqueología Peruana: Homenaje a la Dra. Mercedes Cárdenas Martin*. Luisa Vetter, Sandra Téllez, and Rafael Vega-Centeno, editors, pp. 311–322. Pontificia Universidad Católica del Perú, Universidad Nacional Mayor de San Marcos. Lima, Peru.

HUDTWALCKER, JOSÉ ANTONIO, AND JOSÉ F. PINILLA
2004 Proyecto Arqueológico San Lorenzo 2003-2004 (The San Lorenzo Island Archaeological Project 2003–2004), pp. 55–64. In *Revista de Marina*, 2. Marina de Guerra del Perú, Callao, Peru.

2005 Puerto y Cementerio Ichma en el Complejo Histórico Arqueológico de Caleta La Cruz, isla San Lorenzo (Ichma Port and Cemetery in Caleta La Cruz Archaeological Complex, San Lorenzo Island), pp. 14–28. In *Revista de Marina*, 2, pp. 14-28. Marina de Guerra del Perú, Callao, Peru.

KUBLER, GEORGE
1948 Towards Absolute Time: Guano Archaeology, pp. 29–50. In *Memoirs of the Society for American Archaeology, No. 4, A Reappraisal of PeruvianArchaeology*. Washington, DC.

MAUDE, H. E.
1981 *Slavers in Paradise: The Peruvian Slave Trade in Polynesia, 1862–1864*. Stanford University Press, Stanford, CA.

PIZARRO, PEDRO
1571 *Relación del Descubrimiento y Conquista de los Reinos del Perú (Relation of the Discovery and Conquest of the Reigns of Peru)*, n.p. Expanded and revised from 1986 edition. Pontificia Universidad Católica del Perú. Lima, Peru.

·················

Vicente Cortez
Peruvian Center of Maritime and Underwater Archaeology – CPAMS
900 N Switzer Canyon Drive Apt. 229
Flagstaff, AZ 86001

Carlos Ausejo
Peruvian Center of Maritime and Underwater Archaeology – CPAMS
Jiron Fanning 305 Dpto 302, Barranco
LIMA 4
PERU

Gulf of Mexico Shipwreck Corrosion, Hydrocarbon Exposure, Microbiology, and Archaeology (GOM-SCHEMA) Project: Studying the Effects of a Major Oil Spill on Submerged Cultural Resources

Melanie Damour
Robert Church
Daniel Warren

Christopher Horrell
Leila Hamdan

Schema, broadly defined, is a representative framework or plan. After the 2010 Deepwater Horizon oil spill, the Natural Resource Damage Assessment process began and the scientific community flocked to the Gulf of Mexico to study the spill's impacts. Unfortunately, shipwrecks and other submerged cultural resources were largely ignored. Through Federal and academic partnerships and contracts funded by the Bureau of Ocean Energy Management, a multidisciplinary team of scientists was assembled to examine the spill's impacts on deepwater shipwrecks and their resident microbial communities. Presented here is the project's "schema": its design and objectives, site selection criteria, and development through partnerships.

Introduction

On 20 April 2010, the *Deepwater Horizon* (DWH) mobile offshore drilling unit exploded off the Louisiana coast (National Commission on the BP Deepwater Horizon Oil Spill and Offshore Drilling [NCBPDHOSOD] 2011:8). The subsequent loss of well control led to a steady discharge of hydrocarbons from the Macondo oil reservoir into the Gulf of Mexico. After 86 days of an unabated flow from the wellhead in more than 5,000 ft. (1,500 m) of water, the well was finally capped on 15 July 2010. Nearly 5 million barrels of Louisiana Sweet Crude oil (roughly 57,000 to 67,000 barrels per day) and up to 500,000 tons of natural gas leaked into the environment (Joye et al. 2011, 2014; NCBPDHOSOD 2011).

During the federally coordinated spill response (hereafter "DWH spill"), mitigation methods were implemented to manage the spill, contain or collect oil on the water surface, and prevent or reduce the amount of oil washing onshore. One such mitigation method was the use of chemical dispersants including Corexit 9500, which was sprayed on the water surface and injected at the subsurface wellhead. More than 1.84 million gallons of dispersant were used to mitigate the DWH spill (NCBPDHOSOD 2010). Chemical dispersants, a mixture of surface acting agents (surfactants) and solvents, act as an emulsifier to break apart oil into smaller droplets. Hypothetically, smaller oil droplets should be more rapidly degraded and consumed by marine microorganisms such as bacteria due to enhanced surface area. However, little data support this assertion where Corexit 9500 is concerned (Hamdan and Fulmer 2011). Although microorganisms capable of hydrocarbon degradation are ubiquitous in the Gulf of Mexico (Orcutt et al. 2010) because of natural hydrocarbon seeps, large events such as the DWH spill have the potential to profoundly impact the structure and function of microbial communities on a variety of scales.

Concurrent with the spill-response efforts, the Natural Resource Damage Assessment (NRDA) process commenced to assess the extent of damages occurring as a result of the DWH spill to the environment (National Oceanic and Atmospheric Administration [NOAA] 2015). Authorized by the Oil Pollution Act of 1990, natural resource trustees—designated Federal and State agencies and Indian tribes—undertake NRDA studies to acquire the information needed to conduct these damage assessments. Working collaboratively with scientists, NRDA studies assess damages to natural resources including, but not limited to, marine mammals and protected species, corals, fisheries, and wetlands. The NRDA process for the DWH spill, however, does not assess damages to submerged cultural resources.

In addition to NRDA efforts initiated soon after the spill, the Gulf of Mexico Research Initiative (GoMRI) formed in May 2010 to investigate impacts from the spill on the Gulf's various ecosystems. Funded by BP at up to $500 million distributed over ten years, GoMRI's independent research program is investigating not only the impacts of the spill on the environment but on public health as well (GoMRI 2013). To date, no

GoMRI-funded studies have examined impacts to cultural resources, either terrestrial or submerged.

A Significant Information Gap

Few studies have been conducted to inform archaeologists of the potential impacts of an oil spill on cultural resources. After the 1989 *Exxon Valdez* spill, archaeologists documented the spill and spill-response impacts to archaeological sites. However, these studies were performed in Alaska, a region not analogous to the Gulf of Mexico, and did not investigate submerged cultural resources (Mobley et al. 1990; Haggarty et al. 1991). Focusing on terrestrial sites and those within the tidal zone, Mobley et al. (1990:101) concluded that the three primary sources of impacts on archaeological sites would be "1) chemical and physical impacts resulting from oil in direct contact with artifacts or features, 2) treatment methods employed to remove oil from a shoreline, and 3) human activities incidental to the actual treatment methods." Of these three, the one most likely to occur on submerged cultural resources during the DWH spill would be chemical and physical impacts from oil contact on the sites.

Studies have examined natural processes of wood degradation (Blanchette 2000; Kim and Singh 2000; Björdal and Nilsson 2008; Björdal 2012) and metal corrosion (Beech and Cheung 1995; Little et al. 2008) in the marine environment; however, few addressed how these processes may be affected by exposure to hydrocarbons (Ejechi 2003a, 2003b). In addition to focusing on how specific materials erode or degrade (e.g., wood, metal, bone, etc.), some studies have examined broader questions of how pollutants affect degradation of buried archaeological materials (Nord et al. 2005) or assessed the risk of 20th century shipwrecks releasing onboard hydrocarbons and other pollutants (Michel et al. 2005). Despite the information provided by these studies, it is not sufficiently understood as to how a major oil spill—and chemicals used to mitigate a spill—affect the natural processes of wood degradation and metal corrosion on shipwrecks and, by extension, the long-term preservation of submerged sites.

Oil in the Water and Deepwater Shipwrecks

There are several pathways by which seafloor sediments and the shipwreck remains embedded within them can be exposed to crude oil in the marine environment. First, oil released from the seafloor (natural seeps or a catastrophic discharge such as the DWH spill) could mix with water column particles to form a loosely aggregated material and sink to the bottom (Passow et al. 2012). Second, dispersants applied to a spill (at the surface or subsea) emulsify the oil into smaller droplets; the droplets mix with other particles or are consumed by marine organisms then excreted to form an aggregate material that sinks. A third source is through the controlled burning of oil on the water surface whereby the burned byproduct sinks or untreated surface oil weathers and the heavier petroleum hydrocarbons sink (Kennish 1997; Hassanshahian and Cappello 2013). A fourth pathway not previously hypothesized, yet encountered and documented during recent DWH spill studies (Camilli et al. 2010; Diercks et al. 2010; Passow et al. 2012; Montagna et al. 2013; Fisher et al. 2014; Joye et al. 2014; Valentine et al. 2014), is a subsea plume of an oil-dispersant mixture that was carried by deepwater currents and deposited patches of a flocculent material or "oiled snow" on the seafloor. Whether through a single pathway or combination thereof, oil and dispersed oil have been documented within seafloor sediments and deposited on deepwater corals in the Gulf of Mexico (Camilli et al. 2010; White et al. 2012; Montagna et al. 2013; Fisher et al. 2014; Valentine et al. 2014). As more studies publish their findings, it is becoming increasingly evident that the area of seafloor exposed to oil and dispersed oil from the DWH spill is much larger than originally hypothesized. Importantly, potentially hundreds of historic shipwrecks are also located within these areas.

Development of a Multidisciplinary, Multi-Partner Study

The Bureau of Ocean Energy Management (BOEM) and the Bureau of Safety and Environmental Enforcement (BSEE) are the regulatory bureaus within the U.S. Department of the Interior responsible for oversight of offshore energy exploration and development in Federal waters of the U.S. Outer Continental Shelf (OCS). As a Federal agency, BOEM is required by Section 106 of the National Historic Preservation Act of 1966, as amended, to consider the potential effects of its permitted activities on historic properties. On the OCS, historic properties primarily consist of historic shipwrecks. As mentioned earlier, little information has been available to adequately inform BOEM of the actual impacts of an offshore oil spill on submerged cultural resources.

As a result of the DWH spill and in recognition of this substantial information gap, BOEM funded and initiated a multidisciplinary study in 2013 to address these gaps. The project team is comprised of Federal agencies, universities, private sector contractors, and a nongovernmental organization. Scientists with George Mason University's (GMU) Department of Environmental Science and Policy are conducting molecular and microbial ecological analyses of sediment, microbial symbionts of coral, and shipwreck biofilms. C&C Technologies, Inc. (C&C), working in collaboration with BOEM and BSEE, is performing the archaeological analyses. Subcontractors to C&C include Montana State University (documentaries and podcasts), Droycon Bioconcepts, Inc. (corrosion studies), and the PAST Foundation (public outreach and education) (MBAC 2014; BOEM 2014).

Federal partners in this effort include the U.S. Naval Research Laboratory (NRL), who is conducting physical sedimentology analyses and corrosion studies, and BOEM's sister agency BSEE, who provided funding and participates in overall project management. The U.S. Office of Naval Research (ONR) provided support on University-National Oceanographic Laboratory System vessels through the NRL Platform Support Program. ONR/NRL funds allowed the project to utilize the Research Vessel *Pelican*, operated by the Louisiana Universities Marine Consortium, for two field expeditions in 2014. Other partners and collaborators include Deep Sea Systems International (*Global Explorer* Remotely Operated Vehicle [ROV]), and the University of Georgia (oil fingerprint analyses).

The Gulf of Mexico Shipwreck Corrosion, Hydrocarbon Exposure, Microbiology, and Archaeology (GOM-SCHEMA) project is taking a multidisciplinary approach to study potential impacts of an oil spill on submerged cultural resources and learn more about microbial community structure and function on deepwater shipwrecks (MBAC 2014; BOEM 2014). Microorganisms colonize all exposed surfaces in the marine environment, including shipwrecks (Huggett et al. 2009). As microorganisms are recruited from the surrounding environment, a biofilm forms, which physically and chemically modifies the surface of the shipwreck. A major constituent of biofilms is exopolymeric substances, which assist in creating favorable conditions for settlement of larvae for artificial reef macrofauna including corals, sponges, and mollusks, which later may attract epifauna including crustaceans and demersal fishes (Munn 2011). Microbial community structure and function and the role of biofilms in shipwreck stabilization and artificial reef formation in the deepwater environment, however, are not well understood. The composition and diversity of microbial communities in the marine environment is influenced by physical (e.g., depth, porosity, hydrodynamics), geochemical (e.g., redox conditions, substrate availability), spatial (e.g., latitude), and temporal (e.g., season) factors (Hamdan et al. 2011). Thus, the abundance, types, and functional roles of all microorganisms in a specific environment (microbiome) can provide information about the local environment as well as perturbations from contamination events. Limited knowledge is available on how impacts to microbiome structure, and by extension biofilms, affect the natural processes of wood degradation and metal corrosion on archaeological resources and whether these processes accelerate or decelerate after exposure to oil and/or dispersed oil.

Several questions arose to help inform and shape the project's goals and objectives: Were shipwrecks within the spill area exposed to hydrocarbons and/or chemical dispersant? If so, how did the oil/dispersed oil interact with and integrate within the shipwreck remains and surrounding seafloor? What is the role of microorganisms in wood degradation/metal corrosion and how do we identify long-term impacts related to spill exposure? How does spill exposure affect biodiversity and a shipwreck's, and surrounding seafloor's, ecosystem function over time?

As such, the project's goals were established to

1. assess the biological, chemical, and physical condition of the selected shipwrecks;

2. profile microbial communities using Next Generation molecular approaches to assess population structure;

3. profile coral microbiomes (those residing on shipwrecks) using Next Generation sequencing to assess population structure and compare with pre-spill microbiome structure assessed by other researchers;

4. employ a systems biology approach to understand microbial community interaction with the local environment (shipwreck materials,

physicochemical conditions, contaminants, etc.);

5. identify gene function associated with wood degradation, metal corrosion, and hydrocarbon metabolism to evaluate variation related to the spill;

6. compare the mineralogy and microbiology of rusticles to determine if spill-related degradation products are observed on samples from spill-impacted areas and to determine if site specificity is evident;

7. conduct short-term experiments using wood and carbon steel coupons placed in close proximity to shipwreck sites to monitor population structure of primary colonizers and biofilm recruitment as well as corrosion rates; and

8. identify and quantify temporal variation in shipwreck stability, degradation, and biodiversity at spill-exposed vs. unexposed sites (MBAC 2014; BOEM 2014).

To accomplish these goals, archaeology is paired with microbial ecology, sediment physical property analysis and geochemistry, coral genetics, field experiments, and laboratory mesocosm experiments to simulate conditions after the spill. Samples collected to inform the project include water, sediment, wood debris, metal fragments, and, where available, *Lophelia pertusa* coral polyps and associated microbiota. Additionally, this research project takes a novel approach to examining potential impacts through a multiscalar evaluation of site variation over time—at the microscale, mesoscale, and macroscale.

Microscale variation is evident in a number of ways by examining

1. the structure and function of microbial communities residing on and around shipwrecks;

2. their reaction to environmental perturbations from events such as the DWH spill;

3. the formation of biofilms on hard surfaces in the marine environment (e.g. shipwrecks) and any impacts to biofilms that can affect wood degradation and metal corrosion;

4. the physical and chemical properties of corrosion products (in situ and ex situ experiments and wreck debris); and

5. the physical presence of hydrocarbons and dispersants.

The importance of examining microbial communities for evidence of impact from contamination events cannot be overstated. Microorganisms are the first to respond to contamination as evidenced by changes in the structure and function of the communities present (Hamdan and Fulmer 2011; Hazen et al. 2010; Lu et al. 2012). Impacts are evident when previously cosmopolitan microbial communities exhibit a decline in biodiversity and shift in abundance of phylotypes associated with specific functions, such as hydrocarbon degradation or sulfate reduction. It is important to emphasize that they are likely the first communities to demonstrate recovery as evidenced by a shift in community composition towards a baseline state once contaminants are no longer present.

Mesoscale variations are the visible indicators that site formation processes—the biological, chemical, and oceanographic conditions—are at work upon the shipwreck remains as the site degrades over time. These variations can be identified through archaeological analysis of the shipwrecks and local formation processes affecting them. Identification of diagnostic features on hull structure that demonstrate observable degradation over time is an important aspect of any long-term monitoring program so that future efforts to document degradation at these targeted loci are informative. In order to provide this information, pre-spill data collected during previous archaeological investigations is compared with similar post-spill collected data. In addition, these post-spill data provide new baseline information so that, moving forward; archaeologists can monitor variation in site condition over time through future repetitive and comparative data collection efforts.

Macroscale variation within the Gulf of Mexico's deepwater environment is examined by comparatively analyzing shipwreck microbiomes—the entire ecological community of microorganisms inhabiting a particular body or structure—and the role of deepwater shipwrecks as hotspots of biodiversity comprising whole ecosystems (Church et al. 2007). For this project, scientists are analyzing the microbiomes of shipwrecks within and outside of the spill-impacted area to compare (un-impacted) reference sites with those in differentially spill-impacted areas. By comparing the locally influenced micro- and mesoscale changes occurring at each site, trends within the broader region, and long-term impacts on shipwrecks from the DWH spill, may begin to emerge.

Site Selection

In the Gulf of Mexico, more than 2,000 shipwrecks have been documented through historical/archival research and geophysical surveys, primarily those conducted for oil and gas operations in Federal waters. BOEM and BSEE maintain a non-publicly available shipwreck database and have conducted, funded, or participated in a number of archaeological investigations of shipwrecks in the Gulf over several decades.

Shipwrecks were selected for the GOM-SCHEMA project based on several criteria:

1. availability of pre-spill data for comparison;

2. proximity to the Macondo wellhead, the origin of the 2010 DWH spill (e.g., sites located within and outside of the spill-impacted area);

3. proximity to natural seeps that could potentially contribute hydrocarbons to the local environment;

4. hull type (wood or metal); and

5. water depth.

At least one wooden-hulled wreck (19th century or prior) and metal-hulled wreck (World War II-era) were selected from each of three areas hypothesized to be either "likely impacted," "potentially impacted," or "un-impacted" (Figure 1). Sites in the presumed "un-impacted" area serve as reference sites for comparison. By pairing sites according to hull material, water depth, and proximity to the spill origin, the team is able to comparatively assess how wooden-hulled and metal-hulled shipwrecks and their resident microbial communities are impacted by hydrocarbon and dispersant exposure.

Wooden-hulled shipwrecks selected for the project and their hypothesized degree of impact from the 2010 spill include Ewing Bank Wreck (un-impacted), Mica

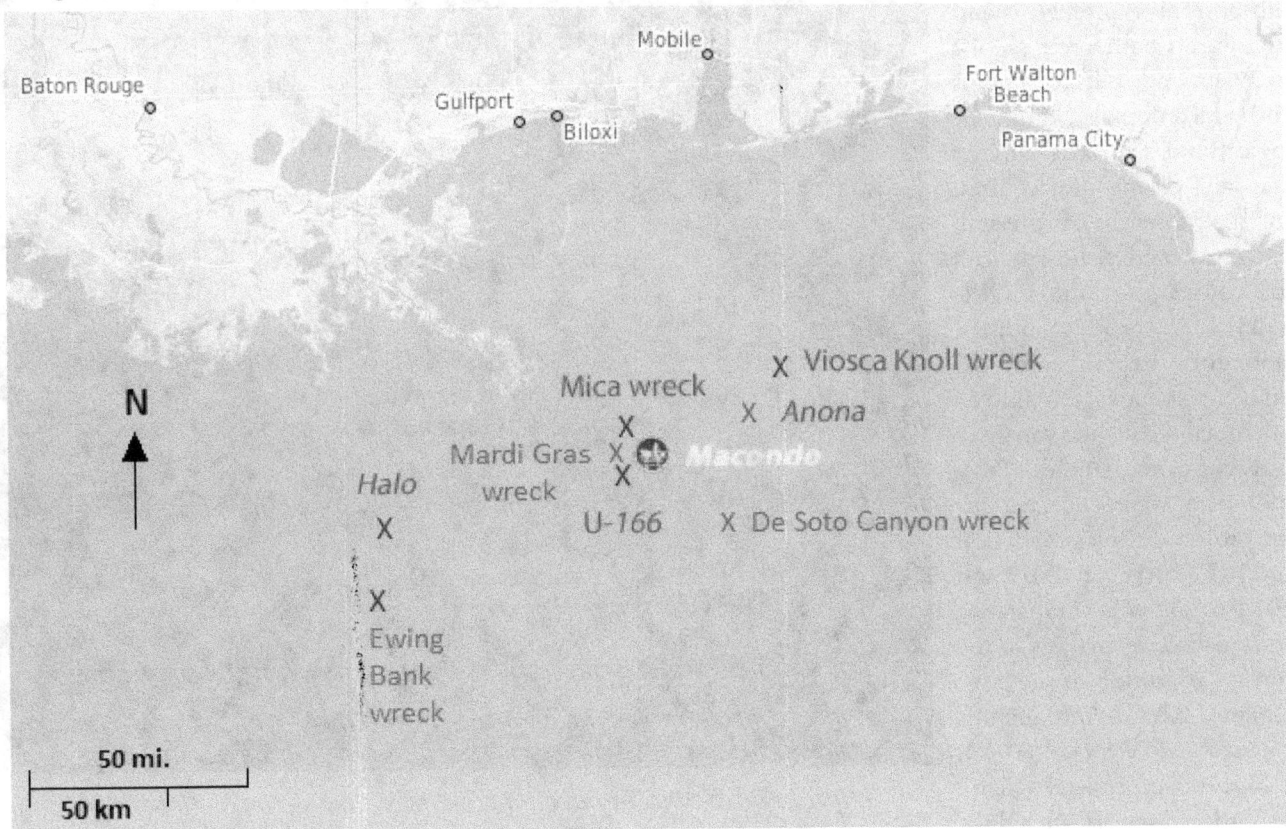

FIGURE 1. MAP OF THE GOM-SCHEMA PROJECT AREA. (MAP BY MELANIE DAMOUR, BOEM, 2014.)

Wreck (likely impacted), Mardi Gras Wreck (likely impacted), Viosca Knoll Wreck (potentially impacted), and De Soto Canyon Wreck (potentially impacted). All wooden-hulled sites date to the mid- to late 19th century with the exception of the De Soto Canyon Wreck, which likely dates prior to the 19th century. Metal-hulled shipwrecks (composed primarily of steel) and their hypothesized degree of impact include *Halo* (un-impacted), *U-166* (likely impacted), and *Anona* (potentially impacted). *Halo* and *U-166* sank in 1942 from World War II-related activity in the Gulf while *Anona* sank in 1944, unrelated to wartime activity. Water depths at selected sites range from approximately 450 ft. (140 m) to more than 7,500 ft. (2,285 m) (MBAC 2014; BOEM 2014).

Development of a Novel Approach to Study Impacts

Pre-spill data from the selected shipwrecks were collected during archaeological investigations and geophysical surveys. Geophysical data included side scan sonar, sub-bottom profiler, and multibeam bathymetry, while ROV surveys collected photos and video footage, and biological and sediment samples at a few of the project sites. In the absence of pre-spill biological and sediment data for comparison, the GOM-SCHEMA project utilized laboratory experiments and other methods to inform microbial ecological analyses and corrosion studies. Post-spill data were collected for the project during geophysical and ROV surveys in 2013 and 2014 to allow a comparative and qualitative analysis of the current condition of the project sites. C&C's Autonomous Underwater Vehicle (AUV), *C-Surveyor VI*, collected high-resolution imagery including side scan sonar, sub-bottom profiler, and multibeam bathymetry as well as photographs for compiling photomosaics.

In addition, the project is employing innovative technology and techniques to digitally record the shipwrecks using 3D laser and 3D acoustic scanning devices. The ULS-500-DR 3D laser scanner by 2G Robotics Inc., installed on C&C's AUV and designed for deepwater use, collects millions of data points along each survey transect to create a 3D planimetric view of the site using point-cloud software. As a supplement to the AUV-collected laser data, the team integrated a Blueview BV5000 3D acoustic scanner on DSSI's *Global Explorer* ROV during the March 2014 cruise to collect profile-oriented acoustic scans to fill in data gaps. When merged together, the resulting 3D models allow archaeologists to observe and document finer details of the shipwrecks that are not usually discernable using traditional remote sensing imagery (e.g., side scan sonar, multibeam bathymetry,

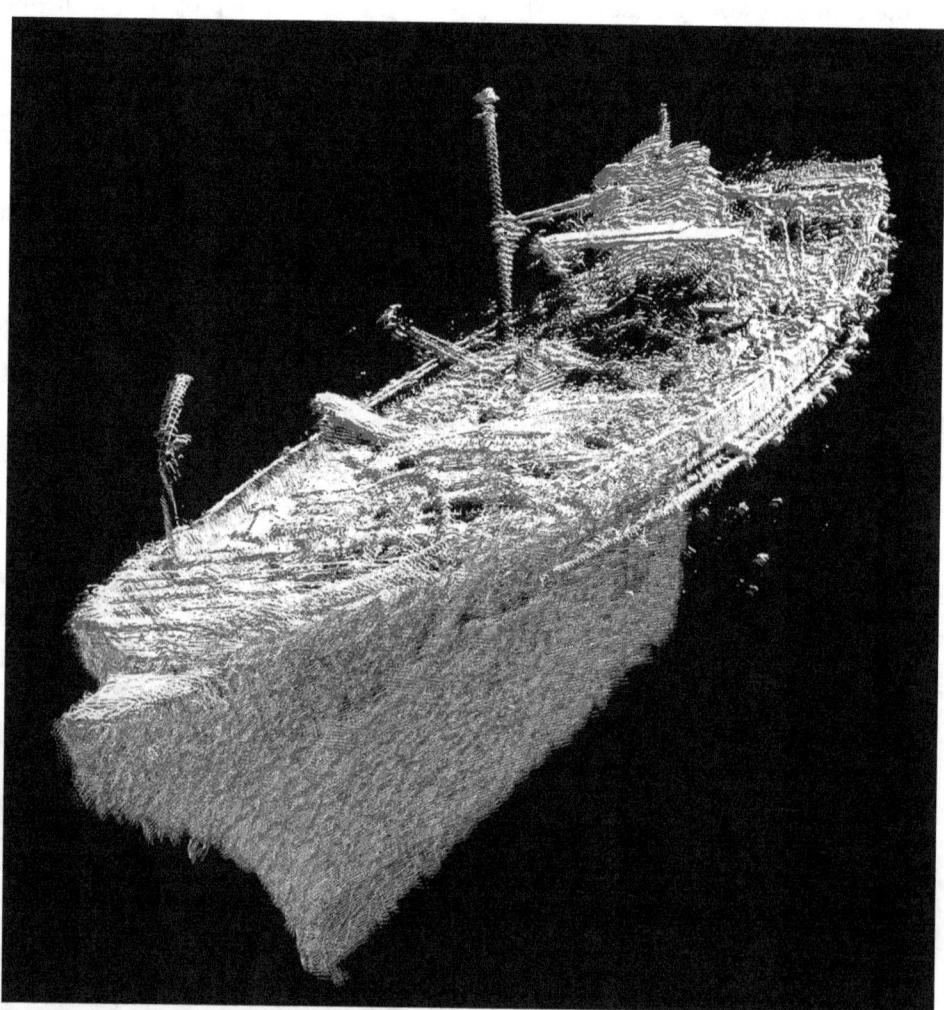

FIGURE 2. POINT CLOUD IMAGE OF THE STEAM YACHT *ANONA* FROM COMBINED AUV-MOUNTED 3D LASER AND ROV-MOUNTED 3D SONAR DATA AT 5-MM RESOLUTION PER SCAN. (IMAGE BY ROBERT CHURCH, C&C TECHNOLOGIES, INC., 2014).

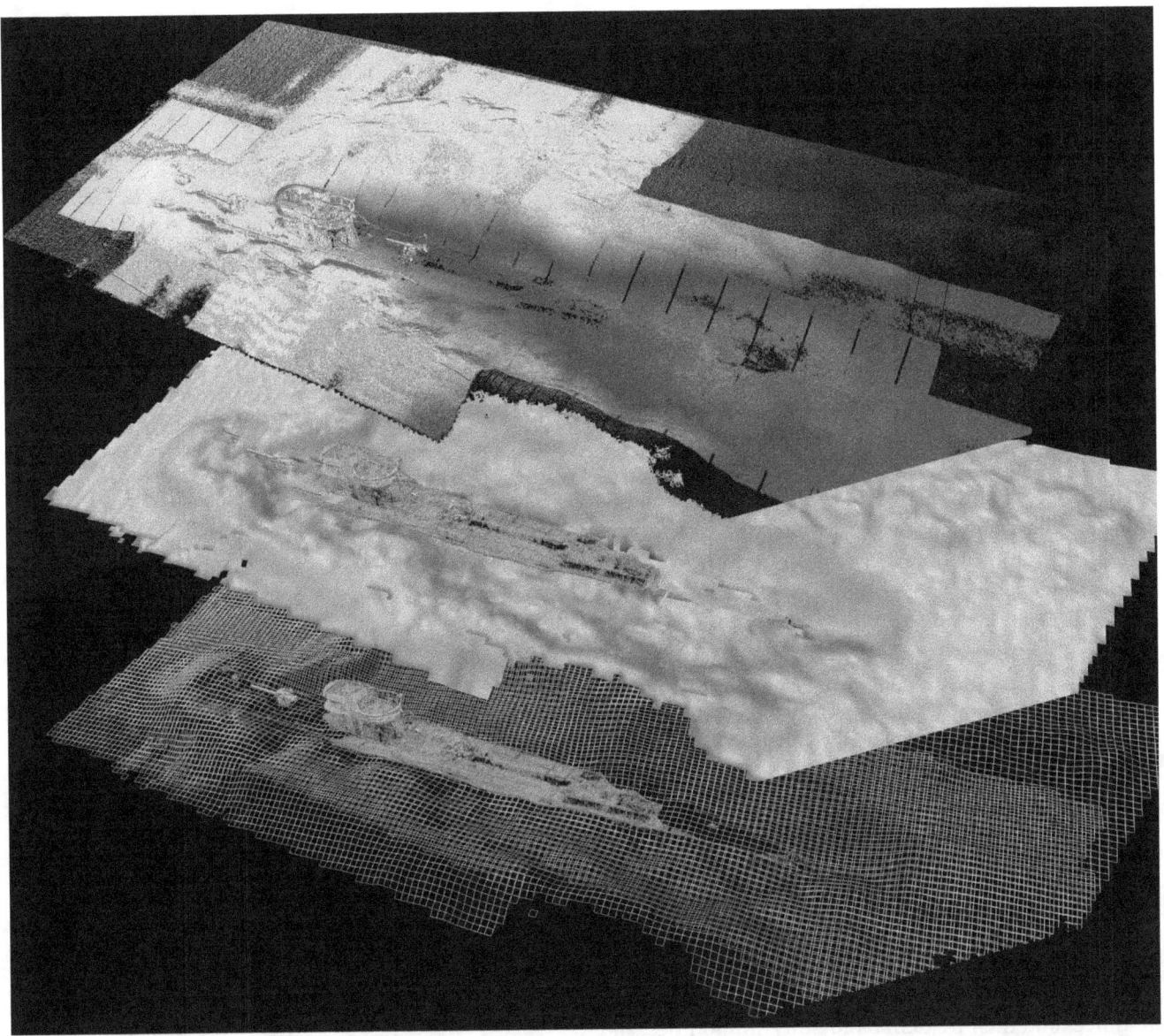

FIGURE 3. POINT CLOUD IMAGES OF THE GERMAN SUBMARINE, U-166, STERN SECTION AND CONNING TOWER. THREE PERSPECTIVES OF 3D LASER DATA AT 5 MM OF RESOLUTION (PORT VIEW). (IMAGE BY ROBERT CHURCH, C&C TECHNOLOGIES, INC., 2014).

etc.) (Figure 2). 3D models provide a valuable dataset for observing and analyzing variation in site condition, especially where degradation could be affected by microbial activity and exposure to hydrocarbons during the DWH spill (Figure 3).

During the March and July 2014 field cruises, the ROV also collected high-resolution photos and video to provide a visual record of the sites' current condition. Another innovative tool that enhanced archaeological analyses was the ROV's paired High Definition (HD) video cameras and passive 3D glasses, which provided a real-time 3D view of the shipwrecks. The addition of depth perception to the high-resolution video footage allows archaeologists to discern features of the shipwrecks and associated artifacts that were relatively indistinguishable in previous ROV surveys using standard 2D video.

Implications for Submerged Cultural Resource Management

The GOM-SCHEMA project's use of 3D laser and acoustic scanning to document shipwrecks is not novel in and of itself as other marine archaeology projects are utilizing this technology for documenting shallow water shipwrecks (Lake Champlain Maritime Museum [2012]; Rush and Söhnlein 2012; NOAA NMS 2013; Moxley 2014). Due to the extreme water depths within the project area, access by divers to manually record the sites in fine detail is not possible. Instead, archaeologists must rely on remotely sensed digital data to monitor site formation processes and degradation. What sets the GOM-SCHEMA project apart in this regard is the use of 3D scanning for *quantitative* analysis of deepwater shipwreck degradation. Archaeologists can measure and quantify degradation at discrete locations on the sites because of the data's sub-centimeter accuracy. With repeated 3D scans of these shipwrecks in the future, we believe 3D scanning will not only allow archaeologists to measure degradation, a process potentially affected by the DWH spill, but will enhance long-term monitoring efforts and inform adaptive management of submerged cultural resources.

In 2015, the GOM-SCHEMA team is completing archaeological and microbial ecological analyses and drafting the final report. Lab mesocosm experiments containing cultivated microbial communities sampled from reference sites are being subjected to oil, chemical dispersant/oil mixture, and dispersant alone to assess microbial response to these contaminants. A fourth mesocosm experiment containing an uncontaminated microbial community is serving as a control for comparative purposes. While many analyses and experiments are still ongoing as of the writing of this article, preliminary results obtained from sediment physical property, geochemical, and molecular biological analyses of cores collected from the sites are strongly suggestive of impacts from the DWH spill in the hypothesized "likely impacted" and "potentially impacted" areas. It is anticipated that the final results will further enhance understanding of oil-spill impacts to submerged cultural resources and their resident biological communities, and facilitate development of best management practices should future catastrophic oil spills occur.

References

Beech, I.B. and C.W.S. Cheung
    1995   Interactions of exopolymers produced by sulphate-reducing bacteria with metal ions. *International Biodeterioration & Biodegradation* 35:59–72.

Björdal, Charlotte G.
    2012   Microbial degradation of waterlogged archaeological wood. *Journal of Cultural Heritage* 13S:S118–S122.

Björdal, Charlotte G. and Thomas Nilsson
    2008   Reburial of shipwrecks in marine sediments: a long-term study on wood degradation. *Journal of Archaeological Science* 35:862–872.

Blanchette, Robert A.
    2000   A review of microbial deterioration found in archaeological wood from different environments. *International Biodeterioration & Biodegradation* 46:189–204.

Bureau of Ocean Energy Management (BOEM)
    2014   Gulf of Mexico Shipwreck Corrosion, Hydrocarbon Exposure, Microbiology, and Archaeology project (GOM-SCHEMA). Project webpage. Bureau of Ocean Energy Management, Gulf of Mexico OCS Region, New Orleans, LA. <http://www.boem.gov/GOM-SCHEMA/>. Accessed 5 January 2015.

Camilli, Richard, Christopher M. Reddy, Dana R. Yoerger, Benjamin A.S. Van Mooy, Michael V. Jakuba, James C. Kinsey, Cameron P. McIntyre, Sean P. Sylva, James V. Maloney
    2010   Tracking Hydrocarbon Plume Transport and Biodegradation at Deepwater Horizon. *Science* 330(6001):201–204. <http://dx.doi.org/10.1126/science.1195223>.

Church, R., D. Warren, R. Cullimore, L. Johnston, W. Schroeder, W. Patterson, T. Shirley, M. Kilgour, N. Morris, and J. Moore
    2007   *Archaeological and Biological Analysis of World War II Shipwrecks in the Gulf of Mexico: Artificial Reef Effect in Deep Water*. U.S. Department of the Interior, Minerals Management Service, Gulf of Mexico OCS Region, New Orleans, LA. OCS Study MMS 2007-015. 387 pp. <http://www.data.boem.gov/PI/PDFImages/ESPIS/4/4239.pdf>.

Diercks, Arne-R., Raymond C. Highsmith, Vernon L. Asper, DongJoo Joung, Zhengzhen Zhou, Laodong Guo, Alan M. Shiller, Samantha B. Joye, Andreas P. Teske, Norman Guinasso, Terry L. Wade, and Steven E. Lohrenz
    2010   Characterization of subsurface polycyclic aromatic hydrocarbons at the Deepwater Horizon wellhead site. *Geophysical Research Letters* 37. <http://dx.doi.org/10.1029/2010GL045046>.

Ejechi, Bernard O.
    2003a   Microbial deterioration of partially submerged service timbers in a tropical inter-tidal zone. *International Biodeterioration & Biodegradation* 51:115–118.

    2003b   Biodegradation of wood in crude oil-polluted soil. *World Journal of Microbiology & Biotechnology* 19:799–804.

Fisher, Charles R., Pen-Yuan Hsing, Carl L. Kaiser, Dana R. Yoerger, Harry H. Roberts, William W. Shedd, Erik E. Cordes, Timothy M. Shank, Samantha P. Berlet, Miles G. Saunders, Elizabeth A. Larcom, and James M. Brooks
    2014   Footprint of *Deepwater Horizon* blowout impact to deep-water coral communities. *Proceedings of the National Academy of Sciences*, Early Edition. <http://www.pnas.org/cgi/doi/10.1073/pnas.1403492111>.

Gulf of Mexico Research Initiative (GoMRI)
    2013   Investigating the effect of oil spills on the environment and public health. <http://gulfresearchinitiative.org/>. Accessed 2/6/2015.

Haggarty, James C., Christopher B. Wooley, Jon M. Erlandson, and Aron Crowell
    1991   The 1990 Exxon Cultural Resources Program: Site Protection and Maritime Cultural Ecology in Prince William Sound and the Gulf of Alaska. Report published by Exxon Shipping Company and Exxon Company, USA. Anchorage, Alaska.

Hamdan, L. J., P. A. Fulmer
    2011   Effects of COREXIT (R) EC9500A on bacteria from a beach oiled by the Deepwater Horizon spill. *Aquatic Microbial Ecology* 63:101–109.

Hamdan, L. J., P. M. Gillevet, J. W. Pohlman, M. Sikaroodi, J. Greinert, and R. B. Coffin
    2011   Diversity and biogeochemical structuring of bacterial communities across the Porangahau ridge accretionary prism, New Zealand. *FEMS Microbiology Ecology* 77:518–532.

Hassanshahian, Mehdi, and Simone Cappello
    2013   Crude Oil Biodegradation in the Marine Environments. In *Biodegradation – Engineering and Technology*, Rolando Chamy and Francisca Rosenkranz, editors, pp. 101–135. InTech. Published online as an open access book. <http://dx.doi.org/10.5772/55554>.

Hazen, T. C., E. A. Dubinsky, T. Z. DeSantis, G. L. Andersen, Y. M. Piceno, N. Singh, J. K. Jansson, A. Probst, S. E. Borglin, J. L. Fortney, W. T. Stringfellow, M. Bill, M. E. Conrad, L. M. Tom, K. L. Chavarria, T. R. Alusi, R. Lamendella, D. C. Joyner, C. Spier, J. Baelum, M. Auer, M. L. Zemla, R. Chakraborty, E. L. Sonnenthal, P. D'haeseleer, H. Y. N. Holman, S. Osman, Z. M. Lu, J. D. Van Nostrand, Y. Deng, J. Z. Zhou, and O. U. Mason
    2010   Deep-Sea Oil Plume Enriches Indigenous Oil-Degrading Bacteria. *Science* 330:204–208.

Huggett, Megan J., Brian T. Nedved, and Michael G. Hadfield
    2009   Effects of initial surface wettability on biofilm formation and subsequent settlement of *Hydroides elegans*. Biofouling 25:387–399.

Joye, Samantha B., Ian R. MacDonald, Ira Leifer, and Vernon A. Asper
    2011   Magnitude and oxidation potential of hydrocarbon gases released from the BP oil well blowout. *Nature Geoscience* 4:160–164.

Joye, Samantha B., Andreas P. Teske, and Joel E. Kostka
    2014   Microbial dynamics following the Macondo oil well blowout across Gulf of Mexico environments. *BioScience* Vol. 64, No. 9:766–777.

Kennish, Michael
    1997   *Practical Handbook of Estuarine and Marine Pollution*. CRC Press, Inc., Boca Raton, FL.

Kim, Yoon S. and Adya P. Singh
    2000   Micromorphological characteristics of wood biodegradation in wet environments: A review. *International Association of Wood Anatomists (IAWA) Journal* 21(2):135–155.

Lake Champlain Maritime Museum
    [2012]   Scanning Sonar System for Submerged Archaeological Sites. <http://www.lcmm.org/mri/projects/scanning-sonar-sloop-island.htm>. Accessed 5 January 2015.

Little, Brenda J., Jason S. Lee, and Richard I. Ray
    2008   The influence of marine biofilms on corrosion: A concise review. *Electrochimica Acta* 54:2–7.

Lu, Z. M., Y. Deng, J. D. Van Nostrand, Z. L. He, J. Voordeckers, A. F. Zhou, Y. J. Lee, O. U. Mason, E. A. Dubinsky, K. L. Chavarria, L. M. Tom, J. L. Fortney, R. Lamendella, J. K. Jansson, P. D'haeseleer, T. C. Hazen, and J. Z. Zhou
    2012   Microbial gene functions enriched in the Deepwater Horizon deep-sea oil plume. *Isme Journal* 6:451–460.

Michel, Jacqueline, Dagmar S. Etkin, Trevor Gilbert, Robert Urban, Jon Waldron, and Charles T. Blocksidge
    2005   Potentially Polluting Wrecks in Marine Waters: An Issue Paper Prepared for the 2005 International Oil Spill Conference. In *International Oil Spill Conference Proceedings: May 2005*, Vol. 2005, No. 1, pp. 1–40. Miami Beach, Florida. <http://ioscproceedings.org/doi/pdf/10.7901/2169-3358-2005-1-1>. Accessed 12 October 2014.

Microbiome Analysis Center (MBAC)
    2014   Gulf of Mexico Shipwreck Corrosion, Hydrocarbon Exposure, Microbiology, and Archaeology project (GOM-SCHEMA). Project webpage. George Mason University, Department of Environmental Science and Policy, Manassas, VA. <http://mbac.gmu.edu/mbac_wp/gulf_wrecks/>. Accessed 5 January 2015.

Mobley, Charles M., James C. Haggarty, Charles J. Utermohle, Morley Eldridge, Richard E. Reanier, Aron Crowell, Bruce A. Ream, David R. Yesner, Jon M. Erlandson, and Paul E. Buck
    1990   The 1989 EXXON VALDEZ Cultural Resource Program. Report published by Exxon Shipping Company and Exxon Company, USA. Anchorage, Alaska.

Montagna, Paul A., Jeffrey G. Baguley, Cynthia Cooksey, Ian Hartwell, Larry J. Hyde, Jeffrey L. Hyland, Richard D. Kalke, Laura M. Kracker, Michael Reuscher, and Adelaide C. E. Rhodes
    2013   Deep-sea benthic footprint of the Deepwater Horizon blowout. *PLoS ONE* 8(8):e70540. <http://journals.plos.org/plosone/article?id=10.1371/journal.pone.0070540>. Accessed 4 December 2013.

Moxley, Juliana
    2014   Explorers map Great Lakes shipwrecks with lasers, sonar, photo sleds and robots. Great Lakes Echo. <http://greatlakesecho.org/2014/11/11/explorers-map-great-lakes-shipwrecks-with-lasers-sonar-photo-sleds-and-robots/#>. Accessed 28 February 2015.

Munn, Colin B.
    2011   *Marine Microbiology: Ecology and Applications* (2nd Edition). Garland Science, Taylor & Francis Group, LLC, New York, NY.

National Commission on the BP Deepwater Horizon Oil Spill and Offshore Drilling (NCBPDHOSOD)
    2010   The use of surface and subsea dispersants during the BP Deepwater Horizon Oil Spill. Staff Working Paper No. 4. <http://media.mcclatchydc.com/smedia/2010/10/06/18/_Staff_Report_No._4.source.prod_affiliate.91.pdf>. Accessed 5 January 2015.

    2011   Deep Water: The Gulf Oil Disaster and the Future of Offshore Drilling. Report to the President. <http://cybercemetery.unt.edu/archive/oilspill/20121211005728/http://www.oilspillcommission.gov/sites/default/files/documents/DEEPWATER_ReporttothePresident_FINAL.pdf>. Accessed 4 January 2015.

National Oceanic and Atmospheric Administration, National Marine Sanctuaries (NOAA NMS)
    2013   State of the Art Sonar Map Reveals New Details of Sunken Civil War-era Warship. Press release, 11 January 2013. <http://sanctuaries.noaa.gov/news/press/2013/pr011113.html>. Accessed 6 February 2015.

National Oceanic and Atmospheric Administration (NOAA) Restoration Center
    2015   Gulf Spill Restoration: Damage Assessment. <http://www.gulfspillrestoration.noaa.gov/assessment/>. Accessed 6 February 2015.

Nord, Anders G., Kate Tronner, Einar Mattsson, Gunnar Ch Borg, and Inga Ullén
    2005   Environmental Threats to Buried Archaeological Remains. *Ambio: A Journal of the Human Environment* 34(3):256–262. <http://dx.doi.org/10.1579/0044-7447-34.3.256>. Accessed 7 February 2015.

Orcutt, B. N., S. B. Joye, S. Kleindienst, K. Knittel, A. Ramette, A. Reitz, V. Samarkin, T. Treude, and A. Boetius
    2010   Impact of natural oil and higher hydrocarbons on microbial diversity, distribution, and activity in Gulf of Mexico cold-seep sediments. *Deep-Sea Research Part Ii-Topical Studies in Oceanography* 57:2008–2021

Passow, U., K. Ziervogel, V. Asper, A-R Diercks
    2012   Marine snow formation in the aftermath of the Deepwater Horizon oil spill in the Gulf of Mexico. *Environmental Research Letters* 7:035301. <http://iopscience.iop.org/1748-9326/7/3/035301/pdf/1748-9326_7_3_035301.pdf>. Accessed 7 February 2015.

Rush, Stockton, and Guillermo Söhnlein
    2012   Manned Submersible Captures 3D Sonar Scans of Shipwrecks. *Sea Technology*. Arlington, VA. <http://www.sea-technology.com/features/2012/0612/3d_sonar_scans.php>. Accessed 5 January 2015.

Valentine, David L., G. Burch Fisher, Sarah C. Babgy, Robert K. Nelson, Christopher M. Reddy, Sean P. Sylva, and Mary A. Woo
    2014   Fallout plume of submerged oil from *Deepwater Horizon*. Proceedings of the National Academy of Sciences, Early Edition. <http://www.pnas.org/cgi/doi/10.1073/pnas.1414873111>. Accessed 2 December 2014.

White, Helen K., Pen-Yuan Hsing, Walter Cho, Timothy M. Shank, Erik E. Cordes, Andrea M. Quattrini, Robert K. Nelson, Richard Camilli, Amanda W.J. Demopoulos, Christopher R. German, James M. Brooks, Harry H. Roberts, William Shedd, Christopher M. Reddy, and Charles R. Fisher
    2012   Impact of the *Deepwater Horizon* oil spill on a deep-water coral community in the Gulf of Mexico. *Proceedings of the National Academy of Sciences* 109(50):20303–20308. <http://www.pnas.org/cgi/doi/10.1073/pnas.1118029109>. Accessed 20 December 2014.

· · · · · · · · · · · · · · · ·

Melanie Damour
Environmental Studies Section
Bureau of Ocean Energy Management
1201 Elmwood Park Blvd.
New Orleans, LA 70123

Robert Church
C&C Technologies, Inc.
730 E. Kaliste Saloom Rd.
Lafayette, LA 70508

Daniel Warren
C&C Technologies, Inc.
10615 Shadow Wood Dr., Suite 100
Houston, TX 77043

Christopher Horrell
Environmental Enforcement Branch
Bureau of Safety and Environmental Enforcement
1201 Elmwood Park Blvd.
New Orleans, LA 70123

Leila Hamdan
Department of Environmental Science and Policy
George Mason University
10900 University Blvd., MSN 4D4
Manassas, VA 20110

Reconstructing the Forward Crew Compartment of the H.L. Hunley Submarine

Benjamin Rennison
Michael Scafuri
Maria Jacobsen

The Civil War shipwreck H.L. Hunley *has been the focus of intensive research from its discovery in 1995. Since its recovery in 2000 and subsequent excavation, archaeologists have employed advanced 3D measurement techniques to document the submarine. The archaeological team has used traditional survey techniques such as photography and illustration to record the vessel, and, employed advanced techniques such as 3D point measurement systems, laser scanning, color structured light scanning, and photogrammetry to collect accurate, high resolution data. Through dynamic research in recording the vessel, a virtual and physical 1:1 reconstruction of the forward crew compartment section of the* H.L. Hunley *submarine was created.*

Introduction

Prior to the recovery and excavation of the American Civil War submarine *H.L. Hunley*, the question arose whether traditional archaeological mapping practices would allow for the accurate recording of its interior due to its size. The vessel is approximately 12.2 m (40 ft.) long and 1.3 m (4 ft.) high, with a maximum breadth of 1.1 m (3.5 ft.) amidships (Figure 1). Due to its size, shape, and compact nature, it became clear that traditional measurement practices such as; measuring artifact positions by triangulating points using a tape measure and known datums, would be difficult to achieve. In order to document the site, a strategy of 3D coordinate measurement was established. By creating a reference system from the submarine itself rather than from geographic world coordinates, a coordinate system was deployed to monitor the positional data of every object within the vessel and the geometric properties of the vessel itself. This was achieved using a xyz point measurement tool known as the Arc Second, Inc, Vulcan measurement system (Lytle 2003) and three-dimensional scanning to document the physical structure of the submarine, the positional data, and surface dimensions of every artifact documented (a system of coordinate metrology more at home with aerospace applications rather than archaeology) (Zou 2010). Once completed, the dataset collected became a 3D site plan capable of dynamically showing every artifact as excavated in situ using a stand-alone 3D CAD modeling software known as Rhinoceros (Green 2002, Watters 2010).

Background

The *H.L. Hunley* submarine was constructed in response to the naval blockade of the Southern states during the American Civil War (Wills 2000). The blockade, commonly known as the Anaconda Plan, was devised by General Winfield Scott and called for a stranglehold to be placed upon the south in order to prevent trading and free movement of troops over the contested waters (Hearn 1998). This in turn necessitated a call to action to develop new craft capable of usurping the North's naval might and the possibility of collecting high bounties for sinking naval

FIGURE 1. 3D MODEL OF THE H.L HUNLEY SUBMARINE SHOWING PERSPECTIVE VIEW WITH SAILORS AND INTERNAL COMPONENTS AND FRONT VIEW OF SUBMARINE POSITION IN WATER DURING OPERATION (IMAGE BY THE WLCC, 2014.).

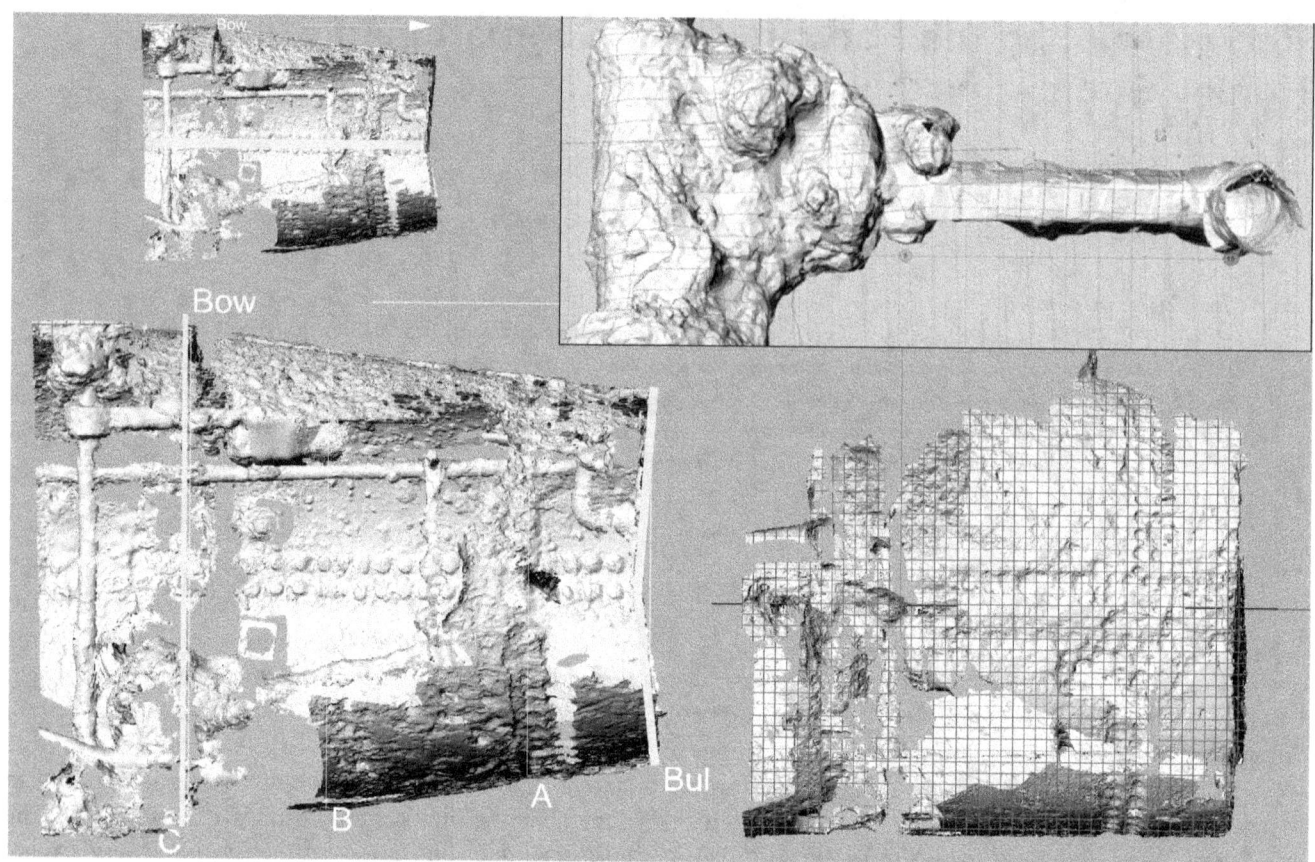

FIGURE 2. PLAN VIEW OF THE SUBMARINE SHOWING STARBOARD SIDE OF SUBMARINE. UPPER IMAGE SHOWS INTERIOR SEDIMENTATION AND LOWER IMAGE DEPICTS PLATE ASSEMBLAGE AND SECTION G1 (IMAGE BY WLCC, 2014)

vessels that were part of the South Atlantic Blockading squadron (Chaffin 2010). The *H.L. Hunley* was the third incarnation of a series of submarines designed and built by Horace Hunley, James McClintock and Baxter Watson for this purpose.

The submarine was constructed in 1863, in Mobile, Alabama at the Park and Lyons machine shop. During August of 1863 the vessel was requested by Confederate General Beauregard to aid the defense of Charleston harbor from the Union's blockading fleet (ORN Ser.I:1:14–728). The submarine arrived in Charleston and was put through a series of trials in order to prove its seaworthiness to General Beauregard. Sadly, it sank on two separate occasions with the loss of 13 crew members. The second sinking claimed the life of Horace Hunley and all crew onboard. General Beauregard, although dispirited, allowed the submarine to be recovered and deployed again with a new volunteer crew. The submarine was put under the command of Confederate Army officer Lt. George E. Dixon, an Army engineer who had worked on and operated the submarine previously. Dixon was convinced that the submarine could successfully attack and destroy enemy ships (Lee 1876). On 17 February 1864, under the command of Lt. Dixon, the 40 ft. long, hand cranked submarine sank the 1240-ton sloop of war USS *Housatonic* in a surprise attack aimed at breaking the naval blockade of Charleston harbor by ramming the ship using a spar-mounted torpedo sinking the enemy and itself.

The submarine remained lost for 136 years until it was located in 1995 by the National Underwater and Marine Agency (NUMA). The submarine was raised from the seabed in August 2000 and transported to the Warren Lasch Conservation Center (WLCC) where it was excavated, removing the remains of all eight sailors on board and their associated artifacts (Conlin 2005). To date, the vessel remains as one of the most intact Civil War era shipwrecks ever found (Neyland 2005).

H.L. Hunley Design and Operation

The vessel's hull is constructed from a series of semi hemispherical rolled wrought iron plates and cast iron bow and stern end caps riveted together to form a cylinder-like shape (Figures 1 and 2). It was heightened using expansion strakes running the length of the ship, attaching to end caps. The vessel carried a crew of eight sailors on board, seven of whom sat upon the port side along a long wooden bench where they were employed to turn a crank running through the center of the submarine to a stepping mechanism that gave motion to the propeller (Figure 1). The eighth man would act as commander at the forward end of the vessel controlling the direction and depth by operating dive planes and the rudder whip staff (Alexander 1902). The depth of the submarine in water could be regulated through the use of a depth gauge and by looking out of two view ports in the forward conning tower, sighting the water level in the submarine. Two cast-iron conning towers, each with heavy hatch covers provided entry into the submarine with rubber gaskets and hatch locking mechanisms to make the vessel watertight. Two water ballast tanks and pumps attached to the hull controlled the amount of water flowing into the submarine at each end of the crew compartment.

Excavation

The excavation of the *H.L. Hunley* crew compartment was conducted between February-December 2001. The submarine was excavated in a large holding tank and cradled in a truss-sling system previously used for the recovery. This meant that the archaeological team was able to drain the tank entirely to gain access to the compartment: a luxury compared to most maritime excavations! As the submarine was recovered mostly intact, access to the submarine was only possible if the vessel could be partially disassembled (González 2004). In order to access the submarine, four plates were removed (Figure 2). The newly opened interior of the submarine revealed interior sections of the crew compartment and internal frame ring stiffeners. These sections were given grid numbers (Grid 1-8) named forward to aft at points where internal frame ring stiffeners were placed, bracketing the position of each sailor under normal operation. With the plates removed, the extent of the site could be fully surveyed, showing that the submarine was entirely filled with sediment (Sharrer et al. 2001).

During the excavation, the human remains of all eight sailors onboard were discovered. Since many of the remains and artifacts were in close proximity to one another, this meant the accurate recording of the site was paramount (Hunter III 2007). To record the artifacts' positions during excavation, normal stratigraphic excavation practices were applied, slowly removing layers of sediment, identifying discernible features of remains and excavating around every object until its form was revealed and removal could take place. Next, prior to removal, the xyz point measurement tool Vulcan was employed. The Vulcan system operates by triangulating points calculated by placing a pole with a steel tip mounted to a sensor around key features of an artifact. During excavation and prior to removal from the site, every artifact was documented using this tool. As a rule, no artifact could be removed without at least three coordinates taken. This enabled the team to collect information for the virtual 3D-based documentation of each artifact and eventual reinsertion into the 3D site plan in Rhinoceros.

For the bulk of this phase (taking place in the interior of the submarine, grids G2-G8), normal excavation practices continued, revealing individual artifacts and human remains as they were uncovered. However, this practice was not suitable for the forward section of G1, as a perceived early hull breech (Figure 2) meant that much of this area was covered in sediment very early on (Neyland 2005). This lead to excellent preservation of the artifacts and human remains, in particular, the broad skeletal assemblage of Lt. George Dixon, the commander of the ship, including much of his torso and other bone assemblages were noted to still be in an articulated state. Correspondingly, in comparison to other members of the crew, the clothing around his body was also found to be in relatively good condition (Rivera 2010). For this reason the decision was made to excavate the section employing a block lift technique (Mardikian 2004). This meant that large composite sections of artifacts could be removed at once in a block and excavated within the confines of the wet laboratory at the conservation center. This provided the excavation crew with the luxury of time and comfort to conduct the excavation posthumously to the site excavation. The method worked well for the excavation and eventual conservation of artifacts; however, the spatial documentation of the artifacts within was not recorded as only the block lift's gross positioning were able to be accurately recorded whilst the block was in situ. The objects recorded within the blocks had settled over time and were not able to be recorded accurately within the wet lab using xyz point measurement. In order to determine the positional data for the artifacts within the block lifts, a decision was made to rebuild the forward section of the submarine's crew compartment known as G1.

Reconstructing the Forward Crew Compartment

The reconstruction of G1 involved both the creation of a virtual model using computer aided design (CAD) and the construction of a physical 1:1 model of the section. Using methods such as 3D modeling, 3D scanning, CAD drawing, illustration, photography, and model building, the archaeological team was able to create a faithful reconstruction of the control room of the submarine (Figure 3). To begin this process, an extensive collection of archaeological data had to be gathered from the project database. This data aided in the reconstruction of the capsule by capturing a moment in time during an excavation that had taken place ten years previous to the G1 study. During this time, it was important to highlight all of the artifacts recovered from the section to create the most complete picture possible of the submarine control room in situ. Using the archaeological reports, the extensive photo rolls and xyz point data, information was gathered to build a portrait of the crew compartment during excavation. The archaeological data collected illustrated an important phase during the submarine's excavation, a time when new discoveries were being made nearly every day in all areas of the submarine. The dataset revealed important information on crucial factors such as artifact positioning and stratigraphic depth at key points when important events were taking place such as the removal of human remains. The data also served to provide positional information for many of the artifacts, achieved by measuring known features within the images, such as scales or in the case when a scale was not available, an artifact could be employed to scale the image. However, traditional archaeological illustrations and photographs could not alone provide the level of information required to build a model including artifact positioning. A 3D site plan was employed.

Modeling the Hull

Since the submarine's recovery in 2000, a range of 3D scans and photogrammetric measurements of the hull's interior and exterior surfaces have been conducted to virtually reconstruct the hull allowing the shape and possible deformation of the hull to be monitored over time (Rennison 2012). The data used included laser scan coordinates collected using a scanning system prior to the hull plate's removal, as well as other scans of specific areas around the submarine. These include the interior of the G1 section as well as the comprehensive scan data collected during the hull's exterior scanning phase using a color structured light scanning system: Breuckmann OptoTop-HE (Watters 2010). For the 3D reconstruction of the G1 compartment, employing virtual data rather than the actual submarine would help to protect

 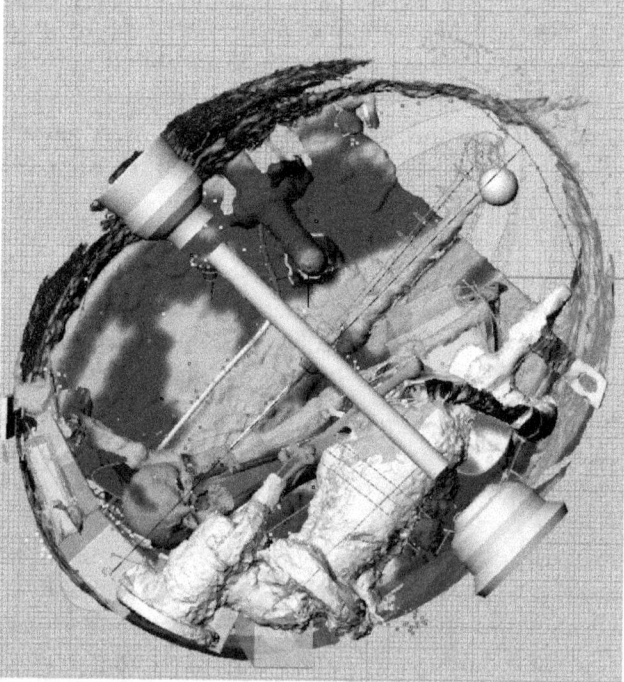

FIGURE 3. VIEW OF 3D RECONSTRUCTION AND 1:1 MODEL OF G1 FORWARD CREW COMPARTMENT (IMAGE BY WLCC, 2014).

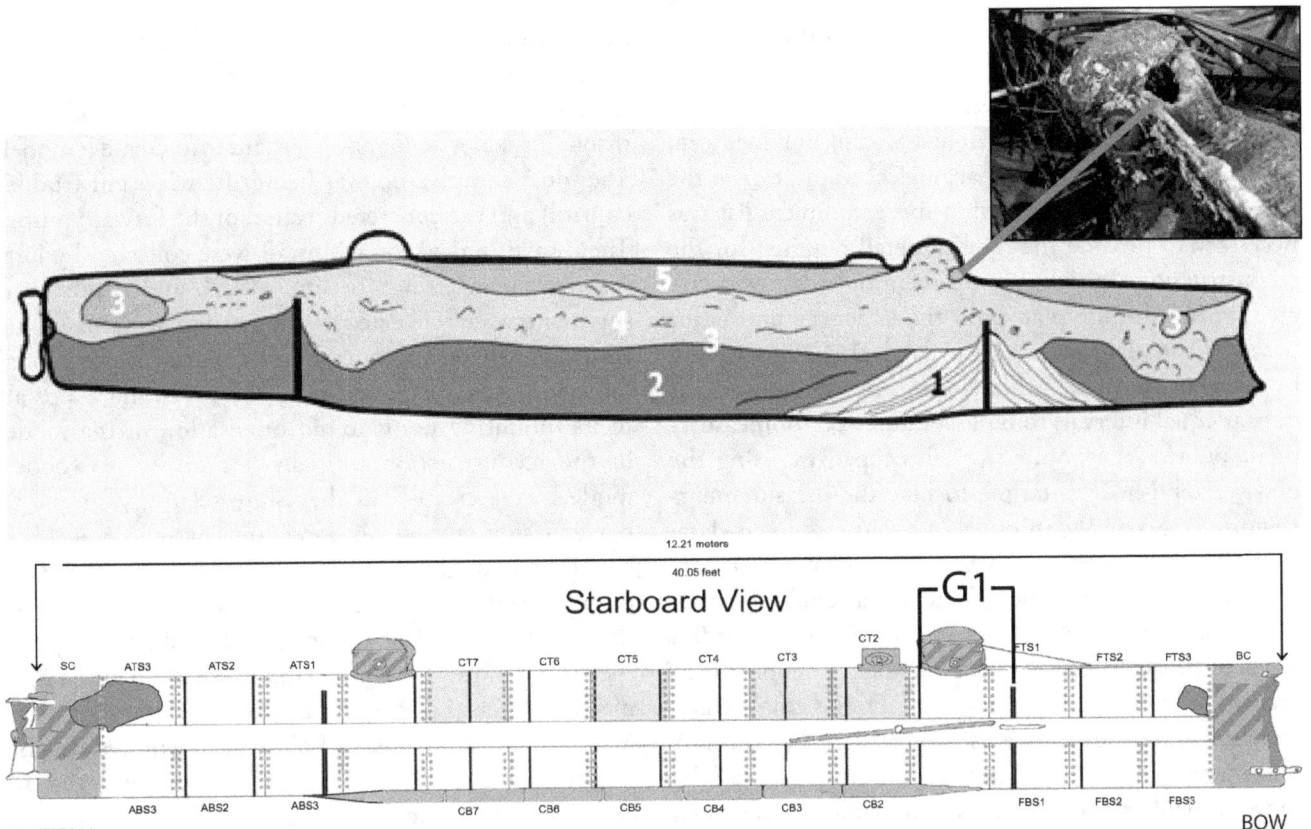

FIGURE 4. 3D CAD IMAGE OF THE DESIGN AND MODELING STAGE OF THE RECONSTRUCTION (IMAGE BY WLCC, 2014).

it from further damage and theoretically, the virtual site plan offered unrestricted access to the submarine for precise data collection and analysis.

The initial steps in the project were to fabricate a physical forward crew compartment section from metal to establish a focal area for the reconstruction as all block lifts, human remain models and artifacts would be placed within it. Dimensions of the hull section were collected using CAD methods for accurate point-to-point measurements. Difficulties, however, ensued when repeated point-to-point measurements had to be collated and differing measurements occurred. For instance, the positioning for a series of rivet heads was measured from 3D scan data collected at different periods during the hull's conservation. The measurements varied on average by +/- 5 mm from each other. Through closer analysis, the discrepancy was determined for two reasons; firstly, due to mesh inconsistencies in the 3D data created during the post processing phase from point data to polygonal mesh; and secondly, due to the nature of the thick concretion, ranging in thickness in this section from 2 mm to 10 mm (Byko 2001). To remedy this, alternative measurements from the physical hull were also collected that the 3D scanning system was unable to collect. This allowed for a type of datum system to be prepared in order to correlate measurements between the hull surface, virtual model, and reconstruction.

To assist in creating dimensions of the hull, a virtual centerline was created to base measurements from (Figure 4). Due to corrosion, the custom-made hull plates were concreted or degraded. This lead to variances in joint seams, thus a centerline was impossible to determine virtually. For this reason it was decided to create an artificial line to base the measurements from within the submarine itself. By identifying max beam and a horizontal position on the actual submarine, hull measurements were taken to correlate with the 3D data. Most importantly, this data was created whilst the submarine was in its recovery position; heeled over at an angle of approximately 45 degrees as it has subsequently been rotated to an upright position (Watters 2013). To counter these challenges, a plumb line was hung to establish a vertical plane and a photograph of the hung line was imported into the Rhinoceros site plan and established virtually.

Developing Contour Profiles

The next task was to develop a list of dimensions to build the hull section. An extensive list of hull measurements was taken by the archaeological team prior to the G1 project. Although useful, a more complete list was necessary to provide the level of detail required for the reconstruction. Initially, new dimensional data was created within the site plan from the laser scan and point based 3D spatial measurement data. This was achieved by creating contour profiles around the sections of 3D data at equal intervals to build a framework of measurement points. The points were developed by using the newly established centerline to take the measurements (Figure 4). Secondly, in order to avoid erroneous data, centerline measurements were taken on the 3D data at points with thin or no concretion at equal intervals along the x axis. Once the centerline was developed, a series of parallel lines spaced 2 in. apart were projected across the hull data. This created a 3D grid from which to base future measurements (Figure 4). The contours also served to act as outlines for building some of the more difficult shaped features and artifacts. One such example was the forward pump.

In order to establish optimum settings for the reconstruction, it was crucial to create an accurate reconstruction of the pump as a range of artifacts and human remains were discovered around or attached to the pump. Two pump designs were modeled. Firstly, one was made using data from the deconcreted pump and secondly, a reconstruction of a section of the heavily concreted pump was created. Next, artifacts requiring reconstruction using the contour method were created by using an artificial x,y coordinate projected down the length of each object and as such, each contour was printed onto paper at each section and cut out to the contour line to create a kind of ribbed framework to build the pump reconstruction from. Once completed, the prints were laid onto 2-in. thick modeling foam and marked out as profiles. Each section was then cut and molded to create a final shape. Once the models were virtually constructed and dimensional data collated, a blueprint of the section was created and a 1:1 physical model of the submarine was constructed (Figure 3).

Artifact Modeling

Next, the artifacts required to fill the submarine's forward section were created. The process involved the collection of 3D scan data, photographs, X-rays, and illustrations, and in some cases, to address fine points in the reconstruction process, actual artifacts were utilized for dimensioning. A number of the artifacts had to go through a series of iterations in order to create a model. The most complex object's being the whipstaff (rudder control) and the concreted section of the forward pump. The dimensions of the whipstaff were collected by lofting the actual artifact in situ. Width and depth measurements were collected by measuring sections of the whipstaff where no concretion was present. Positional information was gathered from the tip of the whipstaff to its mounting point to aid orientation of the model in the reconstruction. Initially a number of wooden models were created, as they were relatively simple to make. Using layered plywood, they were perceived to be strong enough to support the remains of Lt. Dixon found resting upon the artifact. However, once created, the wooden model of the whipstaff could not support the weight of the human remains models. Finally, a rigid metal model was created for inclusion in the reconstruction, which was capable of holding the required weight.

The second complex model created was the reconstruction of the concreted section of the forward pump. Access to the pump was restricted as it had been removed from the submarine and was in conservation in a bath of sodium hydroxide, meaning that the object had to be built entirely from scan data. To achieve this, a collection of polygonal mesh files were assembled and aligned to the submarine's coordinate system. Each of the scans was recorded during different periods of the submarine's conservation and reflected the changes in the pipe post excavation, removal from the sub, and deconcretion. Once the group of scans was aligned, this allowed for a system of datums to be established to base the reconstruction measurements from. The baseline measurement was taken along the length of the pump from its main cylinder to the end of the outflow pipe (Figure 4). This baseline stretched along all main features of the artifact, allowing for coordinates to be collected along its length. In order to provide ample spacing, the features were again measured by creating 1-in. spaced contours along the length of the baseline to reflect changes on the concreted pump section's varying topography (Figure 4, top right). Secondly, profile contours were collected perpendicular to the baseline to establish height changes between the stations. The individual profiles were sectioned in 1 in. stations and each position was printed from the side view to reflect to baseline coordinate and the profile of the contour outline. Next, the profile prints were used to shape 1 in.

sections of foam to recreate the shape at each contour. Once completed, the sections were glued together and the foam was painted for inclusion into the G1 model.

Artifact Positioning

As no original technical drawings of the submarine are known to exist, a series of blueprints had to be created to illustrate major locations of features and artifacts for the reconstruction. Using photographs, scan data and physical survey techniques, a series of drawings were created highlighting the features from oblique angles perpendicular to the areas being measured. The drawings were useful in transforming the data from the site to the reconstruction as they allowed for the clear depiction of the features by removing details such as the heavy corrosion and often dark, irregular surfaces. Collecting the information for the drawings also helped to understand the builders of the submarine, their thought processes and challenges they sought to overcome.

The blueprints also aided the placement of final artifact models. The measurments created were used to establish a series of key points to measure features from. The artifact models were also located using the datum coordinate system referred to previously. Artifact positions were measured within the site plan and corresponding measurment points were created upon both the virtual and physically reconstructed artifacts. The process involved the creation of at least three known datums upon each artifact as well as measuring the positions from each permanent datum within the submarine. Once the measurements were collected, the model artifact was placed within the model by triangluating the points from hull datum to model datum.

Conclusion

The artifact reconstruction of the G1 section is now complete, all relevant models have been created and a working document has been formed to facilitate future research. The next phase of the project is the insertion of Lt. Dixon's human remains assemblage and the development of the artifactual usage hypothesis. The collection of the positional information on the human remains is required as key positional data was lost during the excavation. To achieve this, the block lifts from G1 will be mapped from their x-ray and photographic records and the major remains requiring mapping will be measured and replaced in the model using a physician's skeleton. As shown above in figure 3, some of the remains are tentatively beginning to be placed. Note the position of the cranium and scapula above within the G1 model. Understanding the section is crucial to determining how the submarine operated and the potential reasons for sinking. This phase involves the collection of all of the necessary artifactual information from excavation data to historical usage information. Once the dataset is complete, the model and the virtual data will work together to begin usage hypotheses for submarine operation, navigation, sinking, and importantly, site formation processes post wrecking event.

The use of purely digital reconstruction techniques did not allow for the full interpretation of the G1 section necessitating the creation of a 1:1 model. This project relies heavily upon the application of 3D surface recording systems and 3D modeling software to reconstruct the site. The ability to virtually access a site has revolutionized the world of archaeology and allowed for greater interpretation in reconstructing shipwrecks. In the end, 3D scanning and modeling has made this research achievable and the tools available have provided insight into sites that no longer exist. Here, each instrument within the archaeologist's tool belt works in unison with the other, allowing for close analysis of a challenging site.

Acknowledgements

The authors would like to recognize Dan Dowdey for his 3D modeling work on the *H.L. Hunley* Project.

References

ALEXANDER, WILLIAM. A.
　1902　The True Stories of the Confederate Submarine Boats. New Orleans Picayune, 29 July 1902, New Orelans, LA.Byko, Maureen

　2001　Raising the Hunley: Archaeology meets Technology. Journal of the Minerals, Metals and Materials Society 53(3):12–14.

BELIVEAU, Y. J., FITHIAN, J. E., AND DEISENROTH,
　1996　M. P., "Autonomous Vehicle Navigation with Real-Time 3-D Laser Based Positioning forConstruction." Automation in Construction,(5)

CHAFFIN, TOM
　2010　The HL Hunley: The Secret Hope of the Confederacy. Hill and Wang, New York, NY.

CONLIN, DAVID L. (EDITOR)
    2005   USS Housatonic Site Assessment. Underwater Archaeological Branch, Naval Historical Center, Washington, DC.

GONZÁLEZ, NÉSTOR G.
    2004   Hunting Free and Bound Chloride in the Wrought Iron Rivets from the American Civil War Submarine HL Hunley. Journal of the American Institute for Conservation 43(2):1.

GREEN, JEREMY, SHEILA MATTHEWS, AND TUFAN TURANLI.
    2002   Underwater archaeological surveying using PhotoModeler, VirtualMapper: different applications for different problems. International Journal of Nautical Archaeology 31.2 (2002): 283-292.

HEARN, CHESTER G.
    1993   Mobile Bay and the Mobile Campaign: The Last Great Battles of the Civil War. McFarland.

HUNTER III, JAMES W.
    2007   People Power this Submarine: H.L. Hunley within the Context of Public Archaeology. In Out of the Blue: Public Interpretation of Maritime Cultural Resources, John H. Jameson, Jr., and Della A. Scott-Ireton, editors, pp: 204–222. Springer, New York, NY.

LEE, FRANCIS D.
    1876   Letter from Francis D. Lee to General Beauregard, 15 May 1876. Eustace Williams Papers, no. 3475-z, Southern Historical Collection, The Wilson Library, University of North Carolina at Chapel Hill, NC.

LYTLE, ALAN, KAMEL SAIDI, AND WILLIAM STONE.
    2003   Development of a robotic structural steel placement system. NIST Special Publication 263-268.

MARDIKIAN, PAUL
    2004   Conservation and Management Strategies Applied to Post-Recovery Analysis of the American Civil War Submarine H.L. Hunley (1864). In International Journal of Nautical Archaeology 33(1):137–148.

NEYLAND, ROBERT S.
    2005   H.L. Hunley: Recovery Operations. Naval History and Heritage Command, Department of the Navy, Washington, DC.

OFFICIAL RECORDS OF THE UNION AND CONFEDERATE NAVIES (ORN)
    1894 – 1922   The War of the Rebellion: A Compilation of the Official Records of the Union and Confederate Navies. Series I, Vols. 1–27; Series II, Vols. 1–3, Government Printing Office, Washington DC.

RENNISON, BENJAMIN, SCAFURI, MICHAEL, JACOBSEN, MARIA
    2009   The Alabama Yardstick: Testing and Assessing Three-Dimensional Data Capture Techniques and Best Practices. In Making History Interactive. Computer Applications and Quantitative Methods in Archaeology (CAA). Proceedings of the 37th International Conference, Williamsburg, VA, Frischer, Bernard, Jane Webb Crawford and David Koller, editors, , pp:?–?,. BAR International Series, Archaeopress, Oxford, England.

RENNISON, BENJAMIN
    2012   Photogrammetric Deformation Analysis of the H.L. Hunley Submarine. Paper presented at the Coordinate Metrology Society Conference. New Orleans, LA.

RIVERA, J.
    2010   Conservation of Lt. Dixon's pocket watch recovered from the H.L. Hunley Submarine (1864). Metal 2010. Interim Meeting of the ICOM Committee for Conservation, Charleston, South Carolina, USA, 11-15 October 2010,

SHARRER, ELIZABETH A., DARRAH, SUZANNE G.1, HARRIS, M. SCOTTI, AND JACOBSEN, MARIA
    2001   Marine Macrofaunal Analysis Of The Interior Sediments From The HL Hunley (38ch1651), Charleston, South Carolina. In GSA Annual Meeting, November 5-8, 2001.

WATTERS, CHRISTOPHER
    2010   3D Technology and the H.L. Hunley: Beyond Documentation. Digital Documentation Presidio, San Francisco, CA.

WATTERS, CHRISTOPHER
    2013   A Multidisciplinary Collaborative Effort to Rotate the H.L. Hunley Submarine. Paper presented at the 4th Triennial Big Stuff Conference –Saving Big Stuff in Tight Economic Times, , Ottawa, Ontario.

WILLS, RICHARD
    2004   HL Hunley in historical context. Master's Thesis, Texas A&M University

ZOU, JIHUA
    2010   Indoor Global Positioning Measurement System Application for the Aircraft Flexible Joint Assembly. SAE Technical Paper 2010-01-1857, 2010, doi:10.4271/2010-01-1857.

• • • • • • • • • • • • • •

Benjamin Rennison
Clemson University Restoration Institute
Warren Lasch Conservation Center
Charleston, SC, 29405
ben.rennison@gmail.com

Michael Scafuri
Clemson University Restoration Institute
Warren Lasch Conservation Center
Charleston, SC, 29405
scafuri@clemson.edu

Maria Jacobsen
Clemson University Restoration Institute
Warren Lasch Conservation Center
Charleston, SC, 29405
jacobm@clemson.edu

Oil and Shipwrecks: An Overview of the Sites Selected for the Gulf of Mexico Shipwreck Corrosion, Hydrocarbon Exposure, Microbiology, and Archaeology (GOM-SCHEMA) Project

Daniel J. Warren
Robert A. Church
Robert F. Westrick

In 2013 and 2014, C & C Technologies, Inc. joined a multidisciplinary team studying the impact of the 2010 Deepwater Horizon *oil spill on deepwater shipwrecks in the Gulf of Mexico. C&C's primary objective was archaeological analysis of the selected shipwreck sites for the project. The project includes 19th Century wooden-hulled and 20th Century metal-hulled shipwrecks ranging in depth from less than 150 to more than 2,000 meters. This overview of the project's archaeological objectives, the shipwreck selection process, and the historical backgrounds of the selected study sites establishes the basic framework for the project's archaeological component.*

Introduction

In 2013, the Bureau of Ocean Energy Management (BOEM) contracted C & C Technologies, Inc. (C&C) to perform the archaeological component of a multidisciplinary project examining the impacts of the 2010 *Deepwater Horizon* (DWH) oil spill on shipwrecks. Officially titled "A Comparative Analysis of an Oil Spill on the Biota Inhabiting Several Gulf of Mexico Shipwrecks", the project has since become known as the Gulf of Mexico Shipwreck Corrosion, Hydrocarbon Exposure, Microbiology, and Archaeology (GOM-SCHEMA) project (MBAC 2014).

Archaeological Objectives

The archaeology component of the GOM-SCHEMA project has four main objectives:

1. Collect, process, and analyze 3D data of hull features and associated resident biota from selected shipwreck sites.

2. Conduct systematic ROV visual surveys for comparative analysis with previously collected visual data.

3. Update existing archaeological site plans or produce new plans of the selected shipwreck sites.

4. Using these data, identify changes in site stability and degradation over time.

Shipwreck Site Survey Systems

To investigate the selected shipwreck sites, the GOM-SCHEMA team employed both Autonomous Underwater Vehicle (AUV) and Remotely Operated Vehicle (ROV) technology. AUVs are untethered, self-propelled survey platforms that carry a variety of acoustic and optical sensors. ROVs are tethered vehicles attached and controlled from a surface vessel via an umbilical cable. Like AUVs, ROVs can carry a myriad of cameras and sensors.

The AUV system used for this project was C&C's *C-Surveyor VI (CSVI)*, a Kongsberg HUGIN-style AUV system that has been modified with C&C's proprietary software and collection systems. For this project, *CSVI* collected data from the project sites using side scan sonar, subbottom profiler, multibeam bathymetry, a digital still camera, and 3D laser systems.

The ROV utilized for this project during cruises in March and July 2014 was Deep Sea Systems International's (DSSI) *Global Explorer* system. *Global Explorer* is a medium work class, electric powered vehicle capable of operations down to 3,000 meters (9,842 ft.) water depth and carries numerous recording and sampling systems. For the GOM-SCHEMA project, the ROV was configured with its standard navigations systems, digital and still cameras, 3D digital video system, and a 7-function manipulator arm, as well as project-specific integration of a BlueView 5000 3D scanning sonar deployed during the March 2014 field cruise to collect 3D acoustic scans of select features on the shipwreck sites.

Shipwreck Site Selection

BOEM and the Bureau of Safety and Environmental Enforcement (BSEE), the two bureaus that regulate offshore energy exploration and development in Federal waters, maintain a non-publicly available shipwreck database of known and reported shipwrecks in the Gulf of Mexico. Numerous shipwrecks are located near the DWH spill origin, several of which have been previously investigated by archaeologists. The selection of the shipwreck sites for the GOM-SCHEMA project was based on the following criteria:

1. Availability of pre-spill archaeological data for comparative analyses;

2. Proximity to the *Deepwater Horizon* spill origin (e.g. within or near the hypothesized spill-impacted area and outside the spill-impacted area);

3. Hull composition (wood or metal);

4. Proximity to potential natural seeps; and

5. Water depth.

Using these criteria and taking into account the allotted field times for each cruise; six primary shipwrecks were selected for the project. *U-166* and the Mica Shipwreck are located within the hypothesized spill-impacted area and near the spill origin. *Anona* and the Viosca Knoll Shipwreck are located northeast of the spill origin. Two shipwrecks located outside the spill-impacted area, *Halo* and the Ewing Bank Shipwreck, served as reference sites for comparison. Two additional sites were investigated during the project but limited data were collected in 2014: the Mardi Gras Shipwreck and the De Soto Canyon Shipwreck.

Site Descriptions

U-166

At roughly 8 kilometers (4.9 mi.) from the DWH site, *U-166* is the closest shipwreck to the spill origin and one of two wrecks investigated within the spill-impacted area. Lying in approximately 1,500 meters (4,900 ft.) of water, it represents the only German U-boat lost in the Gulf of Mexico during World War II. The shipwreck was first imaged during an oil and gas survey in 1986, but was not correctly identified and confirmed as *U-166* until an AUV-based oil and gas survey in 2001. During the 2001 investigation, archaeologists determined that *U-166* was sunk by the Naval Patrol Craft (PC) *566* in July 1942 shortly after the U-boat torpedoed and sank the passenger freighter S.S. *Robert E. Lee*, not by a Coast Guard aircraft as had initially been recorded at the end of World War II (Warren et al. 2004; Church et al. 2007).

Since its discovery, seven ROV investigations of the site, including two for the GOM-SCHEMA project, and several AUV-based geophysical and optical surveys have been conducted. In 2001, the site was initially ground-truthed using an ROV, which confirmed the identity of the wreck as *U-166* and provided preliminary data on site size and orientation. In 2003, the *U-166* site was comprehensively mapped during a National Oceanic and Atmospheric Administration, Office of Ocean Exploration (NOAA OE) funded project. This project better defined the site limits and documented over 300 individual artifacts (Warren et al. 2004). Another ROV investigation was undertaken as part of the 2004 DeepWrecks Project, a study funded by BOEM and NOAA and sponsored by the National Oceanographic Partnership Program (NOPP). This project delineated the southern boundary of the site and collected additional digital still and video camera data of the hull and bow sections (Church et al. 2007). In 2010, another NOPP-sponsored study funded by BOEM and NOAA, the *Lophelia* II: Rigs, Reefs, and Wrecks Project (*Lophelia* II), investigated the site a few months after the DWH incident. The 2010 ROV investigation examined the stern and bow sections, imaged the corrosion platforms placed on site in 2003, and collected sediment cores near the bow and stern sections (Brooks et al. 2013).

U-166 represents the remains of a Type IXC German U-boat. The site is oriented roughly north to south and is dispersed over approximately 7.52 hectares (18 acres) of seafloor. Within the site, there are three distinct areas of wreckage: stern, bow, and a debris zone. The stern wreckage is located near the site's eastern periphery. It consists of approximately 55 meters (180 ft.) of hull, encompassing the stern, deck guns, conning tower, and hull area just beyond the forward 105-mm deck gun. The remains of the bow lie near the site's western limit, approximately 140 meters (460 ft.) from the stern section, indicating that *U-166* broke apart near the seafloor. The bow section is approximately 20 meters (65 ft.) long and comprises the forward hull from the prow to just aft of the forward torpedo loading hatch. The area aft of the hatch is heavily damaged and twisted. Debris is scattered throughout the site area but is densest near and to the south of the bow. The 2003 survey's artifact distribution maps indicate the debris field originates approximately 300 meters (985 ft.) south of the bow and shows the path the bow took as it plummeted through the water column before impacting the seafloor (Warren et al. 2004; Church et al. 2007).

During the GOM-SCHEMA project's ROV investigations in 2014, high-resolution 3D acoustic data were collected over the stern and bow areas in addition to video and photographic stills, deployment of new corrosion experiments, and collection of sediment cores. The 2014 3D acoustic data was merged with 3D laser data collected via C&C's AUV, CSVI in 2013. Post-processing indicated that the 3D data's resolution is approximately 5 millimeters, the highest resolution ever collected over the site. The 3D data, in conjunction with the AUV camera and geophysical data, will be used to update the current site plan and provide detailed measurements of key wreck features. These measurements will be used for comparative analysis and to compile new baseline data for the site.

Mica Shipwreck

Located 65 kilometers (40 mi.) southeast of the Mississippi River's mouth, the Mica Shipwreck is the second project site that lies within the DWH spill-impacted area. It rests in approximately 800 meters (2,600 ft.) of water less than 25 kilometers (15 mi.) northwest of the spill origin. The Mica Shipwreck represents a 19th Century two-masted, copper sheathed wooden sailing vessel. The site was accidentally discovered in 2001 when a post-installation pipeline inspection within the "Mica Prospect" found that a pipeline had been inadvertently laid across the midsection of the shipwreck.

Since its discovery, there have been five ROV or submarine investigations of the site and two AUV investigations. The first ROV investigation occurred in 2001 following notification to the Minerals Management Service (MMS, now BOEM and BSEE) of an unanticipated discovery along the pipeline route. MMS archaeologists investigated the site to determine its historical significance and recommended a further data recovery effort at the site. The following year, in 2002, additional investigations took place using the U.S. Navy's research submarine *NR-1*. Over a three-day period in July 2002, scientists from MMS and Texas A&M University (TAMU) used *NR-1* in conjunction with ROVs to collect visual imagery and recover diagnostic artifacts from the site. In 2003, a team of archaeologists from TAMU conducted a four-day, follow-up ROV investigation of the site to collect additional information (Atauz et al. 2006).

The site consists of only the main hull and associated remains. There are no observed debris trails or areas of isolated debris outside the immediate hull. The wreck is oriented with the bow to the north and sits on an even keel. The hull remains measure approximately 20 meters (65 ft.) in length with a maximum relief of 3 meters (9.8 ft.). Several construction features including frames, futtocks, and cant frames are visible, although the site is partially covered by fine silt. Based on these investigations, the Mica Shipwreck is interpreted to be a 110–120 ton vessel dating to the first half of the 19th Century (Atauz et al. 2006).

The GOM-SCHEMA project's field cruises were the first investigations of the site since 2003. During the 2014 investigations, high-resolution 3D laser and acoustic data were collected over the Mica Shipwreck hull. The 3D data in conjunction with the AUV camera and geophysical data will be used to update the site map and examine changes at the site since the investigations 11 years ago. Additionally, sediment core, sheathing, and coral sampling were conducted and corrosion experiments were deployed on site. The findings from this assessment will be used as baseline information for comparison with future survey efforts.

Viosca Knoll Shipwreck

The Viosca Knoll Shipwreck is one of two sites that are located near the periphery of the DWH's spill-impacted area. The wreck is approximately 78 kilometers (48 mi.) northeast of the DWH spill origin, in more than 600 meters (1,900 ft.) of water. The site is a 19th Century copper-sheathed, wooden sailing vessel that was discovered in 2003 during a pipeline survey for Mariner Energy. Since its discovery, three ROV investigations and two AUV investigations of the site have been conducted. The first ROV investigation was conducted in 2006. In 2009, a second ROV investigation took place during the *Lophelia* II project. This project collected video and still photography, and compiled a photomosaic of the site. Project scientists collected sediment cores, placed short- and long-term corrosion experiments, and conducted limited artifact recovery (Brooks et al. 2013).

The site is tentatively interpreted to be the remains of a brig or two-masted schooner and is comprised of extant hull remains and outlying debris covering a roughly 188 by 67 meter (616 x 219 ft.) area of seafloor. The hull measures 37–43 meters (121–141 ft.) in length, with an 8-meter (26-ft.) beam and is oriented with the bow to the southwest and stern to the northeast. The hull is sheathed in Muntz metal and lists approximately 41 degrees to starboard. Because of this list, the starboard side is mostly flush with the seafloor, while the port side is exposed to the turn-of-the-bilge. The stempost is intact and remnants of the head rigging lie on the seafloor under the bow. Ship frames and other construction features, as well as other artifacts are visible in the wreck's interior. The aft portion of the wreck has been heavily damaged due to activities related to nearby oil and gas lease development. Only a portion of the rudder remains at the stern with a possible gudgeon strap lying nearby. On the wreck's starboard exterior, remnants of standing rigging are visible on the seafloor. Additional debris extends out 143 meters (469 ft.) from the wreck. Within this debris field is more rigging, a ship's stove, and a lantern. It has been hypothesized that this mass of rigging and associated debris were moved from the wreck site to clear an entangled anchor cable (Brooks et al. 2013).

ROV investigations for the GOM-SCHEMA project planned to return to the site during the two 2014 field cruises. During the March cruise, however, adverse weather prevented access to the site. The July field cruise successfully collected digital still camera and video data, collected core samples, and placed corrosion experiments on the site. In addition, 3D sonar data collected via ROV supplemented 3D laser data collected by C&C's *CSVI* AUV over the site in 2014. This data will be used to update the current site plan and to determine the level of anthropogenic impacts to the site.

Anona

Anona is the second wreck that is on the periphery of the hypothesized spill-impacted area. It is located 55 kilometers (34 mi.) northeast of the DWH spill origin.

Anona is an early 20th Century steel-hulled steam yacht. It was constructed in 1904 and was once owned by Detroit Industrialist Theodore DeLong Buhl, the son-in-law of Canadian Club Whiskey magnate Hiram Walker. This stately yacht underwent many transformations during a 40-year lifespan, finally ending as a cargo carrier for the Pan-American Banana Producers Association of Montreal, Quebec. In 1944, *Anona* foundered while carrying potatoes to the West Indies, sinking in more than 1,200 meters (3,900 ft.) of water. The site was first imaged during a 1995 oil and gas survey using a deep-tow survey system. At that time the wreck was identified as a probable modern crew boat. In 2002, following a site-specific AUV survey over the shipwreck site, it was determined to be an historic shipwreck later identified as *Anona*. ROV inspections of the site were carried out in 2002 and 2007 during lease development operations near the wreck site. Neither of these investigations were supervised by archaeologists (Church et al. 2007).

The *Anona* site consists mainly of the steel hull remains and a small area of debris adjacent to the hull. The hull measures approximately 43 meters (141 ft.) in length with a 5-meter (16-ft.) beam. It is oriented on a seafloor slope with the bow to the southeast and the stern to the northwest. It is upright on its keel but has a slight starboard list. The hull is constructed of steel plate riveted to steel framing. The bow has a sharp cutwater and a bowsprit support extends out from the stem though the bowsprit is no longer extant. In the forecastle area, a steam-powered windlass sits aft of the bowsprit deck bracket. On either side of the windlass are single davits that acted as catheads for deploying and recovering the two bow anchors. The forecastle deck aft of the windlass is partially intact. The entire forecastle area is littered with extensive amounts of debris. Near the shipwreck's mid-section is a single smokestack and possible boiler remnant. Aft of the stack, the deck is strewn with more debris and several radial lifeboat davits are in their original positions or have fallen across the vessel's aft deck. Another collapsed hatch combing rests between the deck frames in the after deck area. At the vessel's stern the deck planking has disintegrated exposing the internal framing and steerage mechanism. The propeller and rudder are not visible because of silt deposits around the stern (Church et al. 2007).

During the GOM-SCHEMA investigations, high-resolution 3D laser and acoustic data were collected over *Anona*'s hull. In addition, metal fragments and sediment cores were collected and corrosion experiments were deployed. The 3D data in conjunction with the AUV camera and geophysical data will be used to create the first comprehensive site map and provide detailed measurements of key hull features.

Halo

Halo, an early 20th Century steel-hulled tanker, is one of two wrecks that are outside the DWH's spill-impacted area. Located more than 165 kilometers (100 mi.) west of the spill origin at more than 140 meters (460 ft.) of water depth, it is the shallowest shipwreck investigated for the project. Built in 1920 by the

Bethlehem Shipbuilding Corporation, this 6,986 ton tanker had a length of 133 meters (436 ft.), a beam of 17 meters (55 ft.), and a loaded draft of 8 meters (26 ft.). On 20 May 1942 while transporting crude oil, *Halo* was torpedoed by U-506. The shipwreck was discovered in 2000 during an oil and gas pipeline survey for Pogo Producing Company. The only ROV investigation of the site before the GOM-SCHEMA project was conducted during the 2004 DeepWrecks Project. This investigation provided the first comprehensive visual data of the site. Structural features observed during this investigation allowed archaeologists to verify the shipwreck as *Halo* (Church et al. 2007)

The *Halo* site consists of the tanker's hull remains and a limited debris field directly adjacent to the hull. The wreck is oriented with the bow pointing south-southwest and the stern to the north-northeast. It is upright on its keel but has a 5-degree list to port. The vessel's bow is embedded in the sediment while the windlass is partially buried. The foremast remains extend into the water column from the forward deck. A section of catwalk, approximately 6 meters (19 ft.) long, protrudes from the sediment along the vessel's starboard side. The cable handrails are mostly extant, but no grating or wood planking remains attached to the catwalk frame. The superstructure and starboard side of the hull are intact but obscured by biofouling and nets that have become entangled on the shipwreck. The deck and port side hull between the main superstructure and aft deckhouse are severely damaged. Torpedo damage to the vessel's starboard side is not visible and is probably buried below the mud line. There is a breach on the vessel's port side aft deck and the aft deckhouse's main stack is badly damaged. Nets are tangled around the aft starboard quarter, and cover the stern from just forward of the starboard lifeboat davits to the stern starboard hawsehole (Church et al. 2007).

Visibility at *Halo* is usually low due to suspended sediments in the water column. The AUV surveys conducted over *Halo* for the GOM-SCHEMA project did not employ the 3D laser system because of the amount of water turbidity. Instead, the *CSVI* AUV's high-resolution EM 2040 multibeam system and the ROV's 3D sonar were used to map the site acoustically. This dataset provides the first complete image of *Halo* and is now being used to create a more accurate and comprehensive site plan. In addition, sediment cores and corrosion experiments placed on site will inform on the natural degradation processes occurring on sites such as this outside of the spill-impacted area.

Ewing Bank Shipwreck

The Ewing Bank site is the second of two shipwrecks located outside DWH's spill-impacted area. It rests in more than 600 meters (1,970 ft.) of water and more than 190 kilometers (120 mi.) to the west of the spill origin. The Ewing Bank Shipwreck is a 19th Century copper sheathed, wooden sailing vessel. The site was discovered in 2006 during an AUV lease block survey for Remington Oil and Gas Corporation. Since its discovery, four ROV investigations and several AUV surveys of the shipwreck have been conducted. The first ROV site investigation was carried out during the 2008 *Lophelia* II Project cruise. This investigation confirmed the vessel as an historic shipwreck and conducted a basic site reconnaissance that collected the first visual data at the wreck. The 2009 *Lophelia* II Project field investigations carried out a comprehensive site survey including the collection of video and still camera imagery, biological sampling, coring, and limited artifact recovery. This data was used to develop the first wreck site plan and date the wreck's sinking to the latter quarter of the 19th Century (Brooks et al. 2013).

The site is composed of only the hull and associated remains. There are no observed debris trails or areas of isolated scattered debris outside the immediate wreck area. The hull is oriented with the bow facing north-northeast. The wreck is resting upright on its keel but has a 7–10 degree port list. The wreck site covers a roughly 50 meter by 15 meter (164 ft. x 49 ft.) area and consists of three distinct components: the hull remains, the exterior port debris zone, and exterior stern debris area, inclusive of associated materials along the port and starboard stern quarters (Brooks et al. 2013).

The dominant feature at the site is the hull. The hull is extant from the keel to approximately 1 meter (3 ft.) past the turn-of-the-bilge and is sheathed in copper or Muntz metal. Portions of both the stem and sternpost remain intact. The hull is approximately 36.5 meters (119 ft.) long with a beam of 10 meters (33 ft.). The stem extends a maximum of 3 meters (10 ft.) above the seafloor. The list has exposed the starboard hull to the turn-of-the-bilge. The lower portion of the stem is still intact. Aft of the stem, framing, ceiling planking, and other construction features are visible along the wreck's interior. The ship's stone ballast is still intact in the vessel's waist but is obscured by silt. In the stern area, the remnants of a possible keelson and a stern frame are visible. The stern post is partially intact, however, the rudder is gone. A lone gudgeon and pintle remain attached to the stern post. Aft of the stern post is the exterior stern debris zone. This debris area is demarcated by an irregular sediment stain, observed in the AUV imagery, encompassing the stern area. Within this debris area are hull remnants, unidentifiable iron conglomerates, and intrusive materials. On the hull's port exterior, a low relief sediment berm comprises the port debris zone. The berm appears to have built up over time around remnants of the upper hull that collapsed onto the seafloor (Brooks et al. 2013).

During the 2014 GOM-SCHEMA field cruises, the Ewing Bank Shipwreck was revisited. Sections of the wreck were imaged with the ROV-mounted 3D sonar in addition to high-resolution video and still photos. Sediment cores and wood debris were collected and additional corrosion experiments were deployed. The 3D laser and acoustic data in conjunction with the AUV camera and geophysical data will be used to update the current site map and provide detailed measurements of key wreck features. These measurements will be used for comparative analysis, to compile baseline data, and to assess the level of anthropogenic impact at the site.

Additional Shipwreck Sites Investigated

During the July 2014 SCHEMA field cruise, time was allocated for the investigation of two additional shipwreck sites that were within the project area and potentially impacted by the DWH spill; the Mardi Gras Shipwreck and the De Soto Canyon Shipwreck. These two shipwrecks are not part of the primary study, but the assessment of the data collected from the July field cruise will be included in the final project report.

Mardi Gras Shipwreck

The Mardi Gras Shipwreck is approximately 15 kilometers (9 mi.) northwest of the DWH spill origin, in more than 1,200 meters (3,900 ft.) water depth and is within the hypothesized DWH spill-impacted area. The shipwreck is the remains of a wooden sailing vessel believed to have wrecked in the first quarter of the 19th century. The site was first documented as an area of interest following a geophysical survey for the Okeanos pipeline project in 2001. In 2002, a pre-lay inspection of the route by an ROV included an inspection of the debris area. This investigation determined the site to be a historic shipwreck. In 2004, during the DeepWrecks Study, the site was visited at the request of MMS archaeologists. This investigation collected video and still camera data and recovered two artifacts from the site (Ford et al. 2008). In 2006, a third ROV investigation of the site was carried out to document the wreck further. In May 2007, the TAMU Oceanography Department and Center for Maritime Archaeology and Conservation, in conjunction with the MMS conducted an 18-day data recovery investigation (Ford et al. 2008).

The site consists of artifact and hull remains covering a roughly 20-meter (65 ft.) long by 5-meter (16 ft.) wide area on the seafloor. Before the 2007 excavation, a number of artifacts were observed to be scattered across the seafloor along with limited exposed hull remains. Following the archaeological data recovery in 2007, scientists intentionally covered the site with silt (Ford et al. 2008).

The July 2014 investigation during the GOM-SCHEMA project was the first ROV investigation of the Mardi Gras Shipwreck since the 2007 excavation. During this survey, the ROV conducted a video reconnaissance over the wreck to document current site conditions. Because the wreck is within the hypothesized DWH spill-impacted area, sediment core samples and wood debris were collected for further testing. This data will be analyzed and presented as part of the overall project report.

De Soto Canyon Shipwreck

The second additional site visited during GOM-SCHEMA's July 2014 field cruise was the De Soto Canyon Shipwreck located just over 55 kilometers (34 mi.) southeast of the spill origin. The site was first documented in 2012 during an Archaeological and Hazard Site Assessment conducted by C&C on behalf of Shell Offshore, Inc. Review of the AUV geophysical data collected for this project revealed an oval-shaped target approximately 23 meters (75 ft.) long, 7 meters (23 ft.) wide, with 0.7 meters (2 ft.) of relief in more than 2,000 meters (7,217 ft.) water depth (Church et al. 2012). Since the 2012 discovery, there have been two ROV investigations of the site. The first investigation was carried out at the request of BOEM and was not supervised by an archaeologist. This survey collected the first imagery of the site and confirmed it was an historic shipwreck. The second ROV visit was during GOM-SCHEMA's July 2014 field cruise. Project archaeologists supervised a brief systematic ROV survey to determine site boundaries, document construction features, and observe material culture remains. Although, data assessment is still ongoing, the site appears to be the lower hull remains of a wooden sailing vessel. The data collected will be used to produce a site plan to guide future site investigations. A full wreck assessment will be provided in the final project report.

Conclusions

The GOM-SCHEMA project is a unique multi-disciplinary undertaking that has brought scientists together from many disciplines to study the 2010 *Deepwater Horizon* oil spill's impacts on deepwater shipwrecks. For the archaeological component of the project, the team utilized ground-breaking 3D mapping technology; including the use of the first AUV-mounted 3D laser scanning system in addition to an ROV-mounted 3D sonar system to acquire high resolution digital imagery. Data from these new technologies are providing new insights about the study of shipwrecks. Although the data analysis for the project is still ongoing, the final assessments will provide baseline information for future site management.

Acknowledgements

Study concept, oversight, and funding were provided by the U.S. Department of the Interior, Bureau of Ocean Energy Management, Environmental Studies Program, Washington, DC under Contract Number M13PC00021.

The authors would like thank BOEM and BSEE for the opportunity to be part of this project and C & C Technologies, Inc. for the support to pursue this research.

References

Atauz, A.D., W. Bryant, T. Jones and B. Phaneuf
    2006   *Mica shipwreck project: Deepwater archaeological investigations of a 19th century shipwreck in the Gulf of Mexico.* U.S. Dept. of the Interior, Minerals Management Service. Gulf of Mexico OCS Region. New Orleans, LA. OCS Study MMS 2006-072. 116pp.

Brooks, J.M., C. Fisher, H. Roberts, E. Cordes, I. Baums, B. Bernard, R. Church, P. Etnoyer, C. German, E. Goehring, I. McDonald, Harry Roberts, T. Shank, D. Warren, S. Welsh, G. Wolff.
    2013. Exploration and research of northern Gulf of Mexico deepwater natural and artificial hard-bottom habitats with emphasis on coral communities: Reefs, rigs, and wrecks—"Lophelia II" Final report. U.S. Dept. of the Interior, Bureau of Ocean Energy Management, Gulf of Mexico OCS Region, New Orleans, LA. OCS Study BOEM 2013, In Press.

Church R., Baker C.
    2012 Archaeological and Hazard Site Assessment, DeSoto Canyon Area, Gulf of Mexico. Oil and Gas Survey report for Shell Offshore, Inc. C & C Technologies, Inc. Lafayette, LA. 2011.

Church, R., D. Warren, R. Cullimore, L. Johnston, M. Kilgour, J. Moore, N. Morris, W. Patterson, W. Schroeder, and T. Shirley.
    2007. Archaeological and Biological Analysis of World War II Shipwrecks in the Gulf of Mexico: Artificial Reef Effect in Deep Water. U.S. Dept. of the Interior, Minerals Management Service, Gulf of Mexico OCS Region, New Orleans, LA. OCS Study MMS 2007-015. 373 pp.

Ford, B., A. Borgens, W. Bryant, D. Marshall, P. Hitchcock, C. Arias, and D. Hamilton
    2008 Archaeological excavation of the Mardi Gras Shipwreck (16GM01), Gulf of Mexico continental slope. Prepared by Texas A&M University. U.S. Dept. of the Interior, Minerals Management Service, Gulf of Mexico OCS Region, New Orleans, LA. OCS Report MMS 2008-037. 313pp.

Microbiome Analysis Center (MBAC)
    2014 Gulf of Mexico Shipwreck Corrosion, Hydrocarbon Exposure, Microbiology, and Archaeology project (GOM-SCHEMA). Project webpage. George Mason University, Department of Environmental Science and Policy, Manassas, VA. <http://mbac.gmu.edu/mbac_wp/gulf_wrecks/>. Accessed 5 January 2015.

Warren, D. J., R. A. Church, R. Cullimore, L. Johnston.
    2004. ROV Investigations of The DKM *U-166* Shipwreck Site to Document the Archaeological and Biological Aspects of the Wreck Site: Final Performance Report. U.S. Department of Commerce, National Oceanic and Atmospheric Administration, Office of Ocean Exploration. Silver Spring, Maryland.

• • • • • • • • • • • • • •

Daniel J. Warren
C & C Technologies, Inc.
10615 Shadow Wood Dr. Suite 100
Houston, TX 77043

Robert A. Church
C & C Technologies, Inc.
730 E. Kaliste Saloom Rd.
Lafayette, LA 70508

Robert F. Westrick
C & C Technologies, Inc.
730 E. Kaliste Saloom Rd.
Lafayette, LA 70508

The Search for the Lost French Fleet of 1565: Results of the 2014 Survey

Chuck Meide

In July 2014, LAMP launched a search for the lost colonization vessels of Jean Ribault. These were re-supply ships intended for the struggling French colony at Fort Caroline in present-day Jacksonville, Florida. After an abortive attack on rival Spanish forces, they were shipwrecked by a sudden storm in September 1565. LAMP archaeologists conducted geophysical survey and diver testing in Canaveral National Seashore waters. This paper summarizes the methodology and results of the project, which coincides with the 450th anniversary of this pivotal event and the subsequent founding of St. Augustine, the oldest continually occupied European settlement in the U.S.A.

Introduction

In the mid-16th century France was eager to assert her claim to the New World, both to seize the opportunity for material wealth and increased commerce, and to ease religious tensions at home by providing a refuge for Protestant Huguenots (Bennett 2001:13). A series of fleets were sent to colonize the wilderness of La Floride starting in 1562, alternatively lead by Jean Ribault and René de Laudonnière (Ribault 1964; Laudonnière 2001; McGrath 2000; Bennett 2001; Meide and de Bry 2014). The promising start at La Caroline on the River of May (present-day St. Johns River at Jacksonville, Florida) (Figure 1) would come to a bloody endgame shortly after Ribault's 1565 arrival with a re-supply fleet, as the stage was set for a decisive conflict between France and Spain. With the aid of a fierce storm that would destroy Ribault's four largest ships, rival Spanish forces lead by Pedro Menéndez would deal the death blow to France's dream of Florida conquest.

Four hundred fifty years later, the Lighthouse Archaeological Maritime Program (LAMP), the research arm of the St. Augustine Lighthouse & Museum, organized an archaeological search for the lost French ships (Meide 2012; de Bry and Meide 2014; Meide and de Bry 2014, Meide et al. 2015). In anticipation of the 450th anniversary of the founding of St. Augustine and the loss of the fleet, and with funds provided by the State of Florida and NOAA's Office of Ocean Exploration and Research (OER), LAMP partnered with the Center for Historical Archaeology (CHA), the Institute of Maritime History (IMH), and the National Park Service (NPS) to lead an expedition in July and August 2014. The objective of the project was to explore, using geophysical devices and diver investigations, a section of the coast in an effort to identify one or more of Ribault's lost ships. The search area, in Canaveral National Seashore (CANA) waters, was selected because of its proximity to a series of terrestrial archaeological sites associated with the 1565 shipwreck survivors (Meide and de Bry 2014:82-87).

This paper presents an overview of the 2014 survey, summarizing the objectives, methodology, and results of fieldwork carried out between 14 July and 18 August. A total of 175 line miles (324.1 km) of survey was completed, covering the entire survey area that the research vessel could access, leaving only the shallowest surf zone unsurveyed. Data analysis produced a wide array of magnetic anomalies, but few sonar contacts of interest. Diver testing was implemented with a hydraulic probe, followed by dredge excavation in one case. Divers completed more than 300 probes at the three most promising targets. At two of these targets modern wreckage was found, apparently associated with shrimp trawling vessels. While no historic shipwreck remains were identified, there remain a number of other potential targets that can be tested in future phases of this project.

Colony and Conflict in Florida, 1562-1565

After a disastrous 1562 attempt to found a colony at present-day Parris Island, South Carolina, religious war in France delayed any further colonization attempts until 1564 (Meide and de Bry 2014:79). In June of that year, a force of 300 French men and women, mostly Protestant Huguenots, founded the colony La Caroline (known colloquially today as "Fort Caroline") on the River May (Figure 1). The nascent colony was struggling by the summer of 1565. With food supplies exhausted, increasingly hostile Indians, and the requested re-supply fleet nowhere in sight, Laudonnière—who had already faced two mutinies—made the decision to abandon the colony. No sooner had the settlers been loaded onto the two remaining vessels than a fleet arrived, on 28 August.

FIGURE 1. BROAD PERSPECTIVE VIEW OF THE NORTHEAST FLORIDA REGION SHOWING GEOGRAPHIC FEATURES AND SIXTEENTH-CENTURY SETTLEMENT LOCATIONS MENTIONED IN THE TEXT. THE SURVEY AREA MEASURES 5.0 BY 0.4 NAUTICAL MILES (9.26 BY 0.75 KM) AND IS LOCATED ABOUT MIDWAY BETWEEN CAPE CANAVERAL AND PONCE INLET, IN CANAVERAL NATIONAL SEASHORE WATERS. ITS EXACT LOCATION IS NOT SHOWN TO HELP PROTECT THE ADJACENT SHIPWRECK SURVIVOR CAMP ARCHAEOLOGICAL SITES. VIEW IS FACING NORTH (GRAPHIC BY BRENDAN BURKE AND CHUCK MEIDE, COURTESY OF LAMP, 2015).

Ribault had finally returned with the promised re-supply fleet.

Ribault brought with him seven ships with armament, munitions, supplies, livestock, 500 soldiers, and perhaps 500 more seamen and colonists (Lyon 1976:68). However, in close pursuit behind him came Menéndez, with orders from King Philip II to eradicate the French and found a Spanish settlement. Menéndez brought a force comparable to Ribault's, with five ships and 500 soldiers, 200 sailors, and 100 settlers (Lyon 1976:114). The two fleets met only seven days later, on 4 September, and after a brief skirmish the Spanish retreated to the next inlet to the south to hurriedly fortify a position at what is now St. Augustine (Figure 1).

Ribault made a bold decision to launch a pre-emptive strike before the Spanish could entrench themselves. He set sail for St. Augustine with his four largest ships—which had never unloaded the bulk of their supplies—and some 400 soldiers and 200 sailors. At dawn on 10 September the French fleet almost caught Menéndez, who was just able to cross the bar and make landfall. As the French ships were too large to follow, there was a brief stalemate, but within a day a tremendous storm struck. The fateful storm doomed the French colony. Ribault's ships were blown south, where they were all shipwrecked, and Menéndez marched a force north and sacked Fort Caroline. When the beleaguered shipwrecked survivors eventually made their way north, they were intercepted around Matanzas Inlet by Menéndez and famously put to the knife (Lyon 1976:126-128; McGrath 2000:148-155; Griffin 2001).

A more detailed account of the French colonization attempt and the four ships in Ribault's fleet, including transcriptions of surviving cargo manifests, is presented in Meide and de Bry 2014.

Survey Area

The Canaveral National Seashore is the fifth-largest NPS property in Florida, with 57,626 acres along the Intracoastal Waterway and Atlantic Ocean, stretching almost the entire distance from Ponce Inlet to Cape Canaveral (Figure 1). Its eastern boundary extends 0.5 miles (0.80 km) to sea.

While several previous attempts have been made to find Ribault's ships on the beach using geophysical devices (Brewer et al. 1998; Lundin 1999; Lundin et al. 2001; Lawson 2004), no attempt has been made to search for these shipwrecks in the marine environment. The most recent NPS investigation, in April 2004, involved magnetometry, metal detecting, and subsurface testing carried out in some cases immediately adjacent to the 2014 survey area, though only modern materials were unearthed (Lawson 2004).

The area chosen for survey in 2014 was adjacent to a group of archaeological sites, primarily the Armstrong or Oyster Bay Site (8VO3128 or CANA-73), which have been identified as one or more shipwreck survivors' camps associated with the 1565 shipwrecks (Armstrong 2001; Brewer and Horvath 2004; Algoet et al. 2014:199-201, 205; Meide and de Bry 2014:82-87). It is assumed that the survivor camps would be located in relatively close proximity to one or more of the shipwrecks, a correlation that has been demonstrated by Gibbs (2003:132). Researchers selected a search area measuring 5 nautical miles (9.26 km) in length and extending seawards from the beach about 0.4 nautical miles (0.75 km.), centered roughly on the Armstrong Site. Because this area was within NPS jurisdiction, fieldwork was carried out under a U.S. Department of Interior Permit for Archaeological Investigations (CANA 2014-001).

Project Schedule

In order to maximize working time in the survey area, especially considering the prevalence of afternoon thunderstorms in the region, a schedule of three successive liveaboard cruises was designed (Table 1). Living on the research vessel while at sea necessitated a small crew, due to space limitations on the 36 ft. (11 m) *Roper*, but it allowed for operations spanning from dawn until dusk, or even after nightfall.

It was anticipated that the remote sensing survey could be completed in five, ten-hour work days, not

REMOTE SENSING SURVEY, 14-20 JULY 2014		
CRUISE 1	Day 1	Depart St. Augustine for survey area
	Days 2-6	Magnetic and acoustic survey operations covering entire survey area
	Day 7	Depart survey area for St. Augustine
	Crew	Chuck Meide, Brendan Burke, Sam Turner, Brian McNamara
REMOTE SENSING ANALYSIS, 24 JULY – 6 AUGUST 2014		
Analysis		10 working days of analysis at LAMP facilities in St. Augustine with assistance from NPS-SRC, SEARCH, Inc., and Marine Magnetics, Inc.
DIVING OPERATIONS (TEAM 1), 7 – 12 AUGUST 2014		
CRUISE 2	Day 1	Depart St. Augustine for survey area
	Days 2-3	Refinement surveys at selected targets (Targets 1, E1, E3T, E4T, 7)
	Days 4-6	Diving operations (Targets 1 and E3T)
	Day 6	In afternoon, transit to Ponce Inlet for crew switch-out
	Crew	Chuck Meide, David Howe, Sam Turner, Brian McNamara
DIVING OPERATIONS (TEAM 2), 13-18 AUGUST 2014		
CRUISE 3	Day 1	At survey area by morning to commence diving
	Days 2-5	Diving operations (Targets 1, E3T, E4T; media visit on Day 4)
	Day 6	Depart survey area for St. Augustine
	Crew	Chuck Meide, Brendan Burke, Starr Cox, Olivia McDaniel

TABLE 1. PROJECT FIELDWORK SCHEDULE AND CREW ROSTER

including two transit days to and from St. Augustine. Ten work days were then scheduled for acoustic and magnetic analysis. Afterwards, a second field expedition consisting of two back-to-back cruises was planned. This included a transit day to CANA, two days for refinement surveys over the most promising targets, eight days for diver target testing, and a final transit day back to St. Augustine. In between Cruises 2 and 3 the crew was switched out at New Smyrna Beach at Ponce Inlet, so that only the principal investigator worked for more than seven consecutive days at sea during the project.

The flexibility and extra time allowed by housing the researchers on site was critical in meeting all project objectives in the time allowed, especially after a number of delays due to mechanical failure and inclement weather.

Survey Methodology

Procedures were similar to those used on previous LAMP surveys (Turner and Kennedy 2010). The primary tools of the remote sensing survey were a Marine Magnetics Explorer Mini Magnetometer, a Klein System 3900 sidescan sonar, a SyQwest StrataBox subbottom profiler, and a Trimble DSM-232 WAAS-enabled differential global positioning system (GPS). The magnetometer was towed directly from the sidescan sonar towfish, with the length of cable out being adjusted periodically depending on water depth. The sonar fish weighs about 70 lbs (32 kg), enough to keep the magnetometer sensor at its approximate altitude.

Following the recommendations outlined by Bratten (2007) and Enright et al. (2006:147), survey lanes were spaced 20 m (65.62 ft.) apart for the most effective magnetic survey. The survey block consisted of 38 lanes parallel to shore for a total of 190 line miles (352 line kilometers). In practice it was assumed that the linear distance would be somewhat shorter, as the nearest inshore lanes would, depending on the tide, be too shallow for the research vessel to navigate (*Roper* draws 5 ft. or 1.5 m of water when loaded).

As anticipated, the research vessel could not access the shallowest portion of the planned survey area. But the *Roper* was able to complete 34.59 lanes, in waters as shallow as 6.2 ft (1.9 m), covering 91% of the planned survey area.

Remote Sensing Data Analysis

Following the survey, ten working days were reserved for geophysical data analysis before returning to the field. Given this short turnaround, emphasis was focused on magnetic as opposed to the acoustic data, as it was felt that the magnetometer was most likely lead to the identification of historic shipwrecks. After the conclusion of fieldwork, more time was dedicated to acoustic data interpretation, which as anticipated produced negligible results.

LAMP sought the assistance of several other colleagues with considerable experience in the interpretation of magnetic data in order to get multiple perspectives and the most thoroughly analyzed dataset possible. Representatives from three institutions reviewed the data independently from LAMP. The first of these was Doug Hrvoic of Marine Magnetics, Inc., who inspected the raw data and provided advice and assistance to LAMP researchers in the field and during post-processing.

The second independent analyst was Bert Ho, of the NPS Submerged Resources Center (SRC). Ho processed raw data using a method recently pioneered through NPS-SRC and Bureau of Ocean Energy Management. They have developed a series of custom-scripted GIS tools to automate data processing by visualizing and assessing raw magnetic data (Bright et al. 2014). Ho used these GIS tools to contour the entire survey area and identify 94 anomalies.

The final independent magnetometer data analysis was conducted by Jeff Enright of Southeastern Archaeological Research, Inc. (SEARCH). Enright was able to devote significant time to analysis and communication with LAMP researchers in the field and laboratory, and his efforts proved particularly helpful. He generated magnetic contour maps of the survey area, one with the contour level set at 5 gammas and one set at 2 gammas, a resolution he has found the most useful for interpreting 16th-century shipwrecks (namely the 1559 Emanuel Point wrecks) (Meide et al. 2015:27). After analyzing the contoured data, Enright recommended four particular anomalies for further investigation, three of which were also considered by LAMP analysts to be targets of interest.

The principal analyst at LAMP was Sam Turner. Turner used Hypack to scrutinize magnetic data in profile side-by-side with vessel trackline, facilitating the recognition of boat-induced anomalies. Analyzing one survey lane at a time, anomalies—even those as subtle as a few gammas—were characterized as monopolar, dipolar, or multicomponent, with duration and total amplitude calculated for each. A total of 188 magnetic anomalies were identified by Turner in this manner, though 79 were discarded as boat-induced. The 109 remaining anomalies were examined for clustering or alignment on two or more adjacent survey lanes. Spatially adjacent anomalies were defined as targets. This criterion has long been a factor used in the interpretation of magnetic data to identify historic shipwrecks (Arnold 1982:56, 1996:247; Gearhart 2011:96). Anomalies were contoured to better understand their characteristics, particularly polar orientation and magnetic moment (Gearhart 2011:102-109). A number of additional, non-clustered anomalies that displayed characteristics indicative of shipwrecks were also designated targets. A total of 19 targets were defined using these criteria (Meide et al. 2015: 30-38).

Refinement Surveys of Prioritized Targets

Once back in the field, refined magnetometer and subbottom profiler surveys were staged over the highest priority targets to better understand the geophysical signature of each and to obtain precise positioning for target testing. Five targets were selected for refined survey: Target 1, Target E1, Target E3T, Target E4T, and Target 7.

Refinement surveys took place during the first two days of Cruise 2, before diving operations. Before re-surveying, a series of experiments were conducted weighting the magnetometer tow cable in order to sink the towfish without grounding. Differing combinations of lead weights were attached to the tow cable 50 feet (15 m) from the towfish with a digital depth gage attached to the magnetometer to record the depth of the instrument, allowing the fish to be positioned closer to the seabed during re-survey for stronger readings.

The refined surveys were conducted with a lane spacing of 7 m (23.3 ft.), effectively tripling the resolution of magnetic data compared to the overall survey. All lanes were run in the same direction, from south to north, as running the boat with the seas yielded noticeably more consistent data. A typical refinement survey, depending on anomaly size, would include 20 or more lanes measuring 1,000 ft. (305 m). Up to five 230 ft. (70.1 m) long perpendicular lanes were also recorded, spaced 50 m apart. These were run west to east, providing the least "noisy" data, but the wind and swell made these difficult to run and generally of poor data quality.

The magnetic data from refinement surveys was contoured while in the field, ideally before diving began on any given target. These magnetic contour maps were used to precisely position subsurface testing at the margin between negative and positive poles of any given anomaly. These surveys also eliminated one target (E1), which could not be relocated and was assumed to be boat-induced, and lowered the priority of another (Target 7).

Target Testing Methodology and Results

Due to transit days, refinement survey days, a half-day media visit, and a half-day lost to mechanical problems, there were effectively only six days of diving. During that time, a total of 57 dives were completed, for a cumulative bottom time of 38 hours, 51 minutes.

Researchers knew from sidescan sonar imagery that all targets were buried, a typical scenario along Florida's Atlantic coast. Divers therefore used standard methods to systematically probe beneath the seafloor (Turner and Kennedy 2010:12-13). First a buoy was deployed at the central point of the anomaly, and then divers refined the location of strongest magnetism using a handheld magnetometer. Then a hydraulic probe, consisting of a 10 ft. (3.05 m) long section of 1 in. (2.54 cm) diameter pipe, connected by garden and fire hose to a water pump on the vessel, was repeatedly sunk into the sediment its full length at one meter intervals along predetermined transects. The usual pattern was to probe along a 20 m long transect running north-south, and then a perpendicular transect running 20 m east-west, centered on the magnetic contour. Additional transects at various orientations were also probed at each target.

The probe is minimally invasive, liquefying a narrow column of sand as it is thrust downward. Divers can enlarge the hole to reach in and feel for cultural remains up to 80 cm deep. The hole created by the probe quickly fills in with sand once the probe is removed, leaving a shallow divot in the seafloor. These small depressions persist for days, allowing the overall probing patterns to be scrutinized in post-diving sidescan sonar imagery, confirming that probes were placed in their intended locations for each target.

If the target represents a buried wreck, the probing should result in one or more hard or positive returns. Depending on the depth of burial, the next step is to conduct a limited excavation to better understand the nature of the buried object(s). While the probe can be used to jet sediment, a controlled excavation can be executed with a handheld dredge.

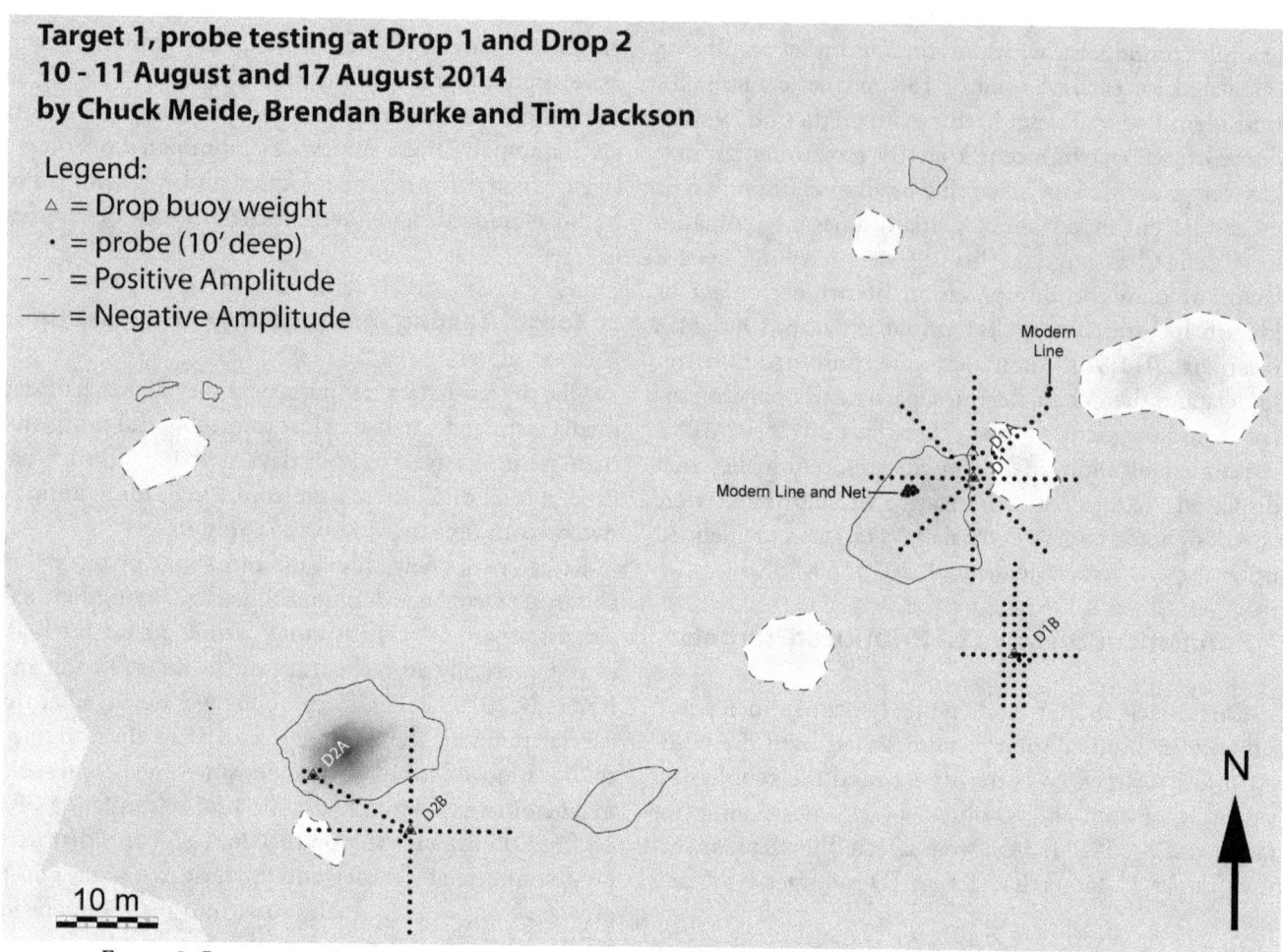

FIGURE 2. PLAN VIEW OF TARGET 1, SHOWING ALL PROBE TESTS CONDUCTED AT DROP 1 (RIGHT) AND DROP 2 (LEFT), SUPERIMPOSED ON THE MAGNETIC CONTOURS. D1 REPRESENTS THE INTENDED LOCATION OF THE DROP 1 BUOY, D1A REPRESENTS ITS ACTUAL LOCATION, AND D1B INDICATES A NEW PROBING LOCATION SELECTED BY DIVERS AFTER THE INITIAL DROP. THIS NOMENCLATURE IS CONSISTENT WITH TESTING AT OTHER TARGETS. NORTH ARROW INDICATES TRUE NORTH (GRAPHIC BY CHUCK MEIDE, BRENDAN BURKE, AND TIM JACKSON, COURTESY OF LAMP, 2015).

The handheld magnetometer used during target testing dives was a Quantro Sensing Discovery proton magnetometer. While this unit has worked with remarkable success in the past, it became increasingly apparent that it was not functioning properly, generating erratic readings and leading divers away from areas of magnetism. The device was thereafter abandoned and the refinement survey contour maps, in conjunction with the highly accurate survey GPS to confirm buoy drops, were used to place divers precisely on magnetic anomalies.

A total of 308 probe tests were conducted at three targets, one of which consisted of two discrete buoy drops or testing locations. Testing results for these targets are presented individually below.

Target 1

Target 1 consists of a linear series of magnetic anomalies running roughly east-west over a distance of around 120 m (Figure 2). Because of the size of this target, two areas of magnetism were chosen for diver testing, designated Drop 1 (D1) and Drop 2 (D2). At D1, the faulty handheld magnetometer initially led divers to probe away from the anomaly (designated D1B in Figure 2). The anomaly was re-tested once this was realized, with four 20 m long transects intersecting at the intended location of D1, for a total of 83 test probes. During probing, divers encountered a significant length of 1 in. (2.54 cm) diameter modern nylon line on the seafloor, mostly buried. At one end, after jetting with the probe, divers observed a section of netting and another line, this one comprised of stainless steel and polypropylene. This composite line has been identified as "polyclad," a type used since the late 1980s on trawlers to line the mouth or opening of the shrimp net. The opening of the net is the part most likely to be snagged on bottom obstructions, suggesting that while this area could represent a lost shrimp boat or simply a lost net, it might also represent a net lost after snagging on a previously exposed shipwreck. Since stainless steel has a negligible magnetic signature, the source of magnetism at this anomaly remains unidentified (Meide et al. 2015:61-65).

The other area of Target 1 tested, D2, is located some 70 m away at the southwestern extent of the target. After a series of circular searches with the handheld magnetometer, the drop buoy was shifted to the southeast (shown as D2B in Figure 2). Four 20 m long transects were probed from this spot, along with another 15 probes sunk between the initial buoy drop (D2A) and D2B. After subsequently plotting these 58 probes, it was seen that many of them were outside the magnetic contour. While 17 probes were placed in the confines of the anomaly, researchers would have repositioned and conducted additional probe tests had time allowed, a goal that could be carried out in a future phase of this project (Meide et al. 2015:65-67).

Target E3T

This target seemed especially promising, due not only to the orientation of its magnetic contour, but also to its proximity to the beach and the Armstrong Site. It appears as a classic dipole (Figure 3), with its negative pole oriented about 337° magnetic from its positive pole, resulting in a magnetic moment direction of around -23°. This is within the range demonstrated by Gearhart (2011) as indicating a complex source anomaly (i.e., likely shipwreck). The strong total amplitude, 692.8 gammas, did seem rather high for a 16th-century shipwreck, but because the Ribault ships were loaded with iron in the form of artillery, ammunition, and supplies, E3T remained a high priority target.

The center of the dipole was defined as D1, and the actual buoy drop (D1A) was located only about 4 meters to the east of this point (Figure 3). Probing began along a north-south transect centered at D1A, and then along a perpendicular transect from west to east. Three hard returns were recorded during the first seven probe tests.

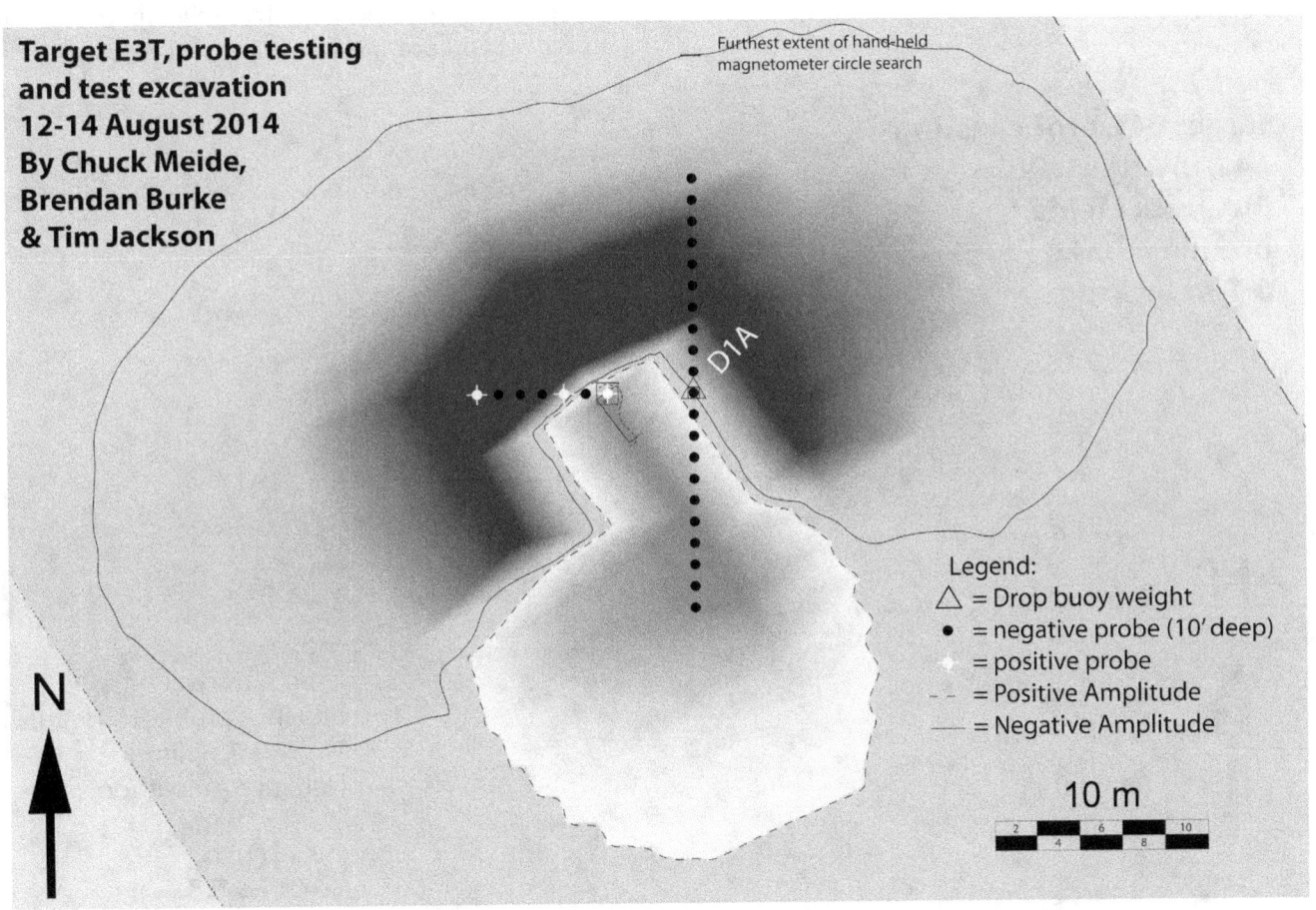

FIGURE 3. PLAN VIEW OF TARGET E3T, SHOWING PROBE TESTS AND EXCAVATION RESULTS SUPERIMPOSED ON THE MAGNETIC CONTOUR. THREE POSITIVE PROBE RETURNS ON THE EAST-WEST TRANSECT RESULTED IN TEST EXCAVATION WHICH EXPOSED A LARGE, METAL BOX, IDENTIFIED AS A FUEL TANK FROM A SHRIMP BOAT, CA. 1940S-1980S. NORTH ARROW INDICATES TRUE NORTH (GRAPHIC BY CHUCK MEIDE, BRENDAN BURKE, AND TIM JACKSON, COURTESY OF LAMP, 2015).

The third positive return was shallow enough so that divers could reach in and feel a concreted object. The following day a 4 in. (10.2 cm) dredge was deployed for test excavation at this location. Excavation revealed a large, concreted, ferrous box-like object (Figure 3). It measured 8 ft. (2.44 m) in length, and at least 38 inches (0.95 m) across. Notable features included 90° corners, a padeye or lifting ring, and a small hole in the edge of the box, confirming it was hollow.

Upon observation of these features, project archaeologists identified the box as a fuel tank from a wrecked shrimp boat, dating from between World War II and the 1980s. Photographs of similar fuel tanks installed in shrimp boat engine rooms exist in the collections of the St. Augustine Lighthouse & Museum. The padeye is similar to those welded on the top of fuel tanks to aid in their lifting and lowering into the boat during installation. Archaeologists believe that the hole is the result of a metal bracket, which once secured the tank, having broken during the wrecking process (Meide et al. 2015: Figures 66-68).

It is believed that Target E3T represents the actual wreck of a shrimp boat rather than the accidental loss or deliberate discarding of a fuel tank. This conclusion was drawn due to the two additional positive probe tests, indicating additional buried material, and also because it seems unlikely that a sizable fuel tank, permanently installed in a trawler, would be removed and disposed of at sea. Once it was realized that the source of this anomaly was modern, or no earlier than the 1940s, the decision was made to abandon further testing after only 28 probe tests and the test excavation (Meide et al. 2015:74).

Figure E4T

Like E3T, this target displayed a dipole contour with an orientation indicative of a shipwreck site, though with its total amplitude of 111 gammas it seemed more likely to represent a 16th-century wreck (Figure 4). The actual location of the dropped buoy (D1A) was only about 3 m north of its intended position (D1). A pair of perpendicular probe transects, oriented to the cardinal directions, was centered on D1A. Then another set of transects was probed, the first oriented at 70° to roughly

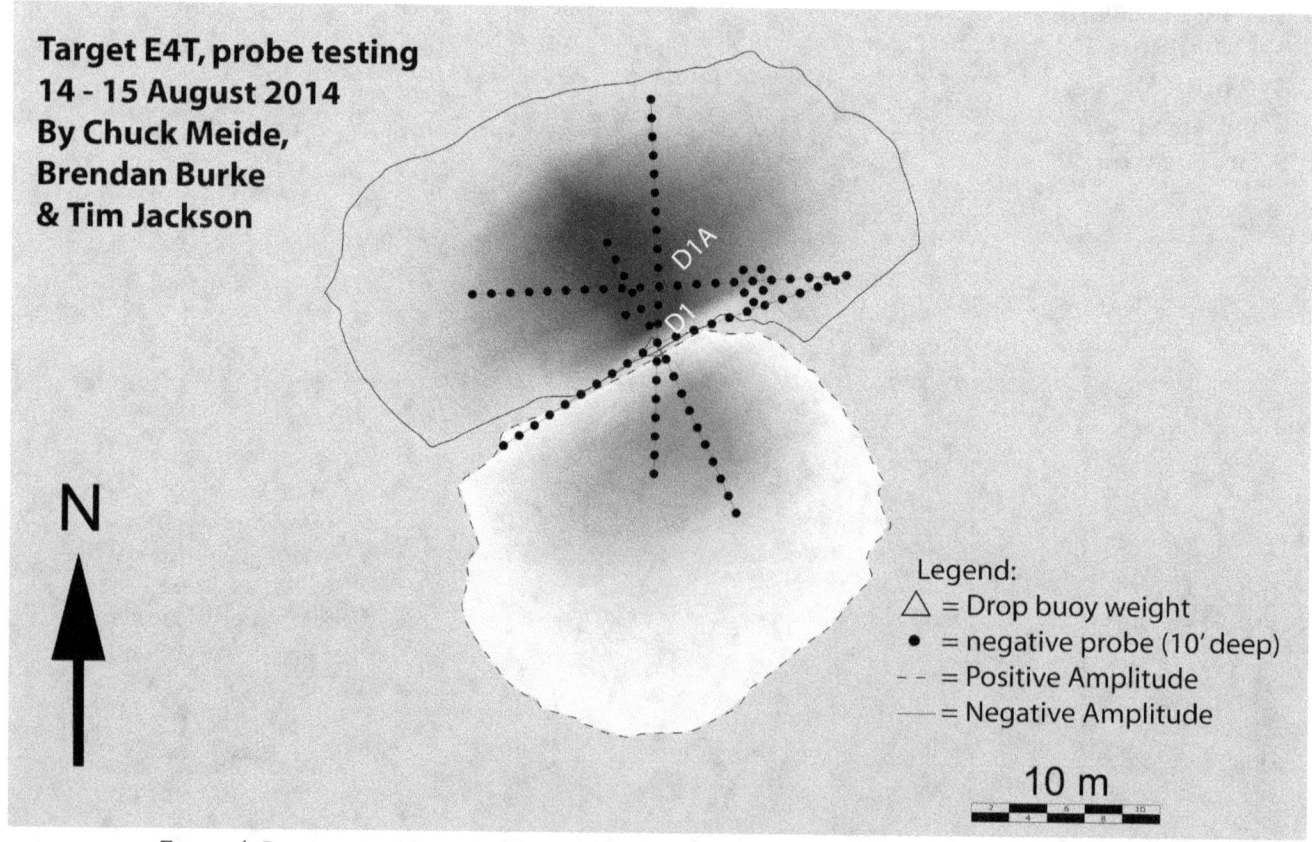

FIGURE 4. PLAN VIEW OF TARGET E4T, SHOWING PROBE TESTS SUPERIMPOSED ON THE MAGNETIC CONTOUR. DESPITE THE 84 PROBE TESTS, NO CULTURAL MATERIAL WAS IDENTIFIED, AND IT MAY BE THAT THE SOURCE OF THE ANOMALY IS BURIED DEEPER THAN THE 10 FT. (3.05 M) PROBE. NORTH ARROW INDICATES TRUE NORTH (GRAPHIC BY CHUCK MEIDE, BRENDAN BURKE, AND TIM JACKSON, COURTESY OF LAMP, 2015).

match the angle between the negative and positive lobes of the dipole, and the second perpendicular to it, intersecting at D1 or the approximate center of the anomaly (Figure 4).

While a possible hard return was reported by divers, additional probe testing at that spot failed to locate buried material. No obvious positive returns were noted out of 84 probe tests at this target. It is not known if the source of the anomaly is buried more deeply than 3 m, or if it consists of sparsely scattered materials that were simply not encountered with the probe (Meide et al. 2015:74-77).

Conclusion

While no historic shipwrecks were discovered, in all other respects the 2014 survey was a success. Virtually all fieldwork objectives were met, despite the usual mechanical and weather delays, during what was an ambitious schedule with little room for error. Researchers fully surveyed all of the search area that could be safely accessed, and placed more than 300 probe tests at three likely targets. Modern materials associated with shrimp trawling were found at two sites, one of which has been abandoned as the site of a modern wreck, the other which could be further tested to determine if the trawl net encountered was there due to snagging on an historic shipwreck. In addition, there remain a number of other potential targets, which can be tested in the next phase of this project. One challenge, exemplified by Target E4T, is how to reach materials that might be more deeply buried than the 3 m probe, which may be the case with 450-year old shipwrecks. At the start of the 450th anniversary year of both St. Augustine and the loss of the French fleet, funding is currently pending from another state grant which could lead to continued research in summer of 2015. There is no better time for archaeologists to pursue these historically significant shipwrecks, and to share their compelling story with the public as the U.S. celebrates its 450th birthday.

ACKNOWLEDGMENTS

This project was funded with Historic Preservation Grant assistance provided by the Bureau of Historic Preservation, Division of Historical Resources, Florida Department of State, assisted by the Florida Historical Commission, and also by NOAA OER. Thanks to the entire LAMP and Lighthouse team along with the NPS (CANA, SEAC, and SRC) for their support of this project. Thanks to Dave Howe and IMH for *Roper*, and to John de Bry (CHA), David Morgan (NPS-SEAC), Dave Conlin and Bert Ho (NPS-SRC), Myrna Palfrey (NPS-CANA), Frank Cantelas (NOAA), Doug Hrvoic (Marine Magnetics, Inc.), Jeff Enright (SEARCH), and the City of New Smyrna Beach for their assistance.

References

ALGOET, GAËTAN, T. L. ARMSTRONG AND ROBERT H. BAER
2014   *A Hundred Giants: The French Huguenot Experience in Florida: 1562-1565, with Pieter Vander Aa's Diverse Voyages of 1705*. Signum Ops, Merritt Island, FL.

ARMSTRONG, DOUGLAS R.
2001   French Castaways at Old Cape Canaveral. Florida Master Site Files Survey Report No. 6189, Tallahassee, FL.

ARNOLD, J. BARTO III
1982   *A Matagorda Bay Magnetometer Survey and Site Test Excavation Project*. Texas Antiquities Committee Publication 9. Texas Historical Commission, Austin, TX.

1996   Magnetometer Survey of La Salle's Ship the Belle. *International Journal of Nautical Archaeology* 25(3 & 4):243-249.

BENNETT, CHARLES E.
2001   *Laudonnière and Fort Caroline: History and Documents*. University of Alabama Press, Tuscaloosa, AL

BRATTEN, JOHN
2007   The Use of Remote Sensing to Inventory Pensacola's Shipwrecks. Paper presented at the first annual Northeast Florida Symposium on Underwater Archaeology, 20 March 2007, St. Augustine, FL.

BREWER, DAVID M., JOHN E. CORNELISON, JR. AND WM. BRIAN YATES
1998   A Beach-Face Magnetometer Survey at Canaveral National Seashore. SEAC Accession No. 1127. National Park Service, Southeast Archeological Center, Tallahassee, FL.

BREWER, DAVID M. AND ELIZABETH A. HORVATH
2004   In Search of Lost Frenchmen. Florida Master Site Files Survey Report No. 9871. National Park Service, Southeast Archeological Center, Tallahassee, FL.

Bright, John C., David Conlin and Sage Wall
2014 Marine Magnetic Survey Modeling: Custom Geospatial Processing Tools for Visualizing and Assessing Marine Magnetic Surveys for Archaeological Resources. OCS Study BOEM 2014-615. U.S. Department of the Interior, Bureau of Ocean Energy Management, Office of Renewable Energy Programs, and the National Park Service Submerged Resources Center.

de Bry, John, and Chuck Meide
2014 The Loss of the Ribault Fleet of 1565. Paper presented at La Floride Française: Florida, France, and the Francophone World, an international conference held at the Winthrop-King Institute for Contemporary French and Francophone Studies, February 20-21, Florida State University, Tallahassee, FL.

Enright, Jeffrey M., Robert II Gearhart, Doug Jones and Jenna Enright
2006 Study to Conduct National Register of Historic Places Evaluations of Submerged Sites on the Gulf of Mexico Outer Continental Shelf. LA OCS Study MMS 2006-036. U.S. Department of the Interior, Minerals Management Service, Gulf of Mexico OCS Region, New Orleans, LA.

Gearhart, Robert
2011 Archaeological Interpretation of Marine Magnetic Data. In *The Oxford Handbook of Maritime Archaeology*, Alexis Catsambis, Ben Ford and Donny L. Hamilton, editors, pp. 90-113. Oxford University Press, New York, NY.

Gibbs, Martin
2003 The Archaeology of Crisis: Shipwreck Survivor Camps in Australia. *Historical Archaeology* 37(1):128-145.

Griffin, Patricia C.
2001 Piñon Inlet and the Massacre of the French. *St. Augustine Archaeological Association* Newsletter 16(1).

Laudonnière, René Goulaine de
2001 *Three Voyages*. Translated by Charles E. Bennett. University of Alabama Press, Tuscaloosa, AL.

Lawson, Charles F.
2004 Trip report on archeological and geophysical survey of four areas at Klondike Beach, Canaveral National Seashore, Volusia County, Florida. April 11-23, 2004. SEAC Acc. 1877. Southeast Archeological Center, Tallahassee, FL.

Lundin, Richard J.
1999 An Overview of Archaeological Research on the French Expeditions to Florida (1562-1568). Paper presented at the Society for Historical Archaeology's 32nd Conference on Historical and Underwater Archaeology, 8 January, Salt Lake City, UT.

2001 Two Case Studies of Geophysical Investigation of Buried, Sub-Beach, Wrecksites on the East Coast of Florida. Paper presented at the Florida Anthropological Society's 53rd Annual Conference, May 12, St. Augustine, FL.

Lyon, Eugene
1976 *The Enterprise of Florida: Pedro Menéndez de Avilés and the Spanish Conquest of 1565-1568*. University Press of Florida, Gainesville, FL.

Meide, Chuck
2012 Á la recherche de la flotte française de 1565. In *Floride, un rêve français (1562-1565)*, Mickaël Augeron, John de Bry and Annick Notter, editors, pp. 133-141. Translated by Annick Notter. Museé du Nouveau Monde, La Rochelle, France.

Meide, Chuck and John de Bry
2014 The Lost French Fleet of 1565: Collision of Empires. In *ACUA Underwater Archaeology Proceedings 2014*, Charles Dagneau and Karolyn Gauvin, editors, pp. 79-92. Advisory Council on Underwater Archaeology, Québec City, Canada.

Meide, Chuck, Samuel P. Turner, P. Brendan Burke, and Olivia McDaniel
2015 The Search for the Lost French Fleet of 1565: Report on 2014 Archaeological Investigations. Report submitted to the National Park Service Southeast Archeological Center by the Lighthouse Archaeological Maritime Program, St. Augustine Lighthouse & Museum, St. Augustine, FL.

McGrath, John T.
2000 *The French in Early Florida: In the Eye of the Hurricane*. University Press of Florida, Gainesville, FL.

Ribault, Jean
1964 *The Whole and True Discouerye of Terra Florida*. Facsimilie reprint of the London edition of 1563. University of Florida Press, Gainesville, FL.

Turner, Samuel P. and Kendra Kennedy
2010 LAMP 2009 Remote Sensing Survey. In *ACUA Underwater Archaeology Proceedings 2010*, Christopher Horrell and Melanie Damour, editors, pp. 11-16. Advisory Council on Underwater Archaeology, Amelia Island, FL.

• • • • • • • • • • • • • • •

Chuck Meide
Lighthouse Archaeological Maritime Program (LAMP)
81 Lighthouse Avenue
St. Augustine, FL 32080

The Shelburne Shipyard Steamboat Graveyard: Four Early Nineteenth-Century Steamboats from Lake Champlain

Carolyn Kennedy

Steamboat construction of the early nineteenth century remains largely forgotten and unstudied. Historical records provide little detail on how construction techniques were evolving in this experimental phase of steam-powered vessels. A survey of Lake Champlain's Shelburne Shipyard revealed the remains of four nineteenth-century steamboats, three of which were built prior to 1840. The four hulls were recorded for comparative study during a field school which took place in the month of June 2014. Their unique and differing features illustrate the innovative approaches utilized by shipwrights specifically adapted to steamboats.

Introduction

The creation of practical engines which could burn fuels and propel vessels against winds and currents was clearly one of history's great benchmarks. North America's steamboat era is considered to have officially begun in 1807 when Fulton and Livingston's *North River Steamboat* made its maiden voyage up the Hudson River. In the decades that followed, steamers rapidly spread throughout the continent, becoming an essential means of North America's transportation, economic, and social systems. Steam's influence was profound, yet paradoxically there are large gaps in our knowledge of early steam technology and vessel construction. The historical records are incomplete, lost, or were simply never generated in the first place. In the rush to develop steam's commercial potential and to out-distance competitors with boats that were bigger, faster, and fancier, most entrepreneurs and builders never bothered to preserve plans, tables of timber scantlings, or other details of their work. We know that steam propulsion transformed North American life, but many aspects of the propulsion systems and the boats still elude us, particularly for the dynamic decades of experimentation and adaptation before 1850.

Fortunately, a material record of early steam navigation was preserved in the form of steamboat hulls accidently sunk or intentionally abandoned beneath North American lakes, rivers, and coastal waters. Since 1980 archaeological studies of the sidewheel steamers *Phoenix I* (1815) in Lake Champlain, *Lady Sherbrooke* (1817) in the St. Lawrence River, *Heroine* (1832) in Oklahoma's Red River, *Anthony Wayne* (1838) in Lake Erie, and the early screw-propeller steamer *Indiana* (1848) in Lake Superior have greatly added to our understanding of the technology of steam machinery and the rapidly-evolving architecture of steamers between 1807 and 1850.

By 1828, there were five competing steamboat companies on Lake Champlain, but most powerful among them was the Champlain Transportation Company (CTC), established in 1826 (Ross 1997:29). Within its first year, the CTC formed a partnership with the Lake Champlain Steamboat Company, the oldest company still in existence at the time. The partnership was favorable to the CTC, but the Lake Champlain Steamboat Company struggled financially. In 1833 all of the older company's property was sold to the CTC. This property included the steamboats *Phoenix II* and *Congress*, and all of the Lake Champlain Steamboat Company's land at Shelburne Harbor, for a total value of $47,000 (Isaiah Townsend, power of attorney to P. Doolittle 1835 [2]:86).

Shelburne Harbor is located in a protected bay in Lake Champlain on the eastern side of Shelburne Point, Vermont. The area is an excellent location for a shipyard due to its protection from prevailing winds and waves. This area served as the location of the CTC's shipyard starting in 1833, and thereafter all of their steamboats were built and retired in this harbor. The retirement of these vessels is the most important consideration for the purposes of this investigation.

In anticipation of a planned archaeological investigation of Shelburne Shipyard to take place in the 2014 field season, Kevin Crisman and Carolyn Kennedy began researching the site's history in 2013. They were greatly assisted by a satellite image that showed four shallow wrecks in close proximity to each other near the southern shore of the harbor (Figure 1). Additional research leading up to the archaeological project was based largely on two semi-reliable sources: *The Steamboats of Lake Champlain 1809-1930*, by Ogden Ross (1997), and the Champlain Maritime Society's 1983 survey of the site (Chase, 1985). These two sources both offered explanations as to which steamboats these old hulls belonged

FIGURE 1. SATELLITE IMAGE OF SHELBURNE SHIPYARD (BING MAPS, 2013).

to, however, neither had clear sources explaining their assumptions. The wrecks were tentatively identified using an old map showing the locations of abandoned steamboats near the CTC shipyard in combination with an early photograph of the steamboat graveyard from circa 1858 (Figures 2 and 3). Though a bit misleading, these sources were the first clues to what remained beneath the lake's surface at Shelburne Shipyard.

The archaeological investigation was hosted by Texas A&M University (TAMU), the Institute of Nautical Archaeology (INA), the Center for Maritime Archaeology and Conservation (CMAC) and the Lake Champlain Maritime Museum (LCMM). A group of ten graduate and undergraduate students from TAMU participated in a field school directed by Crisman and Kennedy. The objective of the 2014 field season was to carry out an underwater survey of the four wrecks, gathering information on the overall dimensions of each, as well as the dimensions and layout of elements such as the keel, endposts, frames, keelson, engine bed timbers, planking and any other significant features associated with the wrecks. This project was to be as noninvasive as possible, with minimal disturbance to sediment overlying the hulls. By the conclusion of the field work, the four hulls were identified, and detailed site plans were drawn up for each wreck.

With the archaeological data in hand, Crisman and Kennedy returned to the historical sources. According to Ross (1997) and Chase (1985), twelve steamboats were retired in the Shelburne Shipyard and its vicinity, ranging in retirement dates from 1838 to 1893. These steamboats were *Franklin* (1827-1838), *Winooski* (1832-1850), *Whitehall* (1838-1853), *Burlington* (1837-1854), *Saranac* (1842-1855), *Francis Saltus* (1844-1859), *R.W. Sherman* (renamed *America*, 1851-1866), *United States* (1847-1873), *Canada* (1853-1870), *Adirondack* (1867-1875), *A. Williams* (1870-1893), and *Herald* (unknown). Out of these twelve, five were located on a map dated to "as early as 1880" in the precise location the satellite image showed four old steamboat hulls (Chase 1985:57). The map identified *Franklin*, *Burlington*, *Whitehall*, *Francis Saltus* and *A. Williams* as five possibilities where four hulls are present today. Since in reality only four wrecks are located in this area, A. Williams was assumed to be an error, since its retirement date of 1893 post-dated the supposed 1880 date of the map.

It was clear that these sources could not be fully relied upon, and therefore initial identifications were tentative. In order to gain a clearer understanding of alternate possible retirement locations for these steamers, they were each thoroughly researched.

Franklin

Franklin was built in 1827, only twenty years after the first successful steamboat. In its first year *Franklin* became the first steamboat on Lake Champlain to achieve a speed of 16.1 kilometers (10 miles) per hour. Not only was *Franklin* the fastest, but was also the largest steamboat built on the lake at this point, at 49.4 m (162 ft.) in length and 6.7 m (22 ft.) in beam, giving her a 7.36:1 length-to-beam ratio (Ross 1997:53).

Franklin established the CTC's reputation for finely decorated, expensive, and beautiful steamboats. The first advertisement printed in the Burlington Free Press described the steamer as "built of the best materials and in the best manner [...] Her cabins are spacious and well lighted, with 84 births for passengers, and no expense has been spared in procuring furniture of the most costly and fashionable description" (Burlington Free Press 1827:3). The CTC was famous for producing very expensive steamboats throughout Lake Champlain's steamboat days, up to and including the launching of *Ticonderoga* in 1906 (Ross 1997:143).

Franklin was allegedly retired in Shelburne Shipyard in 1838, when it was replaced by the CTC's newest and more impressive steamer, *Burlington*. No records have been located that identify the exact location of the hull of *Franklin*, though historical sources placed

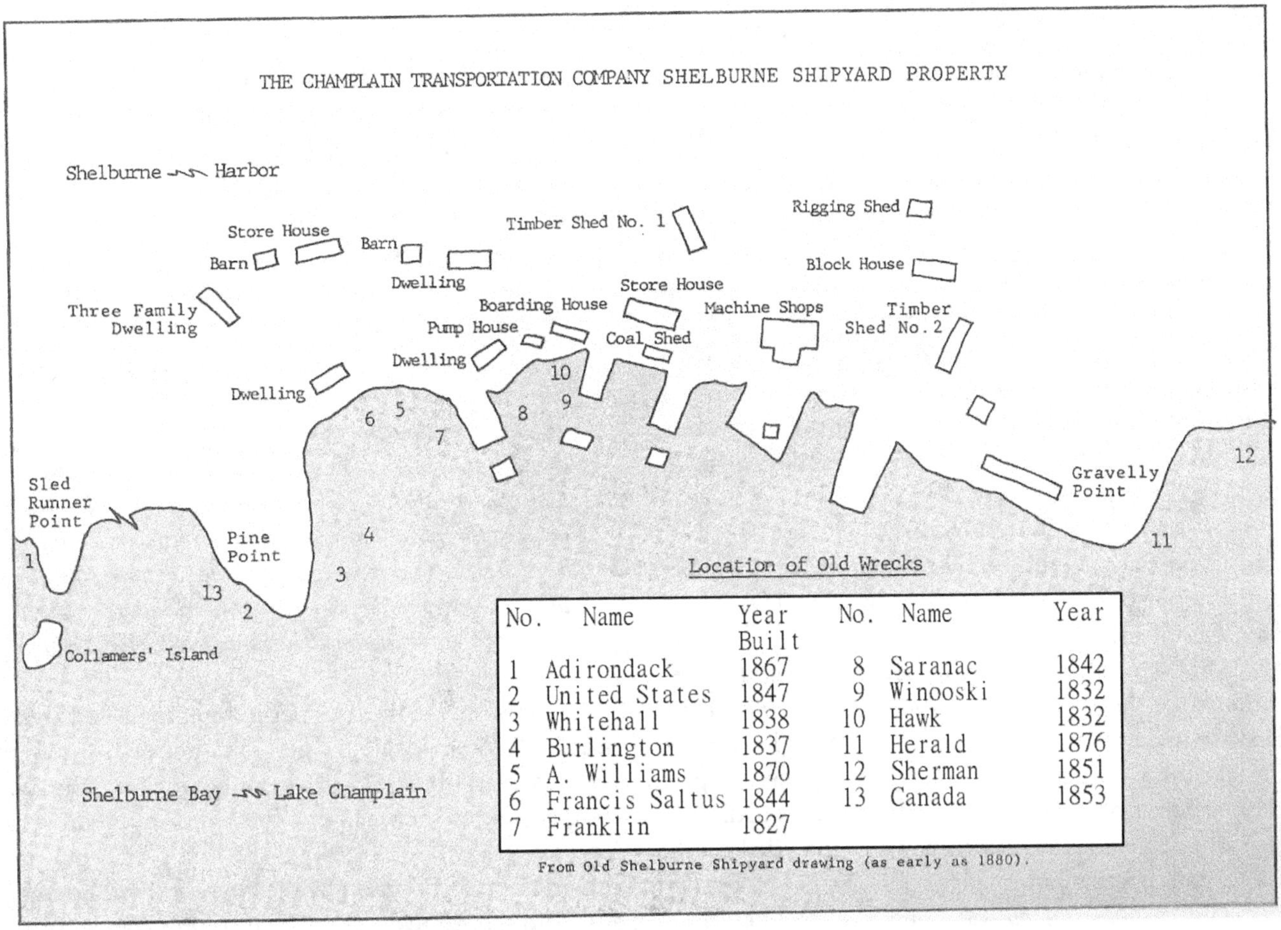

FIGURE 2. OLD MAP OF SHELBURNE HARBOR AND SHELBURNE SHIPYARD WITH POSSIBLE DATE OF 1880 SHOWING WHICH STEAMBOATS WERE BELIEVED TO BE SUNK WHERE. (CHASE 1985:5).

PHOTOGRAPH OF SHELBURNE SHIPYARD CA. 1858, SHOWING TWO ROTTING STEAMBOATS IN THE FOREGROUND WHOSE LOCATIONS AND ORIENTATIONS MATCH PERFECTLY TO WRECK 3 AND 4 IN FIGURE 1 (K. CRISMAN, PRIVATE COLLECTION).

it alongside the wrecks of *Burlington* and *Whitehall* in Shelburne Shipyard (Chase1985:5).

Burlington *and* Whitehall

By 1836, the CTC had bought out all of its competitors and held a monopoly on steam transportation on the lake. The company acquired all of its competitors' boats in these transactions and therefore had not built any new boats since *Franklin*. By this time, many of the existing boats were due for retirement and so the CTC made plans to build a new boat in 1837 (Ross 1997: 61). The resulting steamboat, *Burlington*, was the pride of the CTC and its career epitomized the golden days of steam on Lake Champlain.

Burlington was launched 20 June 1837 from Shelburne Harbor, with very little fanfare. Only a short, four-line blurb announced it in the newspaper (*Burlington Free Press* 1837:2). The boat was launched with its lower hull complete, and its upperworks were finished throughout the summer. By October, *Burlington* was ready to make its maiden voyage, a run the full length of the lake from Whitehall, NY to St. Jean, Quebec. Upper class citizens from Vermont, New York and Canada were invited to ride on this maiden voyage. Included on the list of passengers was Canadian politician, T.S. Brown, who said that *Burlington* was "a perfect specimen of all the arts employed in her construction, she does honor to Lake Champlain on which she floats, and to her liberal proprietors, who to gratify their customers, have spared no expense in adding tasteful decorations to strength and speed" (*Montreal Vindicator* 1837:3).

Brown was not the only one to praise *Burlington*. *Burlington* was the world's finest steamboat of its time, according to the CTC. The *Plattsburgh Republican* enthused, "We have no hesitation in saying that the "*Burlington*" is the most commodious and elegant boat that floats upon the waters of this or any other country" (*Burlington Free Press* 1837:3). Nobody, however, described *Burlington*'s elegance better than the English novelist, Charles Dickens, who took passage aboard the steamboat in 1842 during his travels through North America:

> *There is one American boat – the vessel which carried us on Lake Champlain, from St. Johns to Whitehall, which I praise very highly, but no more than it deserves, when I say that it is superior even to that in which we went from Queenstown to Toronto, or to that in which we travelled from the latter place to Kingston, or I have no doubt I may add, to any other in the world. The steamboat, which is called the* Burlington, *is a perfectly exquisite achievement of neatness, elegance and order. The decks are drawing rooms; the cabins are boudoirs, choicely furnished and adorned with prints, pictures and musical instruments; every nook and corner of the vessel is a perfect curiosity of graceful comfort and beautiful contrivance. Captain Sherman, her commander, to whose ingenuity and excellent taste these results are solely occasion; not the least among them, in having the moral courage to carry British troops at a time (during the Canadian rebellion) when no other conveyance was open to them. He and his vessel were held in universal respect, both by his own countrymen and ours; and no man eve enjoyed the popular esteem who, in his sphere of action, won and wore it better than this gentleman (Dickens1913:167-182)*

In 1835 Peter Comstock began building a new steamboat at Whitehall, NY. The CTC decided to pay off Comstock and buy his new steamboat, eliminating any competition to *Burlington*. The company approached Comstock in 1836, and by 1838 the CTC took over construction of *Whitehall* while it was still on the stocks, and paid Comstock $22,500. Just after the company's takeover, Comstock was put in charge of the construction and was asked to lengthen the hull by 9.1 m (30 ft.) (Miscellaneous Papers 1838[3]: folder 59).

Once it was built, *Whitehall* was to run the same line as *Burlington*, only in reverse. The original schedule had *Burlington* leaving Whitehall every Tuesday, Thursday and Saturday and leaving from St. John's every Monday, Wednesday and Friday. *Whitehall* held the opposite schedule, meaning when *Burlington* left Whitehall, *Whitehall* left St. Johns and vice versa. The two steamboats ran complementary lines for fifteen years, until their retirement, *Burlington* in 1854 and *Whitehall* in 1853. Both were retired side by side in Shelburne Harbor, and completely dismantled by 1855 (Ross 1997:95).

Francis Saltus

During *Burlington*'s reign of the lake, various other steamboats made their appearance as well. Among these were *Saranac* (1842) and *Francis Saltus* (1844). While *Saranac* was being built by the CTC at Shelburne, *Francis Saltus* was under construction in Whitehall, NY.

Having been paid off by the CTC previously, Comstock began building a steamboat of near the same size as *Burlington* and *Whitehall*, no doubt expecting the CTC to pay him off again. The CTC, however, refused to absorb Comstock's plans for a third time, and instead decided to compete with him. Comstock completed his steamboat and launched *Francis Saltus* from Whitehall, NY in 1844.

Within only a year, *Francis Saltus* was sold by Comstock to Grant, Coffin and Church, a firm out of Troy, NY (Ross 1997:79). Throughout its early career, *Francis Saltus* was a thorn in the powerhouse company's side, consistently owned by the company's competitors. After a series of sales that included a short period of ownership by the CTC in 1848, *Francis Saltus* was being operated by the Plattsburgh and Montreal Railroad Company in 1854. The railroad company was running the steamer in direct competition with the CTC's boats, which caused a number of legal battles between the companies. Finally, in 1859, the CTC won their case against the railroad company and claimed ownership once again of *Francis Saltus*, which they immediately retired in Shelburne Harbor (Ross 1997:95).

In the background of Figure 3 on the right-hand side, a nameplate is visible on the pilothouse of one of the steamers. When digitally enhanced, the name *Francis Saltus* can clearly be discerned from the nameplate. Since the photo was most likely taken ca. 1858-1859, it appeared obvious that the June 2014 archaeological investigation of this area would reveal *Francis Saltus'* retirement location adjacent to the hulls believed to be *Burlington* and *Whitehall*.

With all of this information, the identities of the wrecks occupying the depths of Shelburne Shipyard seemed obvious. Within the first few days of surveying, it was clear that these historical sources were mistaken.

Results of the Archaeological Investigation

For fieldwork purposes, the four wrecks were labeled Wreck 1, Wreck 2, Wreck 3 and Wreck 4 (Figure 1). The total lengths of the wrecks were 37.5 m (123 ft. 2 in.), 40.2 m (132 ft.), 48.2 m (158 ft.) and 65.2 m (214 ft.) respectively. These measurements paired with structural components were used to properly identify each hull. Details of larger structural components were recorded, and site plans were drawn for each of the four wrecks (Figure 4).

While the other wreck identities were easily confirmed, Wrecks 1 and 2 proved puzzling. Both measured approximately 40 m (130 ft.) from stem to sternpost and were therefore much smaller than either *Franklin* or *Francis Saltus*. In fact, relatively few Lake Champlain steamboats fell within these measurements.

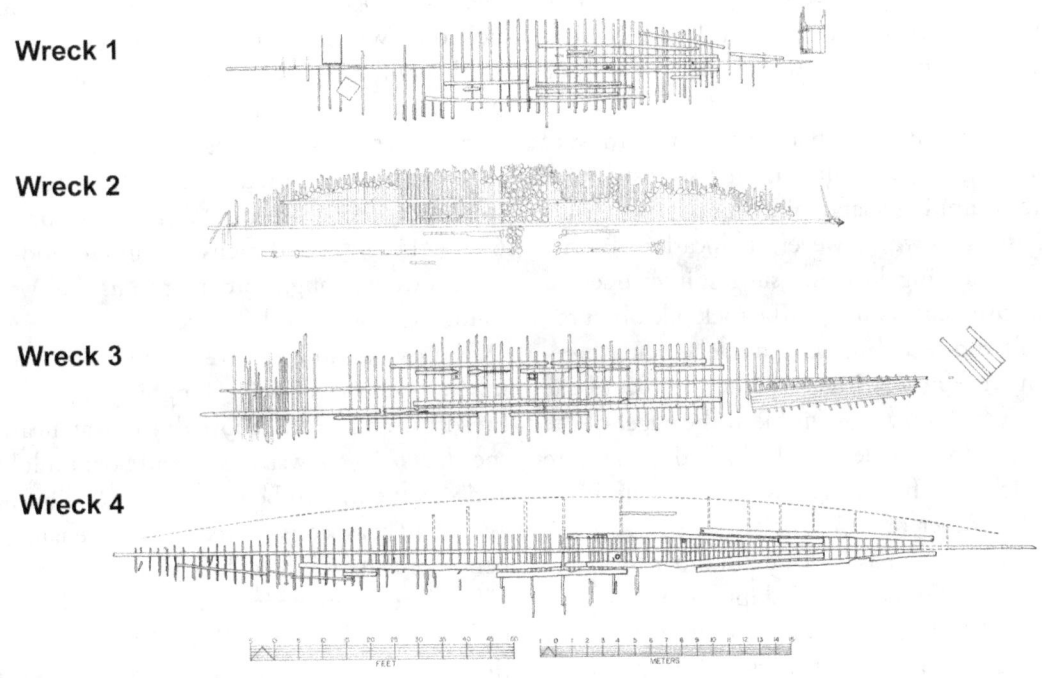

FIGURE 4. SITE PLANS OF WRECK 1 (A. WILLIAMS), WRECK 2 (WINOOSKI), WRECK 3 (BURLINGTON) AND WRECK 4 (WHITEHALL) (DRAWN BY S. KOENIG AND V. MARMARINOU, C. KENNEDY AND M. DECKINGA, R. INGRAM, D. BISHOP AND C. SOWDEN, AND K. CRISMAN AND G. TSAI; INKED BY N. GALLAGHER, 2014).

As the investigation progressed, additional clues to their true identities emerged. The first came during the first week when a diver surfaced holding a ceramic plate fragment from Wreck 1 with the makers' mark 'Burgess & Campbell'. Research revealed that this British company operated between the years 1879 and 1895, a date range which suggested to us that the plate was intrusive trash deposited on an earlier wreck (Barber 1904:58).

More clues followed. Due to its location near a large oak tree on the shore, Wreck 1 was partially obscured by an accumulation of sodden oak leaves. The divers working on this steamer accordingly spent their first few dives fanning away the leafy detritus, and uncovered the rudder at the stern. Both pintles were present with the rudder assembly, one of which was made of a cupreous material. This peculiar choice of metal (iron was the material of choice for early lake vessel fittings) hinted that Wreck 1 was from later in the 19th century, when copper-alloys were cheaper and more widely used in North American shipbuilding (Staniforth 1985:26-27).

With these new clues we went back to our historic map and reconsidered the possibility that Wreck 1 might be *A. Williams*. The final clue came when Arthur Cohn, historian and co-founder of the LCMM, loaned us a late 19th-century photograph of a worn-out steamboat hull, stripped down to the bare bones, labeled *A. Williams*. The hull in the photograph floated directly over the spot where Wreck 1 lies today. The photograph, in combination with the evidence from the wreck itself, led us to the conclusion that Wreck 1 was almost certainly *A. Williams*.

Wreck 2 presented its own challenges, in that most of its length was largely buried under a massive rock pile. The reason for dumping a large pile of rocks specifically on Wreck 2 is unknown, however, its location directly under a modern floating dock may suggest it once served as a base to a 19th-century dock. The rock pile obscured the frame timbers directly adjacent to the keelson, therefore the team working on Wreck 2 opted to record the frame timbers where they were visible at the edges of the pile. Since it was impossible to tell which timbers were floors and which were futtocks, all were given a number, giving a total number of 113 visible frame timbers. A small area of the rock pile was cleared in order to examine what we believed to be the midship frame.

Since Wreck 2 measured 40.6 m (133 ft. 2 in.) from stem to stern, there was no possibility of it being either *Franklin* or *Francis Saltus*. Furthermore, the framing of this wreck was quite unlike the framing of the other three steamboats, leading us to believe that it was older.

Wreck 2's frames were of large dimensions and closely spaced, making it a much heavier hull. The engine bed timbers, on the other hand, were not nearly as massive or numerous as those seen on the other wrecks. All of these features were reminiscent of *Phoenix* (1815), the second steamboat to be built on Lake Champlain. When plans of the two wrecks are compared they are, in fact, very similar.

While *Franklin* originally seemed the clear candidate as the earliest boat shown on the shipyard's wreck map, the lengths simply do not match. Returning to our historical sources, the options quickly narrowed down one likely candidate, the steamboat *Winooski* (1832), a vessel measuring 41.5 m (136 ft.) in length. The resemblance between *Winooski* and *Phoenix* begs the question of whether all of the lake's steamboats built between 1815 and 1832 featured this style of heavy framing.

Winooski, built in 1832 and retired in 1850, was originally built by the Champlain Ferry Company. The Champlain Ferry Company was one of the original five steamboat companies on the lake that was swiftly bought out by the CTC (Ross 1997:45). Since all the building plans for *Winooski* were by another company, the CTC archives were completely lacking of any documents related to its construction. To date, no plans or information have been found.

If Wrecks 1 and 2 initially puzzled us, everything about Wrecks 3 and 4 confirmed their original identifications. Wreck 3 was missing its bow, but the bottom of the hull was otherwise mostly intact to the sternpost; its surviving length of 48.2 m (158 ft) fit within *Burlington*'s recorded original length of 56.4 m (185 ft.) Wreck 4 measured 65.2 m (214 ft) from stem to sternpost, very close to *Whitehall*'s recorded length of 65.5 (215 ft). The dimensions and locations of the two wrecks were enough to convince us that we had indeed found *Burlington* and *Whitehall*.

The two steamboats were built within a year of one other, both were quite long in proportion to their breadths, and both reportedly ran at nearly the same speed. *Burlington* was the second boat built by the CTC, and was the first to be launched at Shelburne Shipyard. *Whitehall* was constructed in Whitehall, N.Y. at the behest of Peter Comstock, a would-be competitor to the CTC. The company forestalled him by buying *Whitehall* before it was launched. The two hulls therefore reflect the design and assembly practices of two different lake shipwrights from the same era, and give us a fascinating look at the rapid development of steamboat designs that took place in the 1830s.

Despite being built within nearly the same year of each other, the framing of the two hulls differed to a surprising extent. *Burlington*'s floors and futtocks were of modest dimensions, nearly square in section, and were more widely spaced than those of Wreck 2 (*Winooski*), except at the very forward end of the hull, where they were laid down in close proximity to one another. *Whitehall*'s frames, on the other hand, were extremely narrow in width (their sided dimension), but had considerable height (their molded dimension); they were closely spaced amidships, and widely spaced at the bow and stern. Clearly, *Whitehall*'s builder was seeking a lighter, shallower, and therefore faster hull, while trying to minimize the weight at the ends that led to hogging (or drooping) that was a chronic problem in long wooden vessels as they aged.

Whitehall also yielded evidence of a hog chain. Hog chains were not really chains, but rather iron rods that ran longitudinally, supported by posts down the length of the hull and tightened with turnbuckles. Their purpose was to hold up the ends of long boats, much like the cables on a suspension bridge. Hog chains reportedly first appeared on steamboats in the late 1830s, and *Whitehall* may in fact be the earliest archaeological example of such a truss system. The intact stern of *Burlington* did not show any evidence that the boat was fitted with a hog chain, but the absence of this vessel's bow structure makes the existence of this feature uncertain.

On all of these Shelburne Shipyard steamboat wrecks, the engine and upperworks have long since been removed. Therefore, reconstruction of these parts will rely heavily on iconographic evidence and contemporary observations. Prior to photography, representations of Lake Champlain steamboats are mostly found in posters or woodcuts commissioned for advertisement purposes. These are problematic because the steamboats represented were often generic images, providing no reliable details about individual construction. Often the representations glossed over details, and so many aspects of construction are left out. This is the case for the known representations of the three earliest steamboats discussed here, *Franklin*, *Burlington* and *Whitehall*. Though it is possible that some of the images are true representations of the steamboat they advertise, they cannot be easily differentiated from unreliable sources.

Contemporary observations can provide many details that iconographic evidence fails to show. Brown was one of the first passengers to ride on *Burlington*'s maiden voyage and his account of the trip includes a detailed description of the steamboat's unique construction features and decorations:

> *The* Burlington *is a most perfect model of "Steamer" architecture, 190 feet long, strengthened by a wooden arch, above which is a wooden frame bracing, similar to that of North River Boats, 25 feet beam, depth of hole [sic] 9 ½ feet, drawing 4 ½ feet water, (all on board,) 51 feet outside the guards, paddle wheels 24 feet high, Fig. head a full length female, or rather "Lady" Fig.; Gentlemen's Cabin below contain 120 berths, well lighted; Ladies' Cabin on deck 20 berths; Promenade deck, supported by slender oak pillars, runs the whole length except a short break running across between the forward gangways. The main deck is superior to any thing I ever saw afloat; block cornice all around, paneled doors, plated handles, with Pilasters and Doric capitals; carved sashes, and about the quarter deck, the panels are all finished with rich carved moulding; stair cases and bar mahogany. Every thing connected with the upper works is made as light as can be, consistent with necessary strength, and all throughout painted white* (Montreal Vindicator 1837:3).

Brown's account is the only known description of the architecture found on board *Burlington*, or any of the other steamers. Since all of this has disappeared from *Burlington*'s remains in Shelburne Harbor, his testimony is very valuable. Brown describes the details of the woodworking in the upperworks, details that without iconographic evidence would be lost.

Brown provides the layout of the cabins, describing the gentlemen's cabins below deck and the ladies cabins on deck. This configuration differed from western river steamboats of the same time period. Western river steamboats had been adapted to have shallower hulls to lessen their draft, but this meant that passengers could not be housed below deck. These steamboats therefore introduced an upper deck which housed the ladies' cabins (Kane 2004:66-67). Brown's description indicates that *Burlington*'s gentlemen's cabins were below the main deck, and the ladies cabins were on the main deck. There is no mention of an upper deck. Since lake steamboats did not need to be adapted with shallower hulls, *Burlington* likely had enough space below deck (in the hold) for passengers.

With the archaeological remains of *Burlington* now documented, plus Brown's stellar description and the archived letters between Doolittle and the machinery contractors, the means to produce a fairly accurate reconstruction of this steamer are available.

Conclusions

Franklin, Winooski, Burlington, Whitehall, and *Francis Saltus* were built during a time when steamboat design was still experimental. Very little documentation about their construction is available, and therefore how steamboats developed in this part of the world is not well known. With the archaeological remains of three of these five steamers, some light has been shed on how steamboat design was developing in the 1830s on Lake Champlain.

Lake Champlain is a historically and geographically important body of water. Samuel de Champlain discovered the lake for Europeans in 1609, and since then Europeans and, later, Americans, used the lake for transportation, social, and economic purposes. Settlers to the Champlain Valley had to adapt to the lakes whims, which could make it calm and beautiful, cold and deep, or stormy and terrifying at any moment. The adoption of steam-powered vessels on this well-used geographical feature was inevitable; however, the unique waters of Lake Champlain provided challenges, and also advantages, to steamboat development. The wrecks in Shelburne Shipyard are incredible sources to use in examining that development.

References

BARBER, EDWIN ATLEE
    1904   *Marks of American Potters*. Patterson & White Company, Philadelphia, PA.

BROWN, T.S.
    1837   *Montreal Vindicator* 24 October: 3. Montreal, QC.

BURLINGTON FREE PRESS
    1827   No title. *Burlington Free Press* 12 October: 3. Burlington, VT.

    1827   No title. *Burlington Free Press* 16 June: 2. Burlington, VT.

CHAMPLAIN TRANSPORTATION COMPANY (CTC) RECORDS.
    Isaiah Townsend, power of attorney to P. Doolittle December 23, 1835 in CTC Archives. Collection A, Carton 2: Folder 86.

CTC RECORDS.
    Miscellaneous Papers January 1-July13, 1838 in CTC Archives. Collection A, Carton 3: Folder 59.

CHASE, JACK.
    1985   Shelburne Bay Project. *A Report on the Nautical Archaeology of Lake Champlain: Results of the 1983 field season of the Champlain Maritime Society*, R. Montgomery Fischer, ed. Champlain Maritime Society, Burlington, VT.

DICKENS, CHARLES.
    1913   *American Notes and Pictures from Italy.* Chapman & Hall, London, UK.

KANE, ADAM.
    2004   *The Western River Steamboat*. Texas A&M University Press, College Station, TX.

PLATTSBURGH REPUBLICAN
    1837   *Burlington Free Press* 27 October: 3. Burlington, VT.

ROSS, ODGEN.
    1997   *The Steamboats of Lake Champlain 1809-1930.* Vermont Heritage Press, Burlington, VT.

SCHWARZ, GEORGE.
    2012   *The Passenger Steamboat Phoenix: An archaeological study of early steam propulsion in North America*. Doctoral Dissertation, Department of Anthropology, Texas A&M University, College Station, TX.

STANIFORTH, MARK.
    1985   The Introduction and Use of Copper Sheathing: A history. *The Bulletin of the Australian Institute for Maritime Archaeology* 9(1):21-48.

• • • • • • • • • • • • • •

Carolyn Kennedy
Department of Anthropology
Texas A&M University
MS 4352
College Station, TX

"Railroaded" - The Wreck of the Schooner Plymouth

David VanZandt
James Paskert
Kevin Magee

An unidentified shipwreck was located in 1996 by CLUE (Cleveland Underwater Explorers) member Rob Ruetschle in Lake Erie, approximately 20 miles off Cleveland, Ohio. CLUE re-visited and surveyed the shipwreck in 2013. After extensive archival research, CLUE identified the wreck as the two-masted schooner Plymouth, *which sank on the night of 23 June 1852, after a collision with the sidewheel steamer* Northern Indiana. *Additional historical research relative to the parties involved revealed a fascinating connection between the reckless operation of the steamer, a political junket, and the powerful influence of the railroads. Ensuing litigation, including personal and political connections to Millard Fillmore, the 13th President of the United States, reinforced right-of-way rules for sailing vessels.*

The Beginning: A Shipwreck Who's Who

On 23 September 2007, while searching for the schooner *Riverside*, the Cleveland Underwater Explorers (CLUE) made a serendipitous discovery of a shipwreck in Lake Erie about 25 miles north of Cleveland, Ohio, USA. Remote sensing data suggested that the wreck was approximately 60 feet (18 meters) in length with a beam of approximately 20 feet (6 meters) and mostly buried in the lake bottom. The initial dive on the wreck on 30 September 2007 confirmed that the wreck was indeed buried with little structure apparent above the lake bottom (Figure 1). Due to the condition of the yet-to-be identified wreck on the bottom, the site was referred to as the "Buried Schooner."

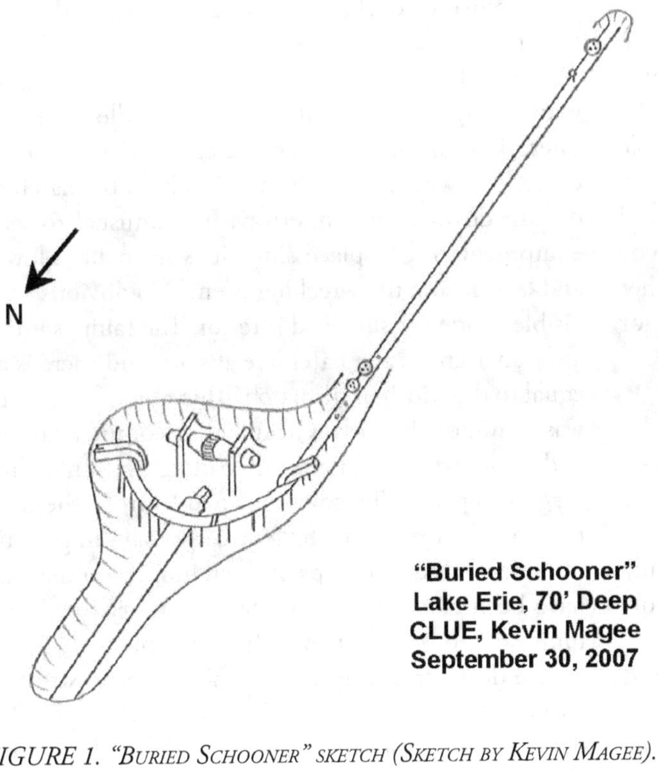

A subsequent reconnaissance survey, performed at the wreck site almost 7 years later on 12 July 2014, showed that additional silt had accumulated leaving the ship almost completely buried. Only a very small portion of the starboard railing, bow railing, and windlass supports remained visible above the lake bottom (Figure 2). Dimensional information obtained by probing suggested a length of about 50 feet (15 meters) and a beam of 16 ft. 6 in. (5.03 meters) at the approximate location of the foremast. This data was comparable to the remote sensing estimates acquired in 2007.

CLUE's historical research failed to identify any documented wrecks with those rough dimensions that potentially could be located in the general area. The closest candidate was the two-masted schooner *Plymouth*, but this was problematic for several reasons. First, the *Plymouth* was considerably larger, and the historical record indicated it should be located some distance further away. Second, CLUE had reason to believe that a wreck discovered on 18 June 1996 by CLUE member Rob Ruetschle, located approximately 20 miles off Cleveland, Ohio, and colloquially known as the "Cleveland Tiller Wreck," may be the remains of the schooner *Plymouth*.

The existence and location of the Cleveland Tiller Wreck were closely held until 2011 when its location was made public by others who subsequently speculated that the wreck might be the two-masted schooner *Mackinaw*. Based on CLUE's historical research, however, this identification was suspect due to the discrepancy between the reported location of the *Mackinaw*'s

"Buried Schooner"
Lake Erie, 70' Deep
CLUE, Kevin Magee
September 30, 2007

FIGURE 1. "Buried Schooner" sketch (Sketch by Kevin Magee).

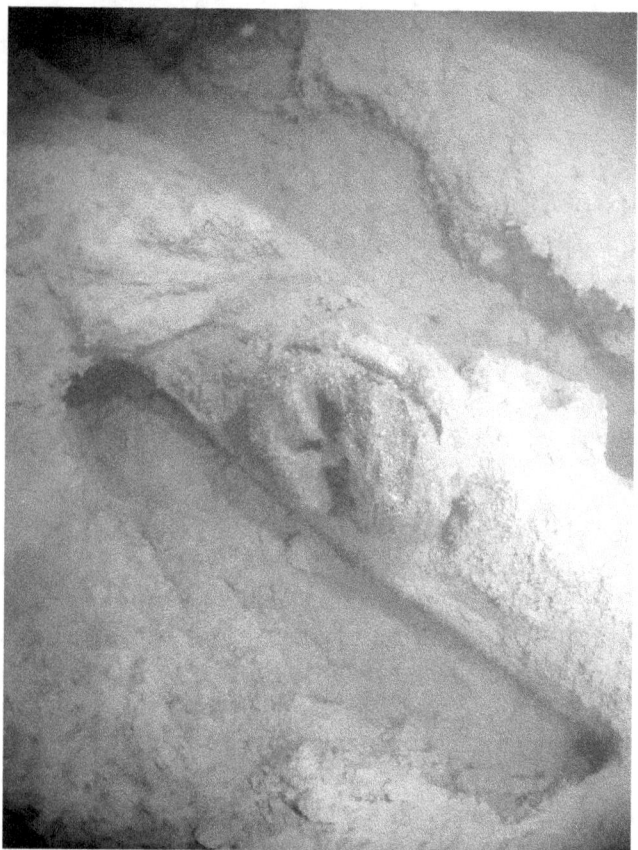

FIGURE 2. "BURIED SCHOONER" PORT RAILING AND DEADEYE ALMOST COMPLETELY SILTED OVER (PHOTO BY DAVID VANZANDT).

sinking and the known location of the "Cleveland Tiller Wreck."

There was not enough archaeological information available from the Buried Schooner to posit a reliable identification. Unable to say what the wreck was, the members of CLUE thought that perhaps it was possible to say what the wreck was not. CLUE thus decided to formally survey and attempt to identify the Cleveland Tiller Wreck. If the Cleveland Tiller Wreck proved to be either the *Plymouth* or the *Mackinaw*, this would either eliminate or reinforce the *Plymouth* as a candidate for the Buried Schooner's identification.

The "Cleveland Tiller Wreck" Survey

On 26 July 2013, David VanZandt and Kevin Magee of CLUE began a reconnaissance survey of the Cleveland Tiller Wreck. The purpose of the trip was to hopefully gather enough data to confidently propose and support an identification of the wreck.

The Cleveland Tiller Wreck's bow points west and stands 5 to 8 feet (1.5 to 2.5 meters) high off the bottom. The bowsprit is snapped off where it passes through the stem's gunwale, but there is a large, elaborate cutwater that juts out 5 feet (1.5 meters) forward of the stem. At the top of this cutwater are curved headboards that connect the cutwater to the hull on either side. There is also a squared notch at the tip of the cutwater that strongly suggests a decorative head of some type may have once been fitted there. Several hearteyes or bullseyes are mounted to the hull near the stem. The overall style of construction of the bow suggests an early 1830-1850 date for the vessel's construction.

The bowsprit is joined to the pawl bitt in front of the windlass. The windlass itself is of a simple design with chain from both hawse holes wrapped around it. On the starboard railing is a 90-degree style cathead with a single pulley embedded in a slot at its tip. The starboard wood-stocked anchor hangs by one of its flukes from the railing aft of the cathead. The stock hangs near the bottom parallel to the hull with the aft portion buried in the lake bottom. The port cathead and anchor are missing from the wreck, and the port anchor chain hangs straight down from the hawse hole into the mud bottom. It is suspected that the anchor is still attached to the chain since it continues down into the mud bottom at least an arm's length. On the port railing, aft of the windlass, are three deadeyes for the foremast. The same configuration is present on the starboard side with the exception that the forward deadeye is missing. No mast or mast hole is evident adjacent to the deadeyes due to the absence of decking in the area and the debris that fills the center of the wreck.

Intact decking is encountered aft of this area along with a cargo hatch located in the middle of the deck. There is a metal bar extended across the hatch at the centerline, which was likely used to hold the hatch cover or tarp down while underway. It is unusual to see this equipment still in place since it is normally blown off and lost during the wrecking event. No obvious cargo is visible inside the silt-filled interior. The railings immediately adjacent to the hatch are absent, and there is a gap equal to the width of the hatch. This style of construction was common in early Great Lakes commercial vessels and designed to facilitate the loading and unloading of cargo using wheelbarrows and planks from the deck to the dock before more efficient cargo handling methods were developed. The gaps in the railings would normally have been closed with rope or temporary planks when underway to prevent people from falling overboard.

The deck aft of the cargo hatch is intact except in an area on the starboard side where a very large gash is evident. The gash appears as a sharp wedge at the side of the hull and transitions into a jagged channel as it penetrates deep into the wreck and crosses the wreck's centerline. The missing deck planks are cleanly cut perpendicular to their direction of travel along the deck, which would have required an extremely strong and focused force to achieve. The gash ends just beyond the exposed centerboard box under the deck. The top of the centerboard box is heavily damaged, and the top of the centerboard inside is exposed. The gash and damage are obviously the result of a collision with another ship, and the wreck appears to have been struck on the starboard side slightly aft of the forward hatch. The collision damage is unique in its narrowness and extreme depth of penetration into the wreck. Most collision damage observed on other wrecks is wedge-shaped and penetrates only a short distance into the wreck's hull.

The railing at the collision site on the starboard side is destroyed, but is again present aft of this location and remains intact all the way to the stern. The port railing is undamaged along its entire length. A set of three deadeyes can be found amidships on both railings, and in the middle of the wreck adjacent to the deadeyes is the stub of the missing mainmast. Just forward of the stub is a large single-barreled hand pump with linkages that attach it to a wooden handle lying on the deck. A simple centerboard winch inside a wooden frame is located in front of the pump. The pump and winch are aligned with each other, but they are offset to the port side relative to the ship's centerline by about a foot (0.3 meter). Offset centerboards were prevalent on ships prior to 1866, after which they were not allowed by the Board of Lake Underwriters.

A metal trough used to funnel bilge discharge from the pump to the chain hole of the centerboard box extends between the pump and the centerboard winch. This is an unusual and novel arrangement since most pumps discharged directly onto the deck to allow the water to run off to the sides.

A small metal rail is mounted to the deck on the centerline in front of the centerboard winch. This metal rail served as a purchase point for the running rigging attached to the foremast boom. On the port side just slightly forward of the winch is a heavily corroded grappling hook lying on the deck.

Immediately aft of the broken mainmast, the decking ends across the width of the wreck, but the outline of a small square hatch coaming can be seen lying on the bottom on the ship's centerline. Wood debris and mud fill the center of the wreck from this point to the stern. The stern is fairly intact, and the starboard railing leads to a five-foot (1.5 meter) long lifeboat davit with two pulleys embedded in slots at its tip jutting out from the wreck. The port davit is missing. The transom is also missing, but two deck beams run across the width of the wreck

Category	*Mackinaw*	*Plymouth*	**Actual**
	Historic Value	Historic Value	Measured Value
Dimensions	112.8' x 23.3' x 9.5'	106' x 23.3' x 8.8'	106.9' +0'/-5' x 23.1' +0'/-1'
Type of Vessel	2-masted schooner	2-masted schooner	2-masted schooner
Head Style	Plain	Scrollhead	Cutwater notch with missing Scrollhead or Figurehead
Cargo	Grain	Grain	Undetermined
Damage	Collision: · Details of damage unknown	Collision: · Starboard side · Amidships · Right angle · Stem driven nearly to the center of the deck	Collision: · Starboard side · 10' forward of amidships · Right angle · Knife-like deck damage past centerboard box
Location	Approx. 10 miles off Cleveland	Approx. 20 miles off Cleveland	21.8 miles off Cleveland

TABLE 1. IDENTIFICATION RESULTS

marking the stern's outline. Standing in the center of the stern is the rudderpost, and attached to it is an impressive eight-foot (2.5 meter) long tiller turned 45 degrees to the starboard side. This feature of the ship is the basis for its informal name "The Cleveland Tiller Wreck." Until the 1850s sailing vessels used tillers, not wheels attached to steering gear, to control the direction of travel.

The top board of the transom lies on a diagonal from the starboard corner down into the mud close to the port side. On top of this beam at the center is a line chock carved into the wood with small wheels embedded at each end to help line move more easily through the slot without damaging either the rope or the chock. Another example of this unusual style of line chock is built into the gunwale at the bow and represents one of the many interesting details observed on this wreck.

Detailed measurements and survey notes were taken on the second dive and again during two follow-up dives on 5 August 2013 with CLUE member Cindy LaRosa and a site plan was developed (Figure 3) along with photographic documentation of the site (Figure 4).

Identification

The identification of the Cleveland Tiller Wreck was accomplished using the VanZandt Historic Shipwreck Identification Method (VHSIM) developed by David VanZandt, one of the authors (VanZandt 2009). The historical data available for the *Mackinaw* and the *Plymouth* was categorically evaluated against the acquired archaeological data from the wreck site. Table 1 describes some of the features used to identify the wreck and how they compare to the known historic values.

The measured length of the wreck was 106 ft. 11 in. (32.59 meters) with a beam of 23 ft. 1 in. (7.04 meters). The *Mackinaw* was 112 ft. 10 in. (34.39 meters) in length with a 23 ft. 3 in. (7.09 meters) beam (Port of Sandusky 1847; District of Buffalo Creek 1851). While the beam measurement is quite close, the length of the measured wreck is too short. Wrecks are frequently measured to be longer than they actually are due to outward sagging of the wreck, sagging of the tape measure, and

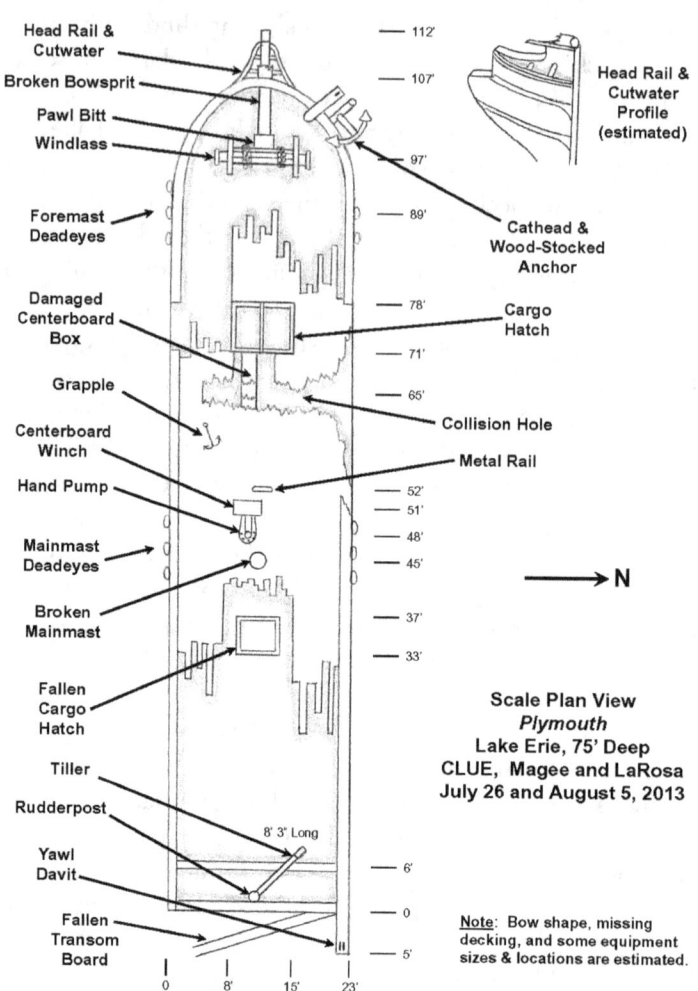

FIGURE 3. "CLEVELAND TILLER WRECK" RECONNAISSANCE SURVEY SKETCH (SKETCH BY KEVIN MAGEE AND CINDY LAROSA).

extra tape measure length used to run it around and over obstructions along the centerline. To measure 6 feet (1.8 meters) shorter therefore makes the wreck unlikely to be the *Mackinaw*. The length of any candidate ship was estimated to be from 101 to 107 feet (30.8 to 32.6 meters). The *Mackinaw* had a plain head, an important item explicitly mentioned in its enrollment (Customs House, Oswego New York 1847), and the wreck instead features a missing scrollhead or figurehead. Furthermore, the location of the "Cleveland Tiller Wreck" is far outside the area described by historical documentation for the *Mackinaw*, again making this ship an unlikely candidate.

The result of the analysis strongly suggests the wreck is indeed the schooner *Plymouth*, and this name can now be confidently applied to this formerly unidentified shipwreck off Cleveland. It sank on the night of 23 June 1852 after a collision with the sidewheel steamer

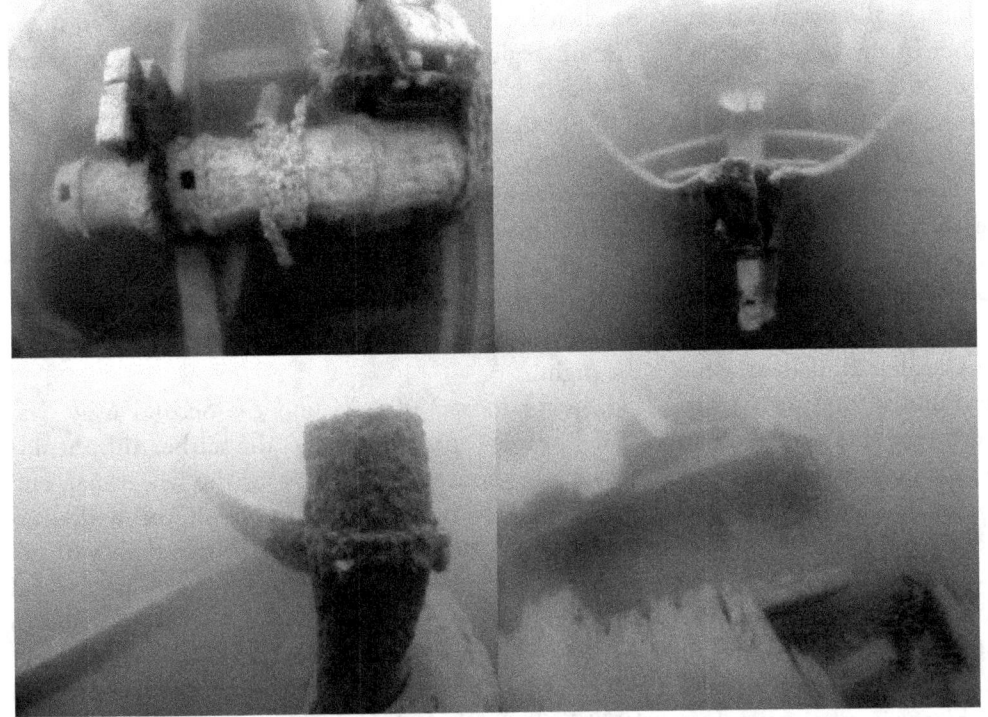

FIGURE 4. "CLEVELAND TILLER WRECK" RECONNAISSANCE SURVEY PHOTOS, CLOCKWISE FROM UPPER LEFT: WINDLASS, BOW HEADBOARDS AND CUTWATER, COLLISION HOLE, AND TILLER (PHOTOS BY DAVID VANZANDT).

The Sinking of the *Plymouth*

In May, 1851 the Atlantic coast and the Great Lakes were connected by rail when the last spike was hammered into the rails connecting the New York and Erie Railroad right-of-way between Piedmont and Dunkirk, New York (Erie Railroad.org 2015a). The first Erie Railroad train to travel the entire distance departed from the eastern terminus at Piedmont on May 14, 1851 and rolled into Dunkirk, the western terminus of the line on the south shore of Lake Erie, the next day, May 15, 1851 (Erie Railroad.org 2015b). It was stipulated in the charter granted to the Erie Railroad by the State of New York that the railroad could never connect to any other railroad leading to any other state (Erie Railroad.org 2015a). The political powers of New York apparently believed that such a stipulation would limit the railroad to intrastate commerce and insure that the Port of New York remained the hub of interstate and foreign commerce. The directors of the Erie Railroad would work within the boundaries of this stipulation but had no intentions of limiting their railroad and revenue to intrastate commerce. Dunkirk, New York had no rail connection, but it did have a connection to the West via the lakes. The selection of Dunkirk as the western terminus of the railroad may have violated the spirit of the charter stipulation but not the literal language. The directors of the Erie Railroad would have their cake and eat it too.

By the spring of 1851, Charles Butler of New York and several associates had gained control of both the Michigan Southern and Northern Indiana railroads and secured the rights through a lease agreement between the two railroads to connect the western end of Lake Erie to Chicago by rail. Butler was a lawyer and philanthropist who studied law in the offices of Martin Van Buren the 8th President of the United States (WP 2015). He accumulated his vast wealth by investing in the railroads

Northern Indiana. The collision was so violent that the steamer's stem was driven "nearly to the centre [sic] of the deck of the schooner" (Blatchford 1870:96). Sidewheel passenger and freight steamers of the early 1850s had sharply raked bows to allow for high speeds, and the unusual and unique collision damage observed on the wreck very closely matches the damage expected from a sharply raked bowed vessel traveling at high speed. The accident location was described as about 20 miles out of Cleveland (The Conneaut Reporter 1852), which coincides nicely with the actual wreck location of 21.8 miles from Cleveland's east breakwall.

Furthermore, the measured dimensions of the wreck are a very good match for the *Plymouth*, which was built in Huron, Ohio, in 1847 (Port of Sandusky 1847). The original enrollment measurements of the *Plymouth* were 106 ft. 0 in. (32.31 meters) in length with a beam of 23 ft. 3 in. (7.09 meters) (Port of Sandusky 1847). This compares very closely with the wreck's measured length of 106 ft. 11 in. (32.59 meters) and beam of 23 ft. 1 in. (7.04 meters). The *Plymouth* also had a scrollhead listed on its enrollment, and this is evidenced by the observed empty notch in the cutwater at the location below where the bowsprit was attached.

and land that helped turn Chicago, Illinois into a city (WP 2015). Charles's brother-in-law and business associate, William B. Ogden, also known as "The Railroad Tycoon Who Built Chicago," later became that city's first mayor (SIUP 2015). In the spring of 1852 not only did the Michigan Southern and Northern Indiana Railroads commence rail service from Monroe, Michigan on the western end of Lake Erie to Chicago, the Michigan Southern established regular steamboat passenger and freight service between Monroe and the western terminus of the Erie Canal at Buffalo and the western terminus of the Erie Railroad at Dunkirk. To do this the Michigan Southern commissioned Buffalo shipbuilder Bidwell & Banta to construct two large and essentially identical steamers, the *Northern Indiana* and the *Southern Michigan*. Launched in the spring of 1852, "they were elaborately fitted out vessels, equipped with every possible comfort and convenience to appeal to the travelling public" (Heyl 1956:173). With the addition of these two fine steamers to the route, one could now travel from New York city to Chicago in relative comfort aboard the trains of the Erie Railroad, the steamboats of the Michigan Southern and the trains of the Michigan Southern and Northern Indiana Railroads. A trip that previously spanned 1600 miles and often took 3 weeks was reduced to less than 1000 miles and 5 days with the Erie, Michigan Southern and Northern Indiana railroads managing everything from beginning to end.

To celebrate the opening of the route the Michigan Southern and Northern Indiana Railroads hosted a "stock holder's excursion" (The Literary World 1852:26) inviting over 400 guests on an all expense paid trip from New York to Chicago. The lists of guests included "notabilities of the Northern States, ladies and their liegemen, chiefly from New York" (New York Daily Times 1852:2). New York (city) guests departed New York on June 21, 1852 aboard a train of the Erie Railroad and arrived in Dunkirk, New York at about noon on June 22. Here they boarded the Michigan Southern operated steamboat *Northern Indiana* upon its arrival from Buffalo with the invited guests from Buffalo and western New York State already on board. The *Northern Indiana* departed Dunkirk mid-afternoon for Monroe with the full complement of guests attended to by their host, none other than Mr. Charles Butler Esquire.

The purpose of the excursion was to pamper, impress and promote travel via railroad and railroad-operated steamer. One reporter noted: "The bill of fare furnished a most gratifying argument in favor of railroads, for by no less potent an agent than steam could the varied excellencies of the fish and flesh and fruits of so many distant regions be brought together. Choice wines flowed in abundance, and the merry buzz of conversation, though not flagging before, still bore testimony to its enlivening effects" (*The Literary World* 1852:26).

The festivities and celebration aboard the *Northern Indiana* that night were short lived however. The lake became rough and many guests retired to their staterooms somewhat unsettled by the onset of mild motion sickness. By midnight almost everyone had retired for the night.

It was almost 1:00 AM and the Second Mate was seated near an open window on the starboard front side of the pilot house conversing with the wheelsman and occasionally focusing his attention on the dark hazy waters of the lake ahead. The night was dark with no moon and somewhat hazy. Suddenly, both the Second Mate and the Wheelsman saw a light that appeared to be very close, perhaps 450 feet, about one to one and a half points ahead off the larboard bow (Blatchford 1870:102). Without hesitation, as Officer of the Deck, the Second Mate ordered the wheel put hard a-port and as the Wheelsman complied the Second Mate ran out of the pilot house through the port side door and climbed to the upper station on top of the pilot house to get a better look (Blatchford 1870:102). From his position on top of the pilot house the Second Mate could now see a schooner and, realizing that a collision was very possible, immediately rang the bells for checking and backing the engines (Blatchford 1870:102).

The steamer was travelling at seventeen miles per hour (Blatchford 1870:95) and the wheels had only made between one and a half and two revolutions in reverse (Blatchford 1870:103), barely slowing the big steamer, when the bow of the *Northern Indiana* struck the schooner amidships on its starboard side at nearly a right angle, with the stem of the steamer driven nearly to the center of the deck (Blatchford 1870:96). "The shock was terrible, the steamer being sharp, and strong, it nearly cut the vessel in two" (The Plain Dealer 1852a:2). The schooner remained impaled on the bow of the steamer for several minutes and the Captain of the schooner and two of the crew jumped aboard the steamer (The Conneaut Reporter 1852). When the vessels finally parted, the schooner remained afloat for another eight minutes, which was just enough time for the remaining seven people on board the schooner to launch the small boat and get away before the schooner sank bow first (The Conneaut Reporter 1852). They were taken on board the steamer "destitute of coats, hats, shoes and other clothing" (The Conneaut Reporter 1852).

The schooner was the *Plymouth* of Buffalo, 106 feet (32.3 meters) long and 197 tons (District of Buffalo Creek 1851), sailing from Huron, Ohio to Buffalo, New York with a cargo of "8300 bushels of wheat, 150 barrels of flour, several tierces of ashes, and two boxes of goods" (The Conneaut Reporter 1852). The wheat was insured for $8,400.00 and the vessel for $8,000.00 by the Buffalo Mutual Insurance Company (The Plain Dealer 1852b:2). The *Northern Indiana* was 300 feet (91.4 meters) long and 1475 tons (Heyl 1956:173) and was on a course from Dunkirk, New York to Monroe, Michigan via the Middle Passage through the Lake Erie islands (Blatchford 1870:95). The damage to the steamer was more severe than what was reported to the passengers and it immediately headed for Cleveland, the closest port of call arriving there with about 4 feet of water in its hold (New York Daily Times 1852:2). The collision occurred "about twenty-five miles northerly from Cleveland" (Blatchford 1870:94) and it took the *Northern Indiana* several hours to reach this port. The reaction of those on board the steamer after the accident is telling in itself:

> *The first night on Lake was unfortunately marked by a stirring gale, that slightly affected the more sensitive of travelers; but even this had its compensations; for in the course of the night the gallant steamer afforded a novel incident to its passengers, by running into and sinking a laden schooner, bound for Buffalo from Toledo. As the crew of the wreck were saved, nobody allowed himself to be otherwise than amused with the exciting piece of bye-play, the officers of the boat alone being conscious that the steamer had suffered so seriously in the collision, as to render it doubtful whether she could ever reach the shore. ... unapprised of the peril they had been exposed to, the passengers quite felicitated themselves on the accident that had given them an unstipulated glimpse at Cleveland, that thrilliest of inland towns (New York Daily Times 1852:2).*

The steamer was subsequently repaired by the carpenters at Cleveland and left for Toledo, Ohio the following day (New York Daily Times 1852:2).

The Court Case and the Railroad

The owners of the *Plymouth* and the owners of a portion of the *Plymouth*'s cargo each filed suit against the *Northern Indiana* in Federal District Court for the Northern District of New York at Buffalo that very same day, June 23, 1852. While the litigation of such suits is typically of no particular interest, this case (the suits were combined at the discretion of the court) proves to be an exception. The railroads could afford to retain and utilize the best litigators available and they indeed did so for this case. The case is of interest because the highly skilled lawyers representing the Michigan Southern Railroad ludicrously promoted, pushed, and pressed an obviously poor case and position for reasons most likely unrelated to the matter in question.

The claimant's attorneys held that the *Northern Indiana* was not liable because the *Plymouth* was not displaying the required lights and did not change its course in time to prevent the collision (Blatchford 1870:97). These arguments were of little substance as both the Second Mate and Wheelsman of the *Northern Indiana* testified that they saw the lights of the *Plymouth* prior to the collision and by regulation it was the duty of the schooner to maintain its course not alter it as argued. When these arguments failed to sway the judge the attorneys for the claimant reversed their position and suggested that the helmsman aboard the schooner "put his helm up after the danger became imminent," effectively changing the course of the schooner and contributing to the collision (Blatchford 1870:100). The helmsman of the schooner testified that indeed he did in desperation put his helm up immediately before the collision and the judge determined that this action did not alter the course of the schooner sufficiently to cause or contribute to the collision (Blatchford 1870:101). The attorneys for the claimant failed to show negligence or misconduct on the part of the schooner.

The attorneys representing the Michigan Southern Railroad and the *Northern Indiana* were now left with the task of demonstrating that the collision was an unavoidable accident and not due to the negligence or misconduct on the part of those in charge of the steamer. Their defense was even weaker than their offense. To the challenge that the steamer did not have a proper look out they responded that the Second Mate was acting as the lookout at the time of the collision. The court replied that the Second Mate "was not, in this case, in a proper position, and his conduct, as proved by his own testimony, is conclusive evidence that he was himself conscious of his neglect" (Blatchford 1870:107).

When challenged to explain why the steamer was traveling at a high rate of speed on a night described by those in charge of the steamer as sufficiently dark, hazy and thick as to "prevent them from seeing the schooner in time to avoid the collision" (Blatchford 1870:94) the attorneys for the claimant replied almost unbelievably that the Michigan Southern Railroad had a contract to carry the U.S. mail and would be subject to penalties if the mail was delivered late. The court noted that:

> *It was suggested by the advocates for the claimants, that rapidity in travel, and in the transmission of the mails, was in accordance with the spirit of the age, and that reducing the steamer's speed in consequence of the darkness of the night, would have subjected her owners to penalties for the non-fulfilment of their contract with one of the Departments of the National Government; and, they asked, if they could not run seventeen miles an hour, how fast could they run (Blatchford 1870:95:108-9)?*

Why would these very knowledgeable and talented attorneys offer such a ridiculous final defense? They had to know their case was weak yet they repeatedly pressed their poor position to the point of insulting the court. As it turns out, Judge Nathan K. Hall, nominated to the position of Federal Judge by U.S. President Millard Fillmore, and confirmed by Congress on 31 August 1852, some two months after the collision occurred, was trying one of his first cases after leaving his duties as Postmaster General of the United States (MC 2015). Is it a coincidence that the argument about delivering the mail was an attempt to sway sentiment from the former Postmaster General under whose tenure the mail contract with the Michigan Southern was awarded?

Nathan Hall studied law under Buffalo attorney (at the time) Millard Fillmore. He was admitted to the bar in 1832 and joined Fillmore's law firm. He was elected to the New York State Assembly and to the United States House of Representatives (Federal Judicial Center 2015). He was a close advisor to President Fillmore and was appointed Postmaster General in 1850 (USH 2015). Later in 1852, he was appointed Federal Judge in the United States Court for the Northern District of New York by the President (MC 2015). Nathan Hall was well connected politically at both the state and national levels.

Apparently the defense offered by the Michigan Southern Railroad attorneys in the case against the *Northern Indiana* was more about measuring the integrity and the willingness of newly appointed Judge Nathan K. Hall to cooperate than it was about avoiding responsibility for sending the *Plymouth* and its cargo to the bottom of Lake Erie. Judge Hall was not swayed and based on the obvious evidence ruled that the *Northern Indiana* was at fault and liable for the damages specified in the libels. Perhaps to flex their muscles or maybe just to aggravate the court, the Michigan Southern Railroad appealed Judge Hall's decision to the Circuit Court of Appeals. The Circuit Court ultimately affirmed the District Court decision.

The term "railroad" eventually came to be used to describe pushing or pressing a position without due consideration for the opposition such as pushing a bill through the legislature without allowing sufficient time for consideration or convicting a person of a crime without sufficient evidence or without granting sufficient time to consider the available evidence. The case of the *Northern Indiana* appears to be an early manifestation of the behavior that ultimately gave birth to this colloquialism.

Epilogue

We have determined that the Cleveland Tiller Wreck is the wreck of the schooner *Plymouth*. The Buried Schooner remains unidentified, although we know for certain that it is not the *Plymouth* and speculate that, due to its location and size, is most likely not the schooner *Mackinaw*. The Buried Schooner's identity remains a mystery, and the *Mackinaw* is out there waiting to be discovered.

About CLUE

CLUE is a non-profit corporation founded in 2001 whose membership includes avocational divers, historians, and archaeologists dedicated to researching, locating, and documenting the shipwrecks and submerged cultural heritage in the Great Lakes with an emphasis on Lake Erie. CLUE is based in Cleveland, Ohio, on the southern shore of Lake Erie.

Acknowledgments

The authors would like to thank the entire Cleveland Underwater Explorers organization for their support and assistance with the *Plymouth* survey. They would also like to thank the Great Lakes Historical Society for their unwavering support over the years for shipwreck searches and surveys.

References

BLATCHFORD, SAMUEL
 1870 *Reports of Cases Argued and Determined in the Circuit Court of the United States for the Second Circuit, Vol. III*, Baker, Voorhis & Company, New York, NY

THE CONNEAUT REPORTER
 1852 Collision on the Lake – Schooner Plymouth Sunk. *The Conneaut Reporter* June 24. Conneaut, OH

CUSTOMS HOUSE, OSWEGO NEW YORK
 1847 Builders Certificate, Mackinaw, 9 May 1847, Records of the Bureau of Marine Inspection and Navigation, Record Group 41, National Archives, Washington, DC.

DISTRICT OF BUFFALO CREEK
 1851 Enrollment No. 42, 10 May 1851, Records of the Bureau of Marine Inspection and Navigation, Record Group 41, National Archives, Washington, DC.

ERIE RAILROAD.ORG
 2015a Dunkirk Branch. <http://www.erierailroad.org/dunkirk-branch/>. Accessed 1 March 2015

 2015b Erie History. <http://www.erierailroad.org/erie-history/>. Accessed 1 March 2015

FEDERAL JUDICIAL CENTER
 2015 History of the Federal Judiciary. <http://www.fjc.gov/servlet/nGetInfo?jid=947&cid=999&ctype=na&instate=na>. Accessed 8 February 2015

HEYL, ERIC
 1956 *Early American Steamers, Vol. II*, Eric Heyl, Buffalo, NY

THE LITERARY WORLD
 1852 An Excursion of a Thousand Miles out West. *The Literary World* 11(2):26-27. New York, NY

MILLER CENTER, UNIVERSITY OF VIRGINIA (MC)
 2015 Nathan K. Hall (1850–1852): Postmaster General. <http://millercenter.org/president/fillmore/essays/cabinet/252>. Accessed 8 February 2015

NEW YORK DAILY TIMES
 1852 The Lakes. *New York Daily Times* June 29:2. New York, NY

THE PLAIN DEALER
 1852a Schooner Sunk. *The Plain Dealer* June 23:2. Cleveland, OH

 1852b The Plymouth. *The Plain Dealer* June 24:2. Cleveland, OH

 1853 Important Decision – The Law of the Lakes. *The Plain Dealer* April 2:2. Cleveland, OH

PORT OF SANDUSKY
 1847 Enrollment No. 91, 13 Aug 1847, Records of the Bureau of Marine Inspection and Navigation, Record Group 41, National Archives, Washington, DC.

SEDGWICK, CATHARINE M.
 1944 By Rail and River to Minnesota in 1854. *Minnesota History* 25(2):103-116. St. Paul, MN

SOUTHERN ILLINOIS UNIVERSITY PRESS (SIUP)
 2015 Railroad Tycoon Who Built Chicago. http://www.siupress.com/catalog/productinfo.aspx?id=2861&AspxAutoDetectCookieSupport=1>. Accessed 15 February 2015

UNITED STATES HISTORY (USH)
 2015 Postmasters General. <http://www.u-s-history.com/pages/h1233.html>. Accessed 8 February 2015

VANZANDT, DAVID M.
 2009 A Systematic Method for the Identification of Historic Era Shipwrecks, Master's thesis, Department of Archaeology, Flinders University, Adelaide, South Australia.

WIKIPEDIA (WP)
 2015 Charles Butler (NYU). < http://en.wikipedia.org/wiki/Charles_Butler_(NYU)>. Accessed 8 February 2015

· · · · · · · · · · · · · · ·

David Michael VanZandt, MMA, RPA
Cleveland Underwater Explorers, Inc.
1226 Lakeland Avenue
Lakewood, OH 44107

James Edward Paskert
Cleveland Underwater Explorers, Inc.
2619 Remsen Road
Medina, OH 44256

Kevin Scott Magee
Cleveland Underwater Explorers, Inc.
4363 West 182nd Street
Cleveland, Ohio 44135

"Reaching Across the Pond: The Archaeological Investigation, Stabilization, and Management of the HMS Fowey Shipwreck in Biscayne National Park."

Joshua Marano

Since 1983, the archeological remains of HMS Fowey *(1744) have been under the management of the United States National Park Service, which has consistently documented the deterioration of the fragile site due to a combination of both human and natural forces. In 2012 Hurricane Sandy, like most major meteorological events in the area, caused significant and irreparable damage to the site. As a result, a major archeological investigation was conducted to document the surviving portions of the wreck in order to develop and implement a stabilization plan to preserve the site* in situ *for future generations.*

Introduction

On 27 June 1748, the British naval frigate HMS *Fowey* (BISC-20, 8Da11948), wrecked within the Legare Anchorage off Elliott Key, Florida while towing the captured Spanish vessel *St. Judea* within what is now the boundary of Biscayne National Park (BISC) (Skowronek and Fischer 2009:5-6). A suspected wreck site in the vicinity was first plotted as a possible archaeological resource in a preliminary 1975 National Park Service (NPS) management document as a potential site with "considerable historical importance" (Fischer 1975). Often referred to as the "Legare Anchorage Wreck," the archaeological remains were later rediscovered by amateur treasure hunter Gerald Klein when he located a shipwreck he believed to be a "nearly intact Spanish treasure galleon" approximately 12 miles due south of Miami in October 1978 (Lakeland Ledger 1979). Klein subsequently filed an *in rem* complaint in the United States District Court seeking the title or salvage award to "a wrecked and abandoned sailing vessel within the Legare Anchorage" (Skowronek and Fischer 2009:27). The approximate position of the wreck, however, was located within the boundary of BISC. As such, the ownership and jurisdiction of the newly found shipwreck was awarded to the United States government in 1983.

The Legare Anchorage site, later identified by NPS archaeologists as the historic remains of HMS *Fowey*, rests in approximately 30 feet of water and is a contributing member of BISC's Offshore Reefs Archaeological District (8Da3219). While the NPS maintained custody of the wreck, once identified as a foreign military craft it was determined that the government of the United Kingdom maintained sovereignty and ownership of the wreck under Articles 95 and 96 of the United Nations Convention on the Law of the Sea and later under the United States Sunken Military Craft Act of 2004. As such, the wreck of HMS *Fowey* became subject of the NPS's first Memorandum of Understanding (MOU) concerning the management of a foreign-owned shipwreck in federal waters. The finalized MOU, signed by NPS director Jon Jarvis and Commodore Eric Fraser of the Royal Navy on August 15, 2013, officially recognized British title to the wreck while outlining the NPS's intention to manage the site and the associated collection. This included discussion of information and personnel exchanges to facilitate joint research on the vessel, as well as provisions for the unlikely event that human remains were discovered on the wreck site (Gadsby and Conlin 2015:7).

The site, which has been both looted and vandalized several times throughout its history (eventually leading to its closure to the public), is now under near constant attack by shifting local currents that are destroying it at an alarming rate. Prior to the vandalization of the site, it was well protected and stable under a dense bed of seagrass. Several acts of vandalism caused extensive damage to that grass bed, from which it has been unable to recover. The species of grass present at the site, primarily turtle grass (*Thalassia testudirum*), is at its ecological limit in terms of depth, and the active currents and frequent heavy seas in the area will not allow the grass to repopulate the area (Tilmant et al. 1982). The vegetation continues to retreat from unexposed portions of the site, even during years when no named storms impact the area. The loss of grass from the site area is greatly exacerbated by even the most minor of meteorological events that, as could be observed following Hurricane Sandy in 2012, can cause significant and irreparable damage to a finite and important archaeological resource. In addition to the threat of total resource loss to erosion, the presence of an array of exposed and easily transportable artifacts, combined with the site's historically significant past, remains an enticing allure to opportunistic relic hunters and illicit salvors. The presence of newly exposed archaeological material may renew attempts to illegally loot the site, which would cause even more rapid destruction.

Given these threats, BISC partnered with members of the NPS's Submerged Resources Center (SRC) and Southeast Archeological Center (SEAC) to complete a multi-component research project to identify and document the extant in situ portions of the site and to develop an appropriate stabilization and management strategy to preserve and protect the site for future generations. The preliminary results of this project were the subject of a symposium entitled "Reaching Across the Pond: The Archaeological Investigation and Management of the HMS *Fowey* (1748) Shipwreck in Biscayne National Park," that was presented at the Society for Historic Archaeology's 2015 Annual Meeting. This document provides an overview of the symposium with highlights of several of the papers presented and serves as a summary of the purpose, research methodology, and objectives of the project. It should be noted that this work does not intend to provide an in-depth technical discussion of the topics addressed within the symposium, but rather, a basic introduction to the site with an overview of some of the topics covered in presentations during this symposium.

Previous Archaeological Investigations

The first professional archaeological investigation of HMS *Fowey* developed out of the legal proceedings of its custody battle. Following the preliminary injunction that ordered Mr. Klein to cease removing materials from the site, the NPS was tasked with locating the wreck using the minimal positional information provided by Klein to the court in order to secure his salvage claim. The resulting survey, conducted between 27 June and 6 July 1980 sought to relocate the shipwreck identified by Klein in an area slightly larger than one square mile. Using a Geometrics G-806 proton procession marine magnetometer, NPS employees located a historic shipwreck matching Klein's description on 4 July 1980. The remaining fieldwork was immediately devoted to a rapid documentation of the site in order to establish the NPS's claim, which provided baseline documentary evidence to positively identify and manage the site. This process included initial reconnaissance and investigation through photography, sketch maps, notes, and film. In addition to this preliminary investigation, a photomosaic and preliminary site plan were produced, and 21 diagnostic artifacts were documented and recovered from the wreck. All of the fieldwork was conducted by SEAC archaeologists, members of the NPS's Submerged Cultural Resources Unit (now known as the Submerged Resources Center or SRC), and Florida State University anthropology students in 1980 (Skowronek 1984).

While the vessel in question was located by the NPS during the 1980 field season, its identity remained a mystery. While the vessel located by Klein was at first thought to be the remains of a Spanish treasure galleon, archaeological evidence did not support Klein's claim. Initially thought to be of Spanish origin, proper identification of many of the artifacts and contradictory historical records cast doubt on this hypothesis. As such, additional archaeological work was conducted on the site in 1983 in order to determine the site's eligibility for inclusion into the National Register of Historic Places and to meet the NPS management goals of preserving the site for the betterment of future generations, while gathering information vital to developing future plans for the site's management and interpretation (Skowronek and Fischer 2009:82).

The 1983 project was minimally invasive in nature, but included a systematic documentation of the site in order to record its exposed vessel structure, diagnostic construction elements, and the vessel's associated artifact scatter. Again, as with the 1980 survey, certain diagnostic artifacts were collected in order to provide information to potentially identify the wreck. While both the archaeological and historical research conducted for the 1983 field project produced a site plan for BISC-20 and effectively concluded that the Legare Anchorage site's approximate age, function, and cultural affiliation was that of a British warship of the mid-1740's and was most likely the remains of HMS *Fowey*, the identification came at a cost. Prior to the close of field operations for the 1983 project, vandals unhappy with the recent court ruling awarding NPS custody of the archaeological remains, drug anchors through the site in an obvious attempt to destroy it. This unfortunate incident seriously damaged the wreck and the seagrass that covered much of the unexcavated site and may have proven to be the single most destructive event to befall HMS *Fowey* since it initially ran aground in 1748 (Lawson and Marano 2013:9). In 1983, NPS archaeologists experimented with several site stabilization techniques including sandbags, ground cloths, and even an attempt with sediment-trapping artificial seagrass. Unfortunately, none of the tests performed adequately, and all began to fail within a few years.

In 1992, Hurricane Andrew tracked almost directly over the site, further destabilizing and damaging already injured portions of the site. During the archaeological condition assessments that followed the storm, BISC-20 was found to be nearly stripped of sediment and much of the hull was exposed in areas that had never been visible before (Davis et al. 1992). The damage to the site prompted a second assessment and documentation of the wreck carried out by the NPS Submerged Cultural Resources Unit in 1993. The 1993 project resulted in an updated site plan that provided somewhat more detail on the timber arrangement of the most intact portion of the ship's hull. The project also prompted several studies into the possibility of reestablishing seagrass at the site as a protective measure. Despite much examination, on-site study, and even a conference devoted to the topic held in the park, researchers concluded that not only was there no likelihood that seagrass could be reestablished, but that BISC should expect the grass still present on the site to continue to erode and that the rate of that erosion should be expected to increase (Zieman 2000; Skowronek and Fischer 2009:179-181). In the years since Hurricane Andrew, NPS archaeologists have consistently monitored the BISC-20 site, usually visiting it several times per year and always after major storm events. Every monitoring event (especially those that followed storms) has reported the same situation: that seagrass beds surrounding the main hull section are eroding away. As the beds erode, new, previously in situ, portions of the wreck are exposed. Smaller materials that are exposed simply wash out of their primary context and are blown across or off the site, and larger materials, like the wreck structure, are abraded, fractured, and re-exposed to wood-boring organisms and bacterial decomposition (Lawson and Marano 2013; Keller et al. 2014).

Project Objectives

While illicit salvage and treasure hunting were once considered the primary threats to BISC-20, these recent archaeological assessment efforts by NPS staff have revealed that the site was increasingly threatened by erosion and sediment loss during even minor storm events. Both cursory and systematic investigations indicate that BISC-20 is routinely losing integrity, as entire portions of the site and its numerous transportable artifacts are exposed and destroyed by the powerful currents flowing over the area. Artifacts, such as an intact sword and pewter plates observed after Hurricane Sandy in 2012, have been found exposed on the seafloor, later to be carried off by strong tidal currents or recovered by opportunistic looters. The site has substantially fewer in situ artifacts then what was originally documented in 1983 (Lawson and Marano 2013; Keller et al. 2014).

While the initial recording and subsequent reassessments of BISC-20 have been vital in the development of the site's overall management plan, there has been substantial loss of archaeological material since the previous projects. Prior fieldwork indicated that a considerable portion of the lower hull of the vessel was intact and buried in the sediment, but following Hurricane Sandy it was difficult to determine if this was still the case since the most recent fieldwork in 1993 had exposed the entirety of the remaining hull structure. In addition, the debris field surrounding the structure remains includes both dislocated materials and in situ artifacts threatened with dislocation during storm events.

In order to develop a plan to stabilize the remains of HMS *Fowey*, a multiple component research strategy was developed. Additional archaeological research, including some amount of minimally intrusive excavation on the periphery of the site, was first required to determine the current maximum extent of the predominate components of the wreck. This plan identified the in situ portions of the main hull and intact historic debris field, as well as dislocated materials in the surrounding environment. The objective of the expanded evaluation and testing of the site completed in August 2013 was to gather information necessary to refine and finalize the means and extent of stabilization efforts at the site.

A newly updated site plan was also completed. While the delineation of the site's extent was a vital initial step in developing a site stabilization plan, additional research was required to determine the nature and intensity of the environmental forces affecting the site. A year-long study was initiated in June 2013 to document and analyze the on-site conditions, the results of which guided the development of an appropriate and sustainable stabilization strategy that was implemented by BISC in August 2014.

Archaeological Testing and Documentation

One of the primary objectives of the expanded evaluation and testing of BISC-20 was to gather the information necessary to refine and finalize the means and extent of future stabilization efforts at the site (Lawson and Marano 2013:13). Given the substantial loss of archaeological material since the site's initial discovery in 1978, the evaluation and documentation of the surviving intact hull structure was paramount. At the time of its first evaluation by professional archaeologists in 1983, the intact structural remains of BISC-20 measured approximately 75 ft. (22.9 m) in length and 30 ft. (9.2 m) in width (Skowronek 1984:21-22). These remains were described as, "the unsheathed starboard bilges of a vessel with a 36-foot beam, from forward of the mizzenmast to the galley at the foremast". As recorded during the 2013 field season, the articulated remains of BISC-20 measure approximately 51.8 ft. (15.8 m) in length and 25.1 ft. (7.65 m) in width. When compared to the extent of the structural remains documented in 1983, the 2013 project documented an overall reduction of in situ archaeological material of approximately 40% (Marano 2015). In contrast with the original interpretations of the site (Skowronek 1984; Steffy 1986), it can now be confidently stated that the remains of BISC-20 represent the interior portion of the starboard side of the vessel from approximately the turn of the bilge to the lower gun deck. The surviving portion of the vessel includes the remnants of the main gun deck, gun ports, oar ports, and a substantial amount of articulated framing and selectively preserved rigging elements. The orientation of the vessel is approximately 145° magnetic with the bow, near the southeast terminus of the site (Figure 1).

In addition to the detailed documentation of the vessel's structural remains, a systematic visual and metal detecting survey was conducted within 100 meters of the surviving hull structure, encompassing the majority of the extent debris field associated with the site. This survey, which included the placement and excavation of 13 50 by 50 cm exploratory excavation units, aided in identifying the maximum extent of surviving archaeological material at BISC-20 and was later utilized to explicitly delineate the archaeological footprint of the site, a vital initial step in developing future stabilization efforts. Additional systematic magnetometer survey of a 1km square area around the site was completed utilizing a Geometrics G882 marine magnetometer with 5 meter line spacing over the site and 15 meter line spacing along the periphery. This survey identified 38 individual anomalies, one of which proved to be a large admiralty-style anchor contemporary to those carried by HMS Fowey at the time of its demise (Figure 2).

FIGURE 1. SITE PLAN COMPLETED DURING THE 2013 ARCHAEOLOGICAL TESTING AND DOCUMENTATION PROJECT (IMAGE COURTESY OF BISCAYNE NATIONAL PARK).

Pre-Stabilization Research, Stabilization Operations, and Post-Stabilization Monitoring

NPS site stabilization studies began in 1981 with the monitoring of sediment transport across the site, utilizing a simple grid system to measure sediment erosion or accumulation as well as periodic current monitoring between May and July of that year. While this study effectively concluded that normal wave action and currents were not strong enough to cause damaging sediment movement at the site, those created by major meteorological events could initiate substantial sediment transport (Tilmant et al. 1982). Results regarding the gross migration of sediments across the site overtime were inconclusive due to the limited duration of the study and did not account for seasonal variations in environmental conditions on the site. While a number of stabilization plans were suggested at the conclusion of

FIGURE 2. A LARGE ADMIRALTY STYLE ANCHOR LOCATED DURING SURVEY OPERATIONS IN 2013 (IMAGE COURTESY OF BISCAYNE NATIONAL PARK).

the 1981 monitoring project, no stabilization plan was ever selected. Between 1983 and 2000, BISC funded and coordinated a number of sea-bottom dynamics studies, sediment and substrate analyses, and seagrass restoration studies at the HMS *Fowey* site (Tilmant et al. 1982; Tedesco and Wanless 1995; Wanless and Risi 1996; Zieman 2000) all with the intention of producing a stabilization plan for the site. While a number of experiments, including the utilization of sandbags, ground cloths, and sediment-trapping artificial seagrass, were attempted throughout the 1980s and 1990s, none of the methods tested performed as designed and all began to fail within a year (Tilmant et al. 1982; Skowronek 1984:20; Tedesco and Wanless 1995; Zieman 2000; Skowronek and Fischer 2009).

Several of these studies also explored the possibility of reestablishing seagrass at the site as a protective measure, though it was eventually determined that successful seagrass recolonization was unlikely, and BISC should expect the erosion of seagrass to continue with an increased rate of loss over time (Zieman 2000; Skowronek and Fischer 2009:179-181). Unfortunately, the majority of these studies were limited in scope and duration and could not identify any long-term trends on the site. As such, none of the permanent stabilization plans discussed by these studies were developed further or implemented.

The stabilization of the HMS *Fowey* site was no simple task, as it is located in a dynamic and exposed seafloor environment. To stabilize both the site and the surrounding environment, factors such as wave and current-induced sediment transport, especially during storms, needed to be incorporated into an overall stabilization plan. One of the primary objectives of the 2013-2014 survey was to assess the environmental conditions affecting the site and composition of its remaining protective sediment. As such, a variety of techniques, including remote sensing, the recovery of sediment samples, and the continuous monitoring of oceanographic and meteorological data, were utilized to document benthic conditions on site.

Members of the United States Geological Survey (USGS) then assisted with the processing and interpretation of these datasets (Keller et al. 2014). The resultant report discussed side scan sonar imaging of the site to delineate the current extent of living seagrass beds, rasterized TIN images of processed bottom classification data (Sonavision RoxAnn GD-X), sediment sample analysis to determine the composition of the existing substrate on site, and the oceanographic forces observed on site for an entire year through the deployment of a Sontek Triton Acoustic Doppler Velocimeter (ADV) current-meter (Keller et al. 2014). After describing the objectives, operating parameters, and site specific methodologies for each of these analyses, the report provided interpretations of the data collected to describe the oceanographic, benthic, and meteorological conditions observed on site and their potential implications for any proposed stabilization strategy, while also providing a review of several stabilization techniques attempted on similar sites around the world. This report concluded that while native sediment at the site moves infrequently under the observed conditions, measurements were not made for a long enough period to represent long-term (tens-of-years) conditions at the site. Waves are generally greater in winter months, which were under-represented in the sampling period due to a relatively benign winter storm season, and no tropical storms or hurricanes occurred during the deployment. These infrequent but intense storms are most likely to mobilize material at the site (Keller et al. 2014:46).

The report was then reviewed by resource managers at BISC, who had by that time initiated the submission of permitting applications with several parties, including the Florida State Historic Preservation Office (SHPO), the Florida Department of Environmental Protection, and the U.S. Army Corps of Engineers. The resultant plan called for the stabilization of structural remains and associated artifacts of BISC-20 through reburial under a continuous pile of sandbags. These would be placed over the remains of the shipwreck, part of the debris field, and unvegetated sand seafloor up to the edges of surrounding seagrass beds. Layers of sandbags would reach a height 50-75 cm at the central portions of the site and taper towards the perimeters, covering approximately 480 square meters (BISC 2013a; 2013b). Following approval of the required permits, BISC issued a formal statement of work and a request for proposals from contractors to complete the project. Adventure Environmental, Inc. (AEI) (project manager) and Tetra Tech, Inc., (subcontracting dive operations) two marine stabilization and restoration firms with extensive experience in previous aquatic habitat repair/restoration projects in the area were eventually awarded contracts to complete the work.

Following an operations plan developed by AEI from the scope of work provided by BISC, reburial of the site was completed in 37 days and included the filling, transport, staging, and individual placement of approximately 13,580 14 in. by 30 in. (35.5 cm by 76.2 cm) custom-made biodegradable cotton bags (Adventure Environmental Inc. and Tetra Tech, Inc. 2014:4). Each bag, which weighed approximately 75 lbs. when filled to capacity, contained locally obtained sediment similar to that identified on site and currently in use in similar, albeit much smaller, environmental restoration projects in the area (BISC 2013a; Keller et al. 2014; Wright et al. 2015). Divers placed filled sandbags in an orderly fashion along the entire shipwreck site. Under the direction and monitoring of BISC resource managers, Tetra Tech divers utilized a combination of SSA and SCUBA diving modes to complete on site operations in 15 days (Figures 3 and 4). Sandbags were placed as a continuous covering over the site, end to end and side to side leaving no gaps between bags with the exception of one large archaeological feature (shot locker) colonized by corals. Bags around the shot locker were placed to the level specified by BISC cultural resource staff, designed to partially cover the artifact but allow coral exposure above the field of sandbags. A minimum of three to four layers of sandbags reaching an estimated height of 40-75 cm were placed over the central portions of the site to ensure adequate coverage and desired anoxic conditions (Wright et al. 2015).

While the stabilization of the HMS *Fowey* shipwreck was completed on 2 October 2014, a multi-component post-stabilization monitoring strategy will be implemented to identify and document any changes occurring on the site. Two water quality monitoring tubes,

FIGURE 3. LARGE COMMERCIAL GRADE POLYPROPYLENE BAGS, KNOWN AS SUPER SACKS, WERE UTILIZED BY CONTRACTORS TO LOWER LARGE NUMBERS OF INDIVIDUAL BABs ONTO THE SITE IN A CONTROLLED MANNER. THESE SUPER SACKS, WHICH COULD CARRY UP TO 35 BABs (APPROXIMATELY 2,625 LBS.) WERE THEN UNLOADED BY DIVERS AND BABs WERE INDIVIDUALLY PLACED BY HAND OVER THE SITE (IMAGE COURTESY OF BISCAYNE NATIONAL PARK).

FIGURE 4. AN IMAGE SHOWING ONE OF THE FIRST LAYERS OF BABS COVERING THE SITE. NOTE THE DELIBERATE PLACEMENT OF BABS AROUND EXISTING SEAGRASS BEDS (IMAGE COURTESY OF BISCAYNE NATIONAL PARK).

modeled after those utilized on Parks Canada's Red Bay Wreck, were installed both over the site's structural remains and within the debris field to ensure the development and maintenance of an anaerobic environment over previously exposed portions of the site (Parks Canada 2007). In order to monitor the size and shape of the mound now covering the majority of the site, bathymetric survey utilizing a single beam sonar, similar to that employed by the state of North Carolina to monitor sediment transport near the *QAR* shipwreck site, was originally planned to be conducted at least annually (Wilde-Ramsing and Rodriguez 2008). Unfortunately, due to the relatively low height of the mound and the sea state usually encountered at the site, this monitoring technique was ineffective and as such, BISC resource managers have resorted to observing the accretion and erosion of sediment on site using monitoring stakes. In addition to these monitoring strategies, the site will continue to be visited regularly to identify and documented any threats or disturbances to the site.

Conclusions

Though BISC is the current home of over 70 known historic shipwrecks, most were stripped of diagnostic cultural materials in the decades before the establishment of the park. The remains of HMS *Fowey* exist as one of the few examples of a submerged archaeological site within the park that presently contains a substantial material culture assemblage associated with a known wreck. The mission statement of the NPS is to preserve unimpaired the natural and cultural resources and values of the national park system for the enjoyment, education, and inspiration of this and future generations (16 U.S.C. § 1). The documentation and stabilization efforts completed between 2013 and 2014 have established a new baseline dataset for monitoring purposes and will protect the site from future erosion and theft.

While these efforts have largely physically removed access to the site, the site has been closed to the public since the early 1990s and provides an interesting case study in the management, interpretation, and protection of sensitive archaeological sites. BISC has worked diligently to promote a multi-component public outreach program, which has included lecture series, museum and laboratory tours, and the creation of an array of educational material to educate the public on the site while promoting transparency and accountability regarding research efforts.

The NPS did not come lightly to the decision to undertake such a large-scale project on one of BISC's most significant historical resources, and a feature entrusted to NPS care by the government of the United Kingdom. It is only after several decades of monitoring significant loss at the site, both from erosion and looting, that this option was implemented. Other options regarding the management of the site, including full-scale excavation of the site, were deemed cost-prohibitive, not in line with the mission of the NPS, and for the positively identified and archaeologically well documented HMS *Fowey*, not currently necessary for the elucidation of archaeological or historical inquiry. The park has therefore determined that the only hope for maintaining the integrity of the wreck for the future, and for mitigating the ongoing erosion and loss of historic fabric and artifacts, is the stabilization program described herein.

References

ADVENTURE ENVIRONMENTAL INC. AND TETRA TECH, INC.
    2014   Restoration Completion Report: Shipwreck Stabilization, Biscayne National Park. Report to Biscayne National Park, Homestead, Florida.

BISCAYNE NATIONAL PARK (BISC)
    2013a   Statement of Work: Biscayne National Park Shipwreck Stabilization, Biscayne National Park, National Park Service, U.S. Department of the Interior, Homestead, Florida.

    2013b   US Army Corps of Engineers Joint Environmental Resource Permit Application, #SAJ2014-00089, Biscayne National Park Cultural Resources, BISC-20 site files, National Park Service, U.S. Department of the Interior, Homestead, Florida.

DAVIS, G. E., L. LOOPE, C. ROMAN, G. SMITH, AND J. TILMANT
    1992   Hurricane Andrew Resources Assessment of Big Cypress National Preserve, Biscayne National Park, and Everglades National Park. Submitted to National Park Service. Copies available from Southeast Archaeological Center, Tallahassee, Florida.

FISCHER, GEORGE
    1975   Preliminary Archaeological Assessment: Biscayne National Monument, Florida. Manuscript on file, National Park Service, Southeast Archaeological Center, Tallahassee, Florida.

GADSBY, DAVID AND DAVID CONLIN
    2015   "…Concerning their Common Heritage…". Archaeological Site Stewardship and International Cooperation in the National Park Service. Paper presented at the 48th Conference on Historical and Underwater Archaeology, Seattle, Washington.

KELLER, JESSICA A., CHRISTOPHER R. SHERWOOD, JOSHUA MARANO, CHARLES LAWSON, AND REBECCA BEAVERS
    2014   Biscayne National Park, HMS Fowey Pre-Stabilization Report, Technical Report No. 33. Submerged Resources Center National Park Service, US Department of the Interior, Lakewood, Colorado.

LAKELAND LEDGER
    1979   Treasure Hunter Wins Right to Keep Galleon. Lakeland Ledger, 28 October 1979, Vol. 74, No. 5, Page 5b, Lakeland, Florida.

LAWSON, CHARLES, AND JOSHUA MARANO
    2013   Research Design for Archaeological Documentation in Advance of the Stabilization of the HMS Fowey Shipwreck Site, (BISC-20, 8DA11948). Submitted to National Park Service. Copies available from Biscayne National Park, Homestead, Florida.

MARANO, JOSHUA L.
    2015   An Archaeological Investigation and Interpretation of the Structural Remains of HMS Fowey, (BISC-20, 08DA11948). Manuscript, National Park Service, Biscayne National Park, Homestead, Florida.

PARKS CANADA
    2007   The Underwater Archaeology of Red Bay: Basque Shipbuilding and Whaling in the 16th Century. Robert Grenier, Marc Bernier, and Willis Stevens, editors. Parks Canada, Ottawa.

SKOWRONEK, RUSSELL K.
    1984   Archaeological Testing and Evaluation of the Legare Anchorage Shipwreck Site, Biscayne National Park, Summer 1983. Submitted to National Park Service. Copies available from Southeast Archaeological Center, Tallahassee, Florida.

SKOWRONEK, RUSSELL K. AND GEORGE R. FISCHER
    2009   HMS Fowey Lost and Found: Being the Discovery, Excavation, and Identification of a British Man-O-War Lost off the Cape of Florida in 1748. University of Florida Press, Gainesville, Florida.

Sunken Military Craft Act. 10 U.S.C § 113 et seq. 2004.

Tedesco, Lenore P. and Harlod Wanless
    1995   HMS Fowey Project, Biscayne National Park Submerged Site Stabilization Sedimentology / Seagrass Dynamics / Bioturbation. Department of Geological Sciences, University of Miami. Manuscript on file, National Park Service, Biscayne National Park, Florida.

Tilmant, James T., Richard Curry, and Richard D. Conant, Jr.
    1982   Biological, Hydrological, and Sedimentary Characteristics of a Historical Shipwreck in Legare Anchorage, Biscayne National Park, Florida. National Park Service South Florida Research Center. Manuscript on file, National Park Service, Biscayne National Park, Homestead, Florida.

United Nations Convention on the Law of the Sea, December 10, 1982, Article 95, 1833 U.N.T.S. 3

United Nations Convention on the Law of the Sea, December 10, 1982, Article 96, 1833 U.N.T.S. 3

Wanless, Harold R. and J. Andrew Risi
    1996   Winter Storm Assessment of the Submerged Wreck Site, BISC-UW-20. Department of Geological Sciences, University of Miami. Manuscript on file, National Park Service, Biscayne National Park, Homestead, Florida.

Wilde-Ramsing, Mark and Antonio Rodriguez
    2008   Using the Queen Anne's Revenge Shipwreck Site as a Testing Ground for a new Method of Artifact Protection and Preservation in Shallow-Marine Environments. North Carolina Underwater Archaeology Branch, Kure Beach, North Carolina.

Wright, Jeneva, Joshua Marano, and Bert Ho
    2015   HMS Fowey 2014 Stabilization Project Report. Manuscript, National Park Service, Biscayne National Park, Homestead, Florida.

Zieman, Joseph C.
    2000   Evaluation of the Fowey Site in Biscayne National Park. Department of Environmental Sciences, University of Virginia, Charlottesville. Manuscipt on file, National Park Service, Biscayne National Park, Florida.

. . . .

Joshua Marano
Biscayne National Park
9700 SW 328th
St. Homestead, FL 33033

"Old Al's Going to Get It," At Least For A While: Recent Riverine Archaeology in Arkansas"

Leslie C. Stewart-Abernathy

To understand Arkansas history, it is constructive to study the use of the extensive network of navigable waterways in and near the State. In the last 30 years, archeologists have documented recovered Native American dugout canoes, as well as researched vessels employed from the Trail of Tears in the 1830s to the end of the Wooden Age in the 1930s. A major step was at West Memphis on the Mississippi in 1988, when record low water permitted professionals and volunteers to use dry-land field techniques to document model barges, a coal barge and a stern wheel steamboat. Particular success has been achieved during recent underwater surveys and bank line exposures of side wheelers and other wrecks including a flat boat, on the Arkansas, Ouachita, and White Rivers. These projects provide tangible evidence of the working rivers before the coming of the massively powerful towboats, and bass boats, of today.

Introduction

There was a saying on the Mississippi to account for anything that happened to go overboard when a steamboat was loading at the bank or underway. "Old Al's going to get it," meaning the item wouldn't go to waste—the giant alligator that was always nearby would take the object (Burnam 1973:53). It was part prayer, part charm, and partly a nod to the realities and dangers of life on the river.

The state of Arkansas has seen "Al get it" many times. There are major rivers that cross it, and its "East Coast" is the Mississippi itself. It has hundreds of miles of navigable streams (Figure 1), particularly when one considers "navigable," to be able to walk beside a small boat, well-loaded, floating in a few inches of water.

The activities of the U.S. Army Corps of Engineers in the 1950s and 1960s transformed Arkansas' waterways, changing many into chains of deep water lakes. Although some archaeological survey was done on Native American sites, no one recorded the evidence of watercraft or indeed most historic sites before they were drowned.

The common form of watercraft today is the aluminum johnboat or the more upscale bass boat, found in abundance on lakes held behind dams on most of the permanent streams. In fact these waterways have been used for over 10,000 years, based on wear analysis of adzes at the Sloan Dalton site in northeast Arkansas (Yerkes and Gaertner 1977). A few dugout canoes have been recorded, including the Peeler Bend Canoe, a 24 ft. dugout of southern yellow pine, found in the Saline River near Little Rock. It was radiocarbon dated to about

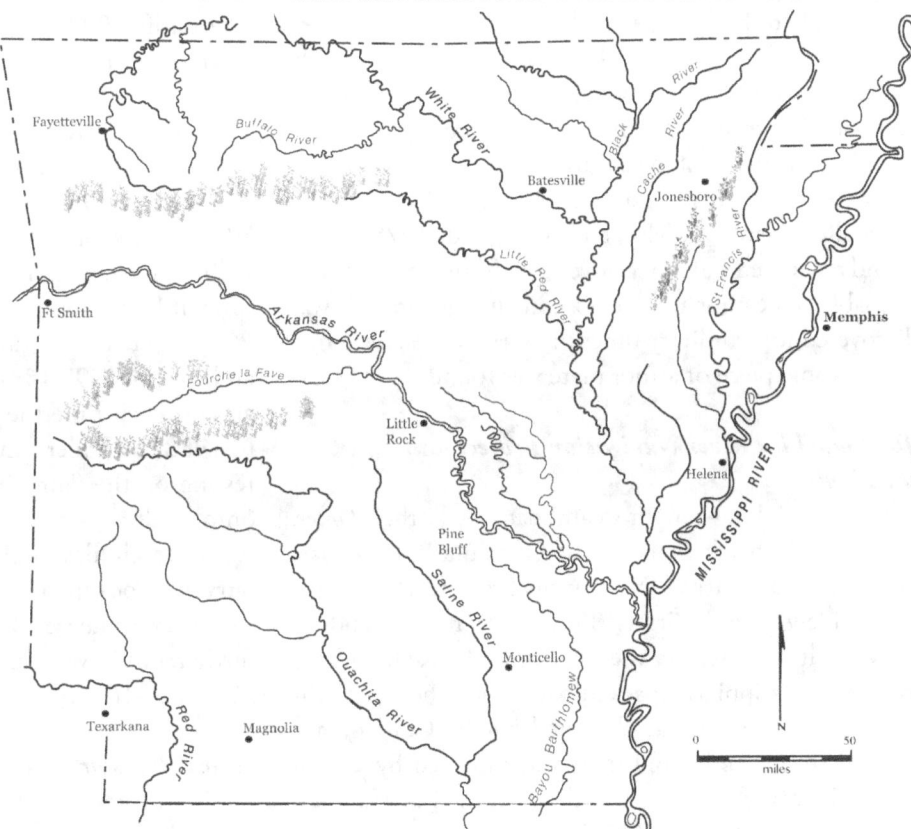

FIGURE 1. MAJOR RIVERS OF ARKANSAS (JANE KELLET, ARKANSAS ARCHAEOLOGICAL SURVEY)

800 years ago (Trubitt 2002). Dugout canoes continued in use into the 20th century.

In Black Water

Fortunately in the last 30 years some attention has been paid to the historic riverine past. I will mention briefly the search for the U.S.S. *Queen City*, and the search for the Homer. In both cases, these were explorations in water with little to no visibility. However, the wrecks remain intact, safely underwater, and mostly buried in the bottom of the rivers.

The U.S.S. Queen City

One of the first underwater explorations by genuine archeologists in Arkansas was the search for the U.S.S. *Queen City* in 1977. The *Queen City* was a sidewheel ferry, refitted in 1863 with thin armor to become "tinclad" Gunboat No. 26. While near Clarendon on the White River, it was captured by Confederate cavalry on 24 June 1864, and burned (Huddleston, and Wood 1995:78, Fig. 36; DeBlack 2003:118-119; Krivor 2004:44-45). This was a particularly embarrassing loss, because it occurred in full sight and hearing of a Union force coming down river but separated from Clarendon by a couple of horse shoe bends

As part of the National Reservoir Inundation Study by the National Park Service, a team of underwater archeologists from the American Archaeology Division at the University of Missouri, Columbia, conducted magnetometer survey and diving on the resulting anomalies (Garrison, May, and Marquardt 1978). They found a wooden hull wreck over 110 ft. in length. It was probably a steamboat, but no conclusive evidence was discovered for a military function of the vessel, although one possible piece of armor plate was found.

The Ouachita River Navigation Project and the Homer

A long-sought steamboat wreck, the *Homer*, was found in black water on the Ouachita River as part of the Ouachita River Navigation Project. The *Homer* was a sidewheeler built in 1859, at 148 ft. long and 28 ft. wide. It was used on the Ouachita, the Red, and the Lower Mississippi as a packetboat. When the Civil War broke out the boat was chartered by the Confederacy to haul troops and supplies. It was captured by Union troops in March, 1864, and then scuttled at Camden (Pearson and Saltus 1993:50-58).

The location was lost until Coastal Environments, Inc. found the *Homer* in 1988. The brick flame bed and the hull below the main deck appear to be intact, but the boilers and the machinery are gone. The cylinder timbers do survive. The *Homer* is in relatively good shape, and remains hidden and preserved under black water (Pearson and Saltus 1993:63-83). Charles Pearson, then Chief Archeologist of Coastal Environments, let me dive on the wreck using the helmet rigged with surface-supplied air and a microphone, but I could not see my hand in front of my face.

In Bright Sunshine

Most of the time in Arkansas boat wrecks appear outside the convenient framework of contract projects or even research projects. They appear instead during low water levels that leave the wreckage in bright sunshine, but subject to further damage. For protection we depend on the authority of the Abandoned Shipwreck Act of 1987 (National Park Service 1990; United States Department of Interior 1990), that gave the Arkansas Commissioner of State Lands the ownership of these vessels, and for documentation we rely on volunteers under my supervision (Davis, Goodman, and Stewart-Abernathy 2002). I would like to discuss four examples briefly, on the Mississippi and White Rivers.

The New Mattie

One of the most obvious is the wreckage of the sternwheel steam towboat *New Mattie*. The boat sank in the White River on 17 February 1900, while fully loaded with cotton bales. The vessel was largely salvaged at the time. It first reappeared in 1976 (Green *Arkansas Gazette* 2, 5, 6 Oct. 1976; Huddleston 1977; Huddleston, Rose, and Wood 1995:153-154; Krivor 2004:49). Bits of it are lost each time the wreck goes back underwater, but in 1988 the boilers on the main deck were still in place resting on the flame bed. The hull had collapsed down onto itself, but at least two rudders remained as well (see research files for 3DE127 at Arkansas Archeological Survey, Coordinating Office, Fayetteville, Arkansas). When examined again in 1999 it had compacted even further, but it was still recognizable (Buchner and Krivor 2001:164-167, Figs. 7.06 and 7.07).

Ghost Boats at West Memphis

The most spectacular set of wrecks to appear so far in bright sunshine were near Memphis, TN, in 1988. Memphis has been a busy river port since the 1830s, and hundreds of vessels of all types have been lost within a few miles of the city. In the summer of 1988 a drought left a part of the river bottom exposed across the river at West Memphis, AR. There were in fact 4 ½ acres of wreckage from the late 1800s and early 1900s (3CT243). We reported on this work in a symposium to this organization at Tucson in 1990 (Stewart-Abernathy 1990) and in an extensive popular report in 2002 (Stewart-Abernathy editor 2002; Stewart-Abernathy 2008).

One vessel was first identified on a morning show on Memphis television as a "Confederate Viking ship," because of what appeared to be a large prow. In fact it was the upstream stem post of a model barge, stripped of its hull planking. It was a double ender, fully exposed, "the pride of the Western boat men" according to one authority in the 1880s (Hall 1884:184). The vessel was almost entirely intact, 137 ft. long, 30 ft. wide, 5.5 ft. deep, and probably the first one seen for five or six decades (Saltus and Stewart-Abernathy 2002:102-118). It had some wire nail fastenings on the deck, so the craft was still in use at least after 1890.

We even found most of a scow bow barge. It had been used to carry coal, and was reconstructed on paper from three huge fragments (Saltus and Stewart-Abernathy 2002:120-128). During low water on the White and other rivers it is common to find wrecks of scow bow wooden-hulled barges. In fact, they probably make up the most common wrecks we know of, above and below the water surface. The documentation of one at West Memphis has proved invaluable in understanding these ubiquitous wrecks.

The most extensive wreckage was of a sternwheel steamboat, the pieces held together still by the twisted, entangled hog chains (Stewart-Abernathy 2002:62-101). With the help of Allen Saltus and Steve James and of course Alan L. Bates (Bates 168), we identified two large sections of hull, one a 60 ft. section flipped upside down and one with a main keelson, a deadman for hog chain fastening, and a sternpost, along with 110 ft. of side framing, the bow, and even smokestacks.

Because the wreckage was momentarily on dry land, we were able to conduct ordinary excavations. This work exposed a bulkhead perhaps from the engine room that had a row of transom windows at the top but without standardized dimensions—each window was hand-made to fit the irregular spacing of the 1 × 4 in. stanchions. Two of these transom windows were blocked by plywood sheets nailed on with wire nails. This bulkhead was laid flat on the sandy bottom of the river, with the interior face up, and used as a salvage platform for the recovery of such items as stirrup bolts for the paddlewheels and an Ashcroft steam pressure gauge with an 1878 trademark. These items were accidentally left in place and then buried by subsequent layers of silt and clay. We were able to document the pieces in detail, but after 26 years we still don't know the name of the steamboat.

The Sidewheeler at 3MO69

Low water in the Fall of 1997 exposed our first sidewheeler, in the White River below St. Charles, 3MO69. With help from Michael C. Krivor of Panamerican Consultants, Inc. of Memphis, volunteers were able to measure the cylinder timbers and axles of the paddlewheels. We knew more of the vessel existed, but that is all we could do at the time. I'll say more about this wreck later.

The Sibley Chute Wrecks

Most of the rivers in Arkansas are tightly controlled by the U.S. Army Corps of Engineers, but portions of two rivers are completely free below the White River Canal that cuts off the Arkansas and the White and connects them to the Mississippi through Lock and Dams 1 and 2. The actual mouth of the White on the Mississippi has become Sibley Chute, and at high water part of the Mississippi flows directly through the Chute, crashing into the bank at one point. In the Fall of 2010, two wrecks were exposed in the collapsing bank. One is probably a steamboat, but the other is a flatboat (Stewart-Abernathy 2011a and 2011b).

We have so far been able to observe the probable steamboat from the bow to about 70 ft. along the hull (see research files for 3DE279 at Arkansas Archeological Survey, Coordinating Office, Fayetteville, Arkansas). Petsch's 1974 (Petsch 1974: Figs. 77 and 78) reconstruction of the hull of the Bertrand has been very helpful for comparison and illustration. The main deck and the upper hull strakes are missing, and there is weathering of the upper ends of the frames. This suggests the hull was exposed to the air for at least some period before complete burial.

The bow stem assembly was revealed when about 15 ft. of the starboard side was undercut and fell away in the Fall of 2010. The lower breasthook assembly can be reconstructed. The hull sits at about a 40° angle heading back into the bank, and rises toward the stern. After the flood of April-May 2011, when the water level went to at least 20 ft. above the top of the bank, about 50 ft. more of the hull was exposed, along with the main keelson and several starboard side keelsons. At that point we were able to measure the width at about 32 ft. from starboard to port chine. Much of the hull seemed to remain in the bank including the port side and several port side keelsons. One interesting feature was a well-made, triangular timber brace that rose from the main keelson, possibly to help support the boiler array. At this point we don't know the name or the date of the vessel. There are no wire nails present for example, as there were on the steamboat bulkhead at West Memphis. Intriguingly, on the bow stem post is carved "I P" although the letters are connected at top and bottom.

The other vessel, now completely gone, appeared to be a flatboat, the first one found in Arkansas waters in spite of the many that were used (see research files for 3DE280 at Arkansas Archeological Survey, Coordinating Office, Fayetteville, Arkansas). Part of the bottom and one side survived long enough to be measured, and we were able to recover an oak peg and boat nails that fastened planking to the side frames. There was enough of the vessel left to document a sloping end wall, two interior bulkheads probably as part of the deckhouse, and the bottom of the hull. Surprisingly, flatboats continued in use his latest as late as 1900. This flatboat may be contemporary with the probable steamboat, but it does lie a few feet lower in the bank. To my somewhat limited knowledge, only two flatboats have been found, this one and one since named America and excavated under the direction of Mark Wagner (Wagner 2005; 2015).

In Bright Sunshine and in Black Water

On one occasion so far, Arkansas has seen a project that combined the techniques of archeology in black water and the much easier task of documenting the much more fragile boat evidence that appears in bright sunshine. That effort was the first part of the White River Navigation Project, conducted by Panamerican Consultants, Inc. from 1999 to 2003 (Buchner and Krivor 2001; Krivor 2004).

The White River Navigation Project

The principal goal of this four year effort was to conduct a sampling of segments of the White River as a test toward transforming the White into a canal to serve the needs of agriculture in eastern Arkansas. To this end Panamerican carried out remote sensing followed by underwater archeology, at selected locations generally south of Interstate 40. One of their discoveries was the largely intact hull known as the "flame bed wreck," found first with the magnetometer and then explored by divers (Krivor 2004:98-104).

Another wreck was yet another steamboat hull in which a cross trench was excavated by divers (Krivor 2004:79-92). This wreck was just south of St. Charles, the site of an important naval engagement in 1864 as Union forces sought to move upstream past the fortified river town. In a vain attempt to block the Union advance, Confederates scuttled three steamboats, the *Eliza G* (also referred to as the *Eliza J*), the *Mary Patterson*, and the gunboat *Maurepas* (Bearrs 1962; Huddleston, Rose, and Wood 1995:68; Krivor 2004:40-41). Unfortunately these vessels were poorly described in the records. The cross trenched hull might be one of these three, particularly the *Maurepas* (Krivor 2004:92).

Fortunately, Panamerican was able to follow up on the 1997 work at 3MO69. Side scan sonar and hydro probing provided much more detail on the wreck of this sidewheeler (Krivor 2004:105-118). Although fast current and debris trapped in the wreckage hindered divers, the work indicates most of the vessel hull is intact and extends well out into the active channel of the White.

Conclusion

It is winter now and the high water season of Spring is coming up. We will continue to watch as more of the probable steamboat at Sibley Chute continues to appear. If the comparison with the *Bertrand* hull reconstruction continues of use, in the next few years we might see evidence of the stern of the vessel, as the Mississippi continues to pour water through Sibley Chute and against that bank. Although, it would not surprise me to see yet more wrecks appear there.

Let me conclude with another context for discovery of boatwrecks in Arkansas. Most wrecks probably lie secure within the bank, as with the *Bertrand* in Nebraska and the *Arabia* in Missouri (Petsch 1974; Hawley 1995; Hawley 1998). Most of these Arkansas wrecks will lie undisturbed. At West Memphis, it took the sinking of a riveted iron barge beside the bank, that then divided some of the Mississippi's force to act against that bank, eventually stripping away several acres of a soybean field to reveal the wrecks 30 ft. below.

But there is one wreck under a bean field that will remain of interest to many outside of the state. That is the *Sultana*, the loss of which in April, 1864, killed more people than died on the *Titanic* (Potter 1992). The *Sultana* site, just north of Memphis, has attained the status of sacred, both for the loss of life, and the knowledge of its approximate location. For now it is secure underneath a soybean field. A museum will open nearby and we shall see what happens to the site after that.

References

Bates, Alan L.
1968 *The Western Rivers Steamboat Cyclopoedium, or, American Riverboat Structure and Detail, Salted with Lore.* Hustle Press, Leonia, NJ.

Bearss, Edwin C.
1962 The White River Expedition June 10-July 15, 1862. *Arkansas Historical Quarterly* 21(4, Winter):305-362.

Buchner, C. Andrew, and Michael Krivor
2001 *Cultural Resources Reconnaissance Study of the White River Navigation Project.* Panamerican Consultants, Inc., Memphis, TN. Submitted to US Army Corps of Engineers, Memphis District, Memphis, TN.

Burnam, Ben Lucien
1973 *Look Down that Winding River.* Taplinger Publishing Co. and Reader's Digest, New York, NY.

Davis, Hester A., Mary Ann Goodman, and Leslie C. Stewart-Abernathy
2002 To the Rescue. In *Ghost Boats on the Mississippi.* Leslie C. Stewart-Abernathy, editor, pp.13-22. Arkansas Archeological Survey Popular Series No. 4, Fayetteville, AR.

DeBlack, Thomas A.
2003 *With Fire and Sword, Arkansas, 1861-1874.* University of Arkansas Press, Fayetteville, AR.

Delgado, James P., and National Maritime Initiative Task Force
1987 *National Register Bulletin Number 20: Nominating Historic Vessels and Shipwrecks to the National Register of Historic Places.* National Maritime Initiative and the National Register of Historic Places, National Park Service, Washington, D.C.

Garrison, Ervan G., J. Alan May, and William Marquardt
1979 Search for the U.S.S. Queen City: Instrument Survey 1977. In *Beneath the Waters of Time: Proceedings of the Ninth Conference on Underwater Archaeology.* J. Barto Arnold III, editor, pp. 45-49. Texas Antiquities Commission Publication No. 6.

Hall, Henry
1884 *Report on the Ship Building Industry of the United States.* Miscellaneous Documents, U.S. House of Representatives, Second Session, 47th Congress, Tenth Census, Vol.13, No. 42, Pt. 8. Government Printing Office, Washington, D.C. (reprinted 1970, Library Editions, Ltd., New York, NY).

Hawley, David
1995 *Treasures of the Arabia.* Arabia Steamboat Museum, Kansas City, MO.

Hawley, Greg
1998 *Treasure in a Cornfield: the Discovery and Excavation of the Steamboat Arabia.* Paddlewheel Press, Kansas City, MO.

Huddleston, Duane
1977 The Wreck of the *New Mattie*. *The Stream of History* 15(2, April), Jackson County Historical Society, Newport, AR.

Huddleston, Duane, Sammie Rose, and Pat Wood
1995 *Steamboats and Ferries on White River: A Heritage Revisited.* University of Central Arkansas Press, Conway, AR.

Krivor, Michael C.
2004 *Remote Sensing Survey and Preliminary Assessment of Submerged Cultural Resources Within the Lower White River Navigation Project.* Panamerican Consultants, Inc., Memphis, TN. Submitted to U.S. Army Corps of Engineers, Memphis District. Memphis, TN.

National Park Service
1990 *Guidelines for the Abandoned Shipwreck Act of 1987 (Public Law 100-298), 55 CFR50116.* Prepared by National Park Service Departmental Consulting Archeologist, Washington, D.C.

Pearson, Charles E., and Allen R. Saltus, Jr.
1993 *Underwater Archaeology on the Ouachita River, Arkansas: the Search for the <u>Chieftain, Haydee</u>, and <u>Homer</u>.* Coastal Environments, Inc., Baton Rouge, LA, report submitted to U.S. Army Corps of Engineers, Vicksburg District. Vicksburg, MS.

Petsche, Jerome E.
1974 *The Steamboat Bertrand, History, Excavation, and Architecture.* National Park Service, Publications in Archeology 11, Washington, D.C.

Potter, Jerry O.
1992 *The Sultana Tragedy: America's Greatest Maritime Disaster.* Pelican Publishing Co., Gretna, LA.

Saltus, Allen R., Jr., and Leslie C. Stewart-Abernathy
2002 The Model Barge and Other Vessels. In *Ghost Boats on the Mississippi.* Leslie C. Stewart-Abernathy, editor. pp. 102-129. Arkansas Archeological Survey Popular Series No. 4, Fayetteville, AR.

Stewart-Abernathy, Leslie C.
1990 Ghost Boats: Archeology on the Parched Bottom of the Big Muddy. Paper presented at the Annual Meeting of the Society for Historical Archaeology and Advisory Council for Underwater Archaeology, Tucson, AZ.

2002 The Steamboat and Its Debris Field. In *Ghost Boats on the Mississippi*. Leslie C. Stewart-Abernathy, editor. pp. 62-101. Arkansas Archeological Survey Popular Series No.4, Fayetteville, AR

2008 Ghost Boats at West Memphis. *Arkansas Historical Quarterly* 67(No. 4, Winter):399-413.

2011a Steamboat and Flatboat: The Sibley Chute Wrecks, 3DE279 and 3DE280. Paper presented at annual meeting of the Lower Mississippi River Conservation Commission, Memphis, TN.

2011b Rat boat? A Squash boat? No, a Flatboat: Chaos and Disaster in Sibley Chute, Arkansas (Barely). Paper presented at South Central Historical Archeology Conference No. 13, Winterville State Historic, Greeneville, MS.

STEWART-ABERNATHY, LESLIE C., EDITOR
2002 *Ghost Boats on the Mississippi: Discovering Our Working Past*. Arkansas Archeological Survey Popular Series No. 4, Fayetteville, AR.

TRUBITT, MARY BETH
2002 Update on the Peeler Bend Canoe: An Ancient Dugout Canoe from Saline County. *Field Notes: Newsletter of the Arkansas Archeological Society* 307:3-5.

UNITED STATES DEPARTMENT OF THE INTERIOR
1990 Final Guidelines, Abandoned Shipwreck Act of 1987 (Public Law 100-298; 43 USC, 2101-2106). *Federal Register* 55(No. 223):50116-50145.

WAGNER, MARK J.
2005 The Flatboat *America* (11PU280): An Early Nineteenth kl;Century Flatboat Wreck in Pulaski County, Illinois. *Illinois Archaeology* 14:90-156.

2015 *The Wreck of the America: A Flatboat on the Ohio River*. Southern Illinois University Press, Carbondale, Il.

YERKES, RICHARD, AND LINA M. GAERTNER
1997 Microwear Analysis of Dalton Artifacts. In Dan F. Morse, *Sloan, a Paleoindian Cemetery in Arkansas*. pp.58-71. Smithsonian Institution Press, Washington, D.C.

. . . .

Leslie C. Stewart-Abernathy
Arkansas Archeological Survey
Winthrop Rockefeller Institute Station
1 Rockefeller Drive
Petit Jean Mountain
Morrilton, AR 71120

A Canoe on a Sand Bar: The Guth Canoe in Northeast Arkansas

Jeffrey M. Mitchem

In Arkansas, only a handful of dugout canoes have been found, all in riverine situations. Severe flooding in northeast Arkansas in 2008 dislodged a dugout in the St. Francis River that ended up on a sandbar. When a local resident discovered it, he transported it to his home and kept it in wet conditions. He contacted the Arkansas Archeological Survey about it, and measurements and a sample were taken for wood identification and possible radiocarbon dating. When the sample was dated, the 1-sigma calibrated range was Cal A.D. 1400-1430. It is now at Cahokia.

Introduction

In the spring of 2008, the floodwaters in northeast Arkansas were the highest in recent memory. The St. Francis River water level was so high that some of the ditches and channels west of the town of Parkin overflowed their banks and kept fields flooded for weeks. Ironically, many of those ditches were dug specifically to help control flooding on the St. Francis and its tributaries after the disastrous flood of 1927 Daniel (1977).

Parts of the region in Cross County were essentially turned into lakes. The fields were covered by several feet of water as far as the eye could see, broken only by stands of cypress and other trees along the field edges. That area is called the Bay Bottoms, and it has no doubt experienced many floods in the past. The 2008 flood caused a lot of hardship for farmers and landowners, and nothing illustrated this more clearly than the plight of a family who resided in a mobile home right next to the waterway: The water was only about a foot from covering their roof and it was that high for weeks.

Coping with flooding is difficult for people today, but it must have been a monumental challenge for the prehistoric inhabitants of Cross County, especially since it probably happened more frequently. While they undoubtedly realized that the floodwaters brought nutrients that helped keep the soil fertile, the difficulties of day-to-day life during a flood would have been staggering. Even though the Parkin site (3CS29) and contemporary villages in the region were surrounded by defensive ditches (Mitchem 2010), these probably would not have kept the inhabitants dry during a major flood. As the water levels rose, the time would come when they would have to abandon their homes and head for higher ground until the waters receded. With no Red Cross or similar agency to provide help, it was up to them to pack up treasured belongings and as much food as they could carry, then canoe across or down the river to wherever higher ground was accessible.

Researchers have long assumed that the native peoples of this region regularly used canoes for travel. The fact that most Parkin phase sites are located along the St. Francis and Tyronza Rivers means that the most efficient way to transport people and materials from one settlement to another would have been by canoeing up or down the rivers. Some of the cypress logs cut into barrel staves at Parkin's early 20th century Northern Ohio Cooperage and Lumber Mill may actually have been old canoes that had become dislodged from the river bottom and were floated down the river with the freshly cut logs. Old canoes are found occasionally elsewhere in the Southeast, and many are in remarkable condition (Hartmann 1996; Ruhl and Purdy 2005; Wheeler et al. 2003).

Known Dugouts from Arkansas

In Arkansas, only a handful of dugout canoes have been recorded. The Griggs Canoe, on permanent display at Toltec Mounds Archeological State Park, was found in the back yard of Mr. and Mrs. A. F. Griggs along the Saline River near the city of Benton (Arkansas State Parks 1980s). It ended up on their land after flooding during the winter of 1982-1983, and they used it as a makeshift cattle trough for several months (Ann M. Early, pers. comm. 2008). They eventually contacted Ann Early (then at the Arkansas Archeological Survey's HSU Station in Arkadelphia), and she arranged for it to be donated to Arkansas State Parks. Made from southern pine, it was constructed using metal tools, so we know it dates from sometime after European contact. Attempts to get a radiocarbon date were unsuccessful. Tree-ring samples were taken, but were not in good enough shape to yield an exact date. Nevertheless, two tentative dates of 1680 and 1840 were suggested (Arkansas State Parks 1980s). Although it was never treated with any kind of preservative, it has remained relatively intact with only moderate surface damage.

The Peeler Bend Canoe has a long and complicated story. In 1999, residents of Benton discovered and removed the dugout from the Saline River. Found near Benton, it was exposed by low water levels (Trubitt 2002). They dug it out of the mud, finding what they thought was an anchor stone nearby. Because it was located in a navigable river, the canoe became the property of the state.

Several problems then became apparent. First was where to store it. And second, how do you preserve it? Researchers at the University of Florida faced these problems with salvaged canoes in the 1970s and 1980s. It takes years of soaking in a solution of polyethylene glycol to get them to the point where they won't disintegrate when they eventually dry out (Purdy 1991:285-311).

Dr. Barbara Purdy was salvaging canoes from all over the state, and gathering great information about their dates and styles, but after they were preserved, there was no room to store or display them in the museum. Eventually space was found in a dark basement at the University of Florida Medical School. At some point in the 1980s the Med School called the museum and said they needed the space, so the canoes needed to go. Graduate students were recruited to help University of Florida employees load the preserved canoes into semi truck trailers. Some were so long that they stuck out the back of the trailers. They were taken north of the city to a state forest owned by the university, where they were stored in open-sided pole barns. The canoes remain there today. Indeed, when over a hundred Archaic Period canoes were found in a lake near Gainesville, Florida in 2000, measurements and samples were taken in place, but none were removed for preservation (Wheeler et al. 2003).

The storage and preservation obligations confronted the Arkansas Archeological Survey and the Historic Arkansas Museum once they took possession of the Peeler Bend Canoe. For temporary storage while trying to find grants to pay for the large amount of polyethylene glycol and a tank to soak the canoe in, the decision was made to sink the canoe in a pond on the property of Mr. Quin Baber. This was done because it is essential that the waterlogged wood not be allowed to dry out. If it dries, the wood cell walls collapse and the object will warp and crack badly or simply disintegrate. Once those types of damage occur, there is no way to restore the artifact to its former condition.

Before being put in the pond, two radiocarbon samples were taken and yielded calibrated date ranges (one-sigma) of cal AD 1160-1260 and cal AD 1200-1280. In 2001, the Historic Arkansas Museum received funding to conserve the canoe. That meant the canoe itself had to be retrieved from the pond and transported to the museum. Dr. Leslie Stewart-Abernathy was in charge of that, donning his mask and snorkel and supervising the raising of the canoe and putting it on a trailer for transport. It took a lot of personnel and cooperation to accomplish this. Unfortunately, it sustained a nasty crack in the side during its initial recovery, but overall it was largely successful (Early and Stewart-Abernathy 2009).

After about a year and a half of soaking, the canoe was stabilized and removed from the solution. Then the problem became where to display it. No museum in the state had room for a 24-foot long canoe. For a year or so, it was put on temporary display at the Historic Arkansas Museum while trying to find another location for it. In 2004, they were contacted by the Tunica RiverPark Museum in Mississippi, a new museum funded by the casino industry, and they agreed to loan it to them. It remained on view there for several years, but is now in storage, awaiting another venue with the space to display it.

The story of the third Arkansas canoe is a bit murkier, and certainly the opposite end of the spectrum of the Peeler Bend one. It was secretly dug up from the mouth of the Caddo River sometime in the 1990s, then hidden away for years (Ann M. Early, pers.comm. 2008). Eventually it was donated to the Arkansas Archeological Survey's SAU Station. It was then loaned to the Sam Noble Museum in Norman, Oklahoma. Eventually it was returned, but it had literally fallen to pieces. After being documented, the pieces were turned over to the Clark County Historical Association for display in their museum.

All three of those canoes were probably made and used by Caddo Indians, although the Griggs Canoe may well have been made by Europeans (Arkansas State Parks 1980s). Measurements of the Griggs and Peeler Bend Canoes show that they are both about the same dimensions, and their discovery provides tangible evidence that the rivers in Arkansas were the highways of the past.

The Guth Canoe

In late spring of 2008, the floodwaters in Cross County finally receded. Wynne resident Matt Guth decided to go for a boat ride on a western meander of the St. Francis River that is sometimes called St. Francis Bay or Cross County Ditch. As he was traveling downriver, he came upon a large wooden object on a sandbar in the river. He recognized it as a canoe, and returned with friends to recover it and move it to his house in Wynne. Fortunately, he knew to keep it wet, so he put it in a shady spot on tarps where it could be wet down as needed.

Mr Guth started contacting various institutions to find out whether it was authentic, how old it was, and other information. Eventually he called the author, and he came to Parkin Archeological State Park to talk about it. The first concern was ownership. It turned out that because it was found on a sandbar, the owner was the finder. If it had been in the river itself, it would have belonged to the state. If it had been found on one of the banks, it would have belonged to the adjacent landowner. This was actually a relief, because if it had been considered state property, the Arkansas Archeological Survey would have been responsible for it, with all the storage problems and costs that go along with that.

At Mr. Guth's invitation, a visit was made to record the canoe and take samples. The quality of preservation was remarkable, with one end completely intact and the other missing one small part (Figure 1). A crack in the bottom ran almost the entire length. There were clear tool marks (Figure 2), plus charred areas that revealed that it had been made by the burn-and-scrape method.

Measurements and photographs were taken, and a small sample was removed for species identification. A larger portion was collected for possible radiocarbon dating, for which a handsaw had to be used (Figure 3). The difficulties and expense involved in properly conserving the canoe were pointed out to Mr. Guth, and he was informed that the state of Arkansas had no interest in buying it. Based on the remarkable state of preservation, it appeared to date from the late

FIGURE 1. THE GUTH CANOE SHORTLY AFTER DISCOVERY. (PHOTOGRAPH BY AUTHOR, 2008).

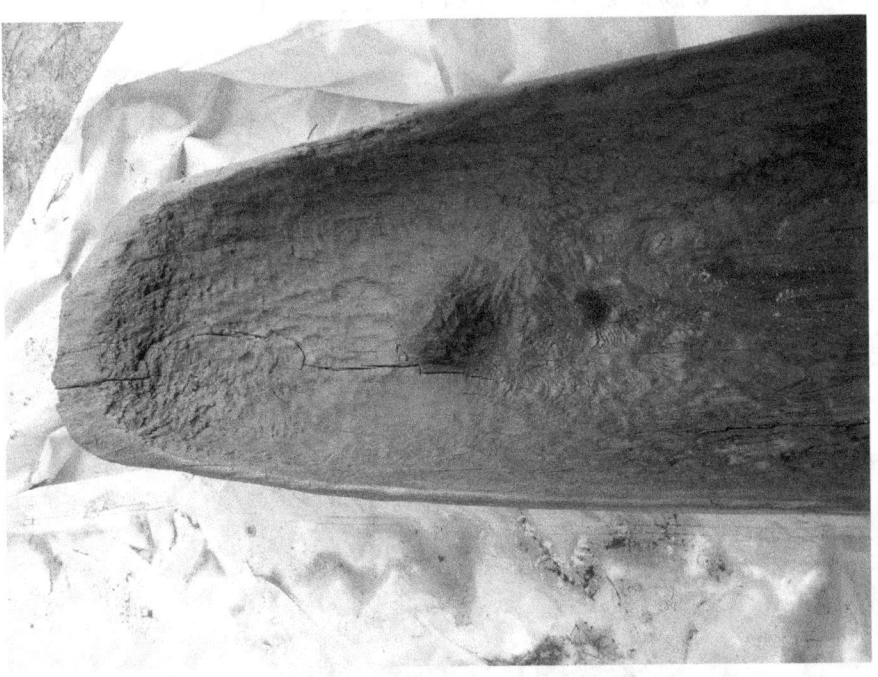

FIGURE 2. CLOSE-UP OF THE GUTH CANOE SHOWING TOOL MARKS. (PHOTOGRAPH BY AUTHOR, 2008).

19th or early 20th century, so he was advised that attempting a radiocarbon date was not worth trying.

Dr. David Stahle of the Department of Geosciences at the University of Arkansas was quickly able to identify the species as baldcypress (*Taxodium distichum*). In addition, he noted that the photographs revealed that the rings and wood anatomy were perfectly preserved and

FIGURE 3. TAKING A WOOD SAMPLE FROM THE GUTH CANOE FOR RADIOCARBON DATING. (PHOTOGRAPH BY AUTHOR, 2008).

FIGURE 4. END OF THE GUTH CANOE SHOWING TREE-RINGS. (PHOTOGRAPH BY AUTHOR, 2008).

that he could count at least 110 annual rings (Figure 4) (David W. Stahle, pers. comm. 2008).

Mr. Guth shared location information and a site form was completed for the find location. It was assigned site number 3CS314. He was advised to keep it wet continuously, and he said he might build a tank to hold it until he could find someone who wanted it.

Several months later, Mr. Guth decided he wanted to pay to have a radiocarbon date run on the sample that had been collected. He was reminded that it was probably too recent, but he decided he wanted to submit it anyway. The sample was shipped to Beta Analytic in December, 2008. To say that the results returned in January were surprising would be an understatement. The radiocarbon age was 530 ± 50 14C years B.P. (GuthCanoe 1; Beta-253301, wood, corrected). The calibrated (1-sigma) date range was cal A.D. 1400-1430 (Talma and Vogel 1993). So the dugout estimated to be only one or two hundred years old is probably at least 500 years old.

The location where the canoe was found, along with the date, indicates that it is undoubtedly a Parkin phase vessel. It is the only known dugout from northeast Arkansas. It is 6.65 m (21 ft. 9 13/16 in.) long, 30 cm (11 13/16 in.) high, and 57 cm (22 7/16 in.) wide at the widest point. As mentioned before, the degree of preservation is remarkable. This is probably partly due to the fact that it was made of baldcypress, which is renowned as a type of wood resistant to rotting. The canoe was probably buried for centuries under mud and silt in the river bottom, which also contributed to its preservation. The increased water flow in 2008 during the floods must have dislodged it and moved it downstream until it came to rest on the sandbar.

After the radiocarbon results were received, Mr. Guth stated that the canoe was still in good condition and that he was trying to find a home for it. He said that some interest had been expressed from Illinois and elsewhere. In February of 2009, Mark Esarey of Cahokia Mounds State Historic Site in Illinois contacted the author about a canoe purportedly from

Arkansas that an archaeological society was considering buying and donating to the park. He was told the history of the Guth Canoe, and he was also informed of the probable difficulties and costs involved in conserving it. State Archeologist Ann Early also wrote him about her experiences getting the Peeler Bend canoe preserved (see above).

Later in 2009, the Illinois State Archaeological Society purchased the canoe and indeed donated it to Cahokia. Transportation of the canoe was accomplished by members of the Cahokia Archaeological Society, who also constructed a tank in which it was soaked for several years. It is now preserved, and is included in an exhibit entitled "Wetlands and Waterways: The Key to Cahokia." (Cahokia Mounds Museum Society 2009; Iseminger 2010; Stratmann 2013).

Although it would have preferable to have it remain in Arkansas, its acquisition by Cahokia is a good thing, because they are committed to properly conserving it and it will be displayed in one of the finest archaeological parks in the country. Fortunately, it was thoroughly documented before it went away.

References

Arkansas State Parks
   [1980s] *The Griggs Canoe: A Treasure from Arkansas's Past*. Brochure, Toltec Mounds Archeological State Park. Also electronic document, http://www.arkansasstateparks.com/images/pdfs/Toltecgriggscanoe.pdf, accessed September 24, 2009.

Cahokia Mounds Museum Society
   2009 Dugout Canoe Donated. *The Cahokian*. Summer. pp. 12.

Daniel, Pete
   1977 *Deep'n as It Come: The 1927 Mississippi River Flood*. Oxford University Press, New York, NY. Reprinted 1996 by University of Arkansas Press, Fayetteville, AR.

Early, Ann M., and Leslie Stewart-Abernathy
   2009 The Peeler Bend Canoe. Presentation at the "Picture the Past" film and lecture series, Winthrop Rockefeller Institute Research Station, Arkansas Archeological Survey. Morrillton, AR.

Hartmann, Mark J.
   1996 Development of Watercraft in the Prehistoric Southeastern United States. Doctoral dissertation, Department of Anthropology, Texas A&M University, College Station, TX.

Iseminger, William
   2010 The Guth Dugout. *Central States Archaeological Journal* 57(4):204-206.

Mitchem, Jeffrey M.
   2010 Mississippian Fortifications at Parkin and Neeley's Ferry, Northeast Arkansas. Paper presented at the 67th Annual Meeting of the Southeastern Archaeological Conference, Lexington, KY.

Purdy, Barbara A.
   1991 *The Art and Archaeology of Florida's Wetlands*. CRC Press, Boca Raton, FL.

Ruhl, Donna L., and Barbara A. Purdy
   2005 One Hundred-one Canoes on the Shore – 3-5,000 Year Old Canoes from Newnans Lake, Florida. *Journal of Wetland Archaeology* 5:111-127.

Stratmann, Gene
   2013 Canoe Conservation Update. *The Cahokian*. Winter. pp.12.

Talma, A. S, and J. C. Vogel
   1993 A Simplified Approach to Calibrating C14 Dates. *Radiocarbon* 35(2):317-322.

Trubitt, Mary Beth
   2002 Update on the Peeler Bend Canoe: An Ancient Dugout Canoe from Saline County. *Field Notes: Newsletter of the Arkansas Archeological Society* 307:3-5.

Wheeler, Ryan J., James J. Miller, Ray M. McGee, Donna Ruhl, Brenda Swann, and Melissa Memory
   2003 Archaic Period Canoes from Newnans Lake, Florida. *American Antiquity* 68(3):533-551.

· · · · · · · · · · · · · · · ·

Jeffrey M. Mitchem
Arkansas Archeological Survey
PO Box 241
Parkin, AR 72373-0241

A Comparative Study on the Speed of Dutch and British Ships, 1750–1830

Patricia Schwindinger

Several previous studies have quantitatively analyzed ship speed, but there is not agreement on whether ships gained speed 1750-1830. Using logbooks digitized by the CLIWOC project, this study finds that both speed and speed–length ratio increased. The average speed–length ratio per voyage increased by 0.17, in part from the introduction of copper plating in the late 1700s, while the speed–length ratio of the best day's run increased by 0.12. British ships travelled faster than Dutch merchant ships, but not Dutch naval ships; this suggests the difference stems from the policies of Dutch merchant companies.

Introduction

The speed of sailing ships reached its peak in the clipper ships of the 19th century, but speed was a feature sought in both naval and merchant ships before their development. Designing a ship for speed was not a simple task, however, as improvements could negatively impact the ship's performance in other areas, such as capacity for cargo or weatherliness (Nowacki 2006). In addition, the forces of hydrodynamics and propulsion that affect ship speed are complicated and were poorly understood at this time (Chapelle 1967). Although attempts at scientific approaches to ship design date at least as early as the 17th century, it was not until well into the 19th century that any truly usable theories were available to shipbuilders (Unger 1997). Nonetheless, the long experience of shipbuilders, combined with comparisons between ships of desirable qualities, led to improvements in theoretical knowledge and ship design prior to the 19th century (Nowacki 2006). Historical records indicate that sailing performance improved throughout the 17th and 18th centuries (Unger 1997).

A quantitative analysis of ship speed is possible using the Climatological Database for the World's Oceans (CLIWOC), a database of 1,674 historical logbooks from four countries dating from 1750 to 1850. The European Union funded project, which sought to obtain meteorological data for the study of Earth's climate, provides over 280,000 individual noon entries from logbooks, as well as information on the ships that recorded them (Können and Koek 2005:119). This analysis will focus on the Dutch and British ships, which together account for 137,000 of the daily entries, as these provide more information on the ships themselves than do the French and Spanish data. The end date of 1830 was chosen because there were few British voyages in the database after this date.

Previous Research

Previous efforts to quantify any improvement in ship speed in the 18th and 19th centuries have produced mixed results. Walton (1966) uses port records to analyze shipping speed for ships travelling from the Caribbean to New York or New England from 1686 to 1775. He measured the speed of ships using the number of days between their recorded exits from one port to their arrivals in the next, and found no particular trend in voyage lengths. Morgan (2004) looked at transatlantic voyages from Bristol to the Caribbean and British America from 1749 to 1779. He also fails to find any clear trend in the length of the voyages, as it increases slightly for ships sailing to Virginia and to Jamaica via Ireland, but decreases by 9.5% for ships sailing directly to Jamaica from Bristol. He cautions that since ships were only making a single voyage per year at this time, one should not read too much into the importance of voyage length. However, he does not distinguish between types of cargo carried, and this could have affected the demand for speed in his sample.

North (1968:967) specifically argues against any improvement in ship speed from 1600 to 1850 as a result of technological improvement in ship design. He states that "ships constructed in the seventeenth and early eighteenth centuries were capable of speeds equal to those achieved by nineteenth-century sailing ships," apparently on the basis of the fact that the Mayflower made the return voyage to England in thirty days while the average voyage time of packet boats 1820–1860 was 24 days. North attributes any decrease in voyage time during this period to decreased time in port, as well as the increasing safety of the seas as a result of a decline in piracy. Although he argues that ships increase in size gradually until 1800 and rapidly after that, he seems unaware that there is a link between ship size and ship speed (North 1968:958).

Other studies have found an increase in speed. For instance, Ville (1986) finds evidence of technological improvement in British colliers moving coal from the northeast coast of Britain to London, resulting in increased speed and maneuverability in these ships over the period from 1700 to 1850. Klein (1978) finds a general decrease in transatlantic shipping times for French slave traders sailing to Saint Domingue over the course of the 18th century, as well as a clear relationship between the length of time at sea and number of deaths among slaves taken as cargo (Klein 1978:85–89, 192).

Rönnbäck (2012:481-482), in a statistical analysis of 2,866 transatlantic slave voyages drawn from the Transatlantic Slave Trade Database (TSTD2 2010), found a general increase in ship speed of around 0.3–0.5% per year during the early modern period, amounting to a 30-day decrease in voyage time from 1700 to 1800. He finds a greater increase during the War of Spanish Succession (1702–1713) and less of a decrease during the French Revolutionary Wars (1793–1802). Rönnbäck also notes that larger ships are faster, which he attributes to larger sail area. However, he finds no statistically significant difference in speed between nationalities, although most of his database is either British or French, with only 4% of ships Dutch. He also finds no evidence of differences between specific routes, little difference between types of rigs, and a difference significant only at the .10 level for the age of ships (Ronnback 2012:481–483). He cautions that since the slave trade had a particular need for speed, it may not be representative of shipping as a whole (Ronnback 2012:484).

One previous study uses the CLIWOC database in order to take a more direct measurement of ship speed than the total voyage length used by earlier studies (Kelly and Ó Gráda 2014). The analysis was carried out separately for British East India Company (EIC) ships, Royal Navy ships (excluding those over 80 guns), and Dutch frigates. Ship speed was measured in knots from the course made good, which was calculated trigonometrically using each day's entries of longitude and latitude. Year, wind speed, wind angle, longitude, and latitude were used as explanatory variables, with the latter two included to account for the effect of currents. Each category of ship was analyzed separately for each wind speed. For British EIC ships and Dutch frigates, they concluded that ship speed was relatively steady from 1750 until the 1780s, when the introduction of copper plating causes a sharp increase of 10% in speed.

From the 1780s to the 1820s, the speed of ships increases steadily by about 20%, with a slight dip during the Napoleonic War. Little change is evident from 1830 to 1850. Royal Navy ships were found to be slower on average than British EIC ships, but they followed a similar pattern over time as the merchant ships, with additional dips in speed during all three periods of war covered by the data. An overall increase of about 1.5 knots in moderate breezes is evident in the data for all three categories over the period 1750–1850. No comparison was made between ships of different sizes or types, and no comparison between Dutch and British ships was made.

Nationality

Historical sources reveal that Dutch ships, particularly Dutch merchant ships, had a poor reputation during this time. The Dutch East India Company (VOC) was struggling financially, and successive changes in leadership and organization did little to alleviate the deepening debt in which the company found itself (Bruijn et al. 1987:20). To make matters worse, in 1722 and 1737, they lost three entire fleets, each in a single day. The twenty four ships lost represent 10% of the total losses of the company over the entirety of its existence, a serious blow to the company (Bruijn 1980:261). Meanwhile, English power was expanding at the expense of Dutch power.

These financial constraints were not without impact on the ships themselves. The 'deep-waisted Indiamen' were considered sluggish and unhandy compared to English and French ships (Boxer 1982:116). Cornelius de Jong van Roodenburg, a Dutchman, writes in a series of letters in 1793–1794 that Dutch sailors were poorly paid, given meager rations, and worked too hard. When it comes time for him to return home, he opts to take passage on a British ship (Boxer 1982:114).

On the way back, they pass a VOC ship, *Sybille Antoinette*, who reports that of her crew of 130, only 16 were fit to climb the ropes, the rest being sick with scurvy. De Jong writes, "It is incomprehensible that on the Company's vessels so little preventative measures against this terrible disease are being taken. We were just as long at sea and yet not in that miserable state" (Boxer 1982:116). Although the nature of scurvy was not truly understood at this point, the importance of fresh fruits and vegetables were known (Carpenter 1988:43–74), and the British Navy had officially adopted the policy of issuing orange juice to sailors in 1790 (Tröhler 2005:519).

Others voiced similarly low opinions. For example, Dirk van Hogendorp, aboard the naval vessel *Utrecht*, complained in 1783 that their pilot believed that the sun revolved around the earth, the moon was created anew each day, and it was not only impossible to calculate longitude at sea but an impiety to attempt it (Hogendorp [1783]:129). Not that this prevented the vessel from arriving at its destination. By coincidence, the 1783 voyage of *Utrecht* was included in the CLIWOC database: they made the round trip voyage in 182 days, averaging a respectable 80.8 nm per day and a best day's run of 190 nm.

Although it is difficult to imagine such an attitude among a navigator, a British passenger on board the Dutch *De Held Woltemade* in 1780 notes with surprise that the captain was a liberal-minded man:

> [He] laughed at the old system of navigation pursued by their [Dutch] ships, which although known to be erroneous was persevered in, merely because it had been so for more than a hundred years. ... His mod of conducting the fleet was precisely the same as in our service, and no British commander could carry sail in a better style than he did (Hickey 1919:230).

Overall, a picture emerges of an organization that, threatened by the intrusion of British and French competition, relied increasingly on strict, formal guidelines at the expense of efficiency. The 1747 revision of the prescribed route yielded a stricter set of instructions at a time when other companies were issuing more liberal instructions and relying on the judgment of their navigators (Bruijn 1980:260; Bruyns 1992:146). Not everyone complied with the new regulations. Captain J.S. Stavorinus, a Dutch captain, notes in his memoirs that in 1778 that he and the four ships he was sailing with ignored the rules and followed the shorter course he knew was being used by ships of other nationalities, while noting in their logbooks the course they were expected to follow (Bruijn 1980:260). After the dissolution of the VOC, Bruijn (1980:260) notes that total passage times for Dutch merchants decreased noticeably.

Data

This analysis uses the speed–length ratio of ships as the measure of their speed. Since longer ships are inherently faster, this ratio allows for a more equivalent comparison of ships of different sizes than speed alone (Chapelle 1967:29). It is calculated as the ratio of the speed in knots to the square root of the length of the ship. Two speed–length ratios were calculated, one using the average speed of the ship over the course of the voyage, which I refer to as the average speed–length ratio, and the other using the best day's run of each voyage, which I call the maximum speed–length ratio.

Speed was calculated using the field "Distance," which was distance travelled in the past 24-hour day (noon to noon). British ships recorded their distances in nautical miles while Dutch ships typically used *duitse mijlen* or, more rarely, leagues. The *duitse mijl* equals four nautical miles (Degroot and Hoffmann 1987:15), while a league equals three nautical miles. Although not all entries specified which measurement was used in the original logbook, it was a simple matter to separate those using *duitse mijlen* from those using nautical miles, as they were an order of difference apart. In a few cases, the original unit of measurement was recorded incorrectly, which was also easily determined. All measurements were converted to nautical miles.

Ship length was measured in feet. The Dutch foot (*voet*) equaled 0.29 m (Carrington 1864:3) while the British Imperial foot equals 0.30 m, a small enough difference that no conversion seemed necessary. For many ships, particularly the Dutch East India Company (VOC), length was provided in the field "OtherShipInformation." For roughly half (57%) of the British Royal Navy ships, I added length to the database using *Ships of the Royal Navy* (Colledge 1987). In addition, for a number of the VOC ships, it was possible to extrapolate the length from the tonnage (tonnage was more frequently given in the CLIWOC database) using the standard contract lengths established by the VOC (Bruijn, et al. 1987:37–55).

Where the same name was used for multiple ships through time, a common practice for both the Dutch and British, every effort was made to distinguish between the ships. If tonnage and/or number of guns changed significantly, if the listed type of ship differed, or if significant gaps occurred between entered voyages, the ships were considered to be distinct. As a general rule of thumb, ships were assumed to have lifespans of no more than 30 years. This provided a final list of 238 British ships and 49 Dutch ships of known length.

Company and nationality of ownership were both designated in the database. For this analysis, ships were grouped as "Navy" or "Merchant" based on the company provided. The Dutch ships included a few whaling ships which were classed as "Other." Where company was not specified, they are listed as "Unknown."

Voyages where the best day's run exceeded 400 nm were excluded, as this is an unlikely record for ship of this time period, and were therefore assumed to be typographical errors. Voyages with less than 10 days in motion were also excluded.

Analysis

Both the average and maximum distances travelled per day increased substantially from 1750 to 1830, gaining on average 25 nm and 44 nm per day, respectively ($p < .0001$, $n=2672$ voyages). However, the length of ships also increases during this time period, with an average increase of 28.3 feet, as shown in Figure 1.

Using the speed-length ratio to account for the increase in length, there is still a clear increase in ship speed. According to the quadratic

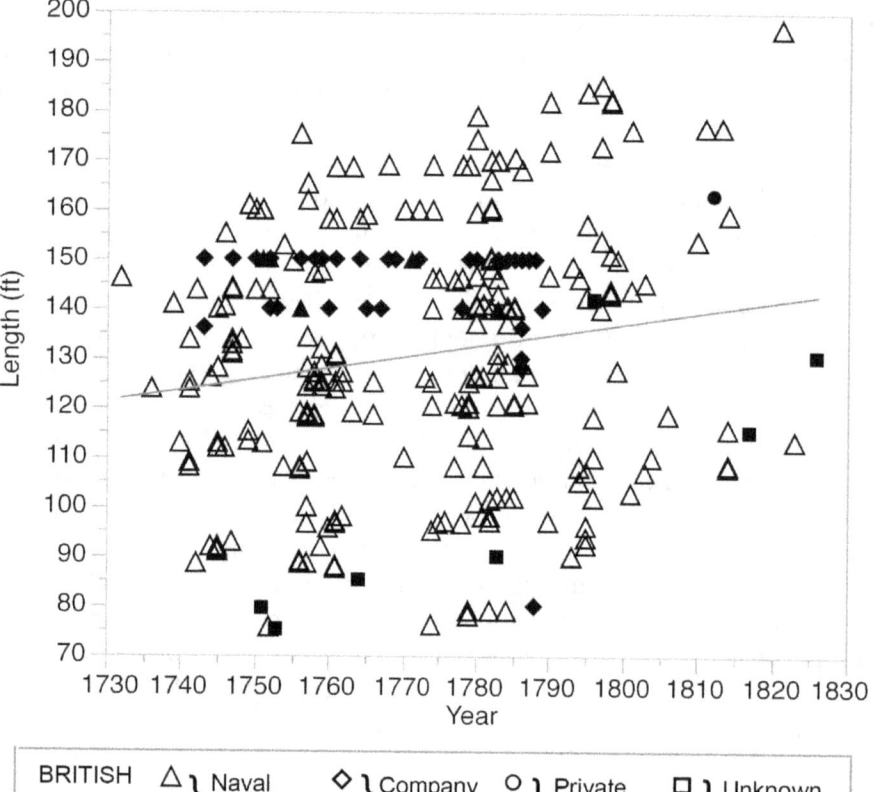

FIGURE 1. LENGTH OF BRITISH AND DUTCH SHIPS 1750–1830. THE YEAR THE SHIP WAS BUILT WAS USED IF IT WAS KNOWN; IF NOT, THE YEAR OF THE FIRST VOYAGE IN THE CLIWOC DATABASE WAS SUBSTITUTED (N=309).

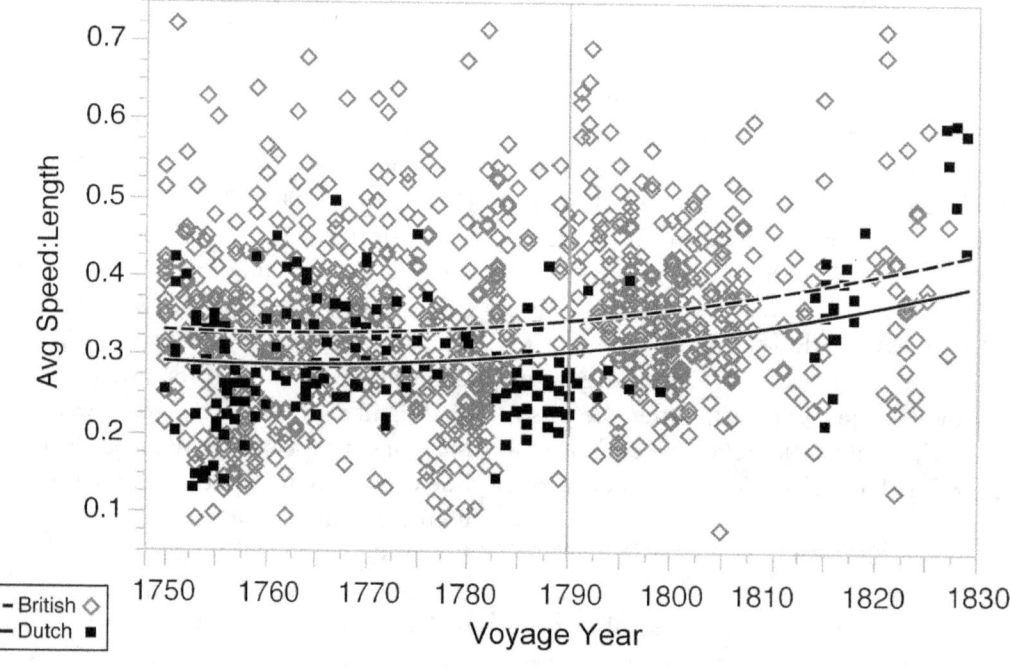

FIGURE 2. AVERAGE SPEED–LENGTH RATIO OF DUTCH AND BRITISH SHIPS 1750–1830 (N=1090). BY 1790 ALL BRITISH SHIPS-OF-THE-LINE WERE COPPER PLATED; THIS YEAR IS MARKED. THE DIFFERENCE BETWEEN DUTCH AND BRITISH SHIPS IS SIGNIFICANT WITH $P <.0001$.

model shown in Figure 2, there is an overall gain in of 0.17 between 1750 and 1830, which means that a ship 100 feet long travelled on average 40.8 nm further per day in 1830 than one of the same length did in 1750. Moreover, British ships are faster than Dutch ships ($p < .0001$), with speed–length ratios on average 0.04 higher, indicating they travelled 9.6 nm further per day on average.

The line begins to bend upwards around 1800. One possible influence is the collapse of the Dutch East India Company (VOC) in 1800. Figure 3(a) shows the dramatic increase in speed, measured as average distance travelled per day, for Dutch merchant ships after 1800, which is consistent with Bruijn (1980:260). Average distance travelled was used, rather than speed–length ratio, because there were few lengths available for Dutch ships after 1800. Figure 3(b) plots the speed of Dutch naval vessels during this same time period—no similar trend is present, suggesting that the speed of Dutch ships prior to 1800 was limited by the organizational constraints imposed on them by the companies that owned them.

The regression of average speed–length ratio over voyage year was repeated omitting each possible combination of Dutch Merchant and Unknown ships. The quadratic term remained significant in all models, but nationality lost its statistical significance if Dutch merchants were excluded. Likewise, no statistically significant differences between the average or maximum speed–length ratios of Dutch and British naval ships were found (n=954, although only 40 are Dutch voyages).

Another explanation must therefore account for the quadratic term seen in Figure 2. Most likely this is the result of the introduction of copper plating, which Kelly's analysis found accounted for a third of the gain in speed observed from 1750 to 1850 (Kelly and Ó Gráda 2014).

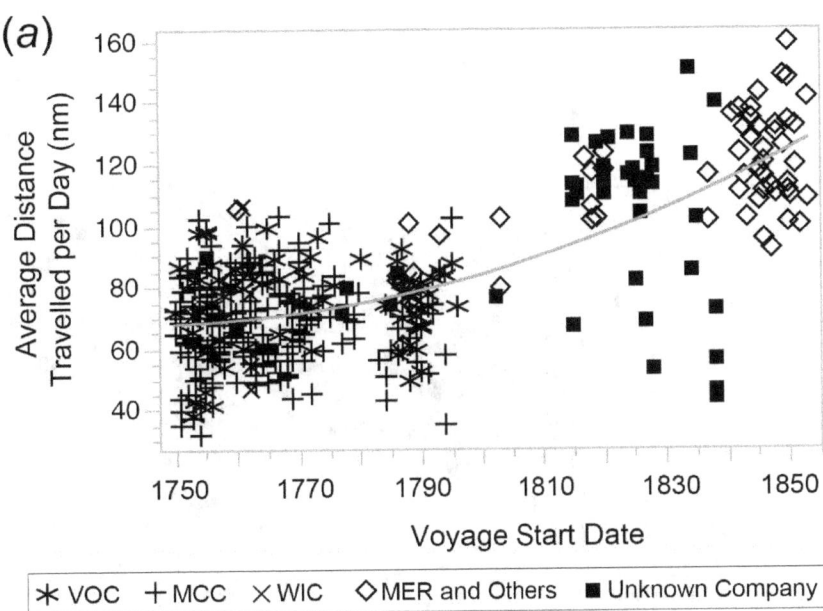

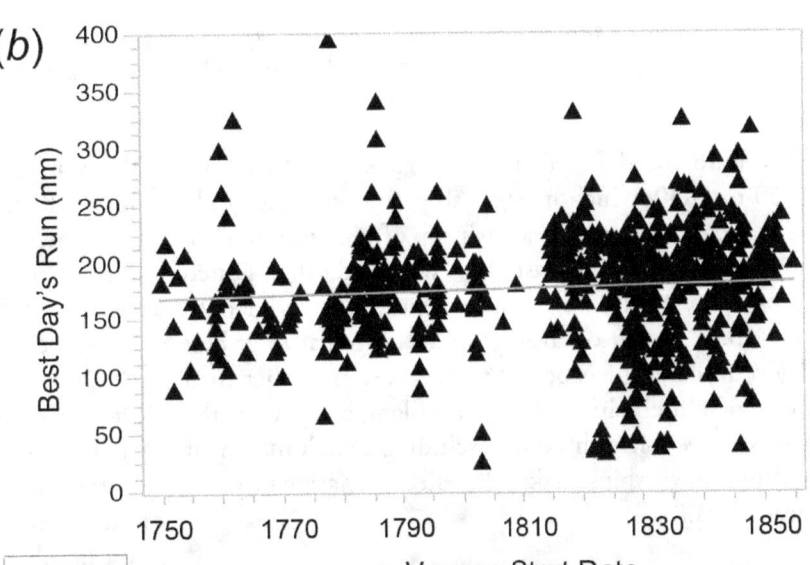

FIGURE 3. AVERAGE DISTANCES TRAVELLED PER DAY BY DUTCH (A) MERCHANT AND (B) NAVAL SHIPS 1750–1850 (N=380).

The year 1790 is marked in Figure 2, as by this year all British ships-of-the-line were copper plated (Bingeman et al. 2000:222).

The maximum speed–length ratio of all voyages also increases over this period, but a linear model was a better fit than a quadratic model (Figure 4). If copper plating was responsible for the quadratic term in the average speed–length ratio, it is not surprising that it is absent here, as a recently de-fouled ship could achieve the same speed as a similarly designed copper-plated ship.

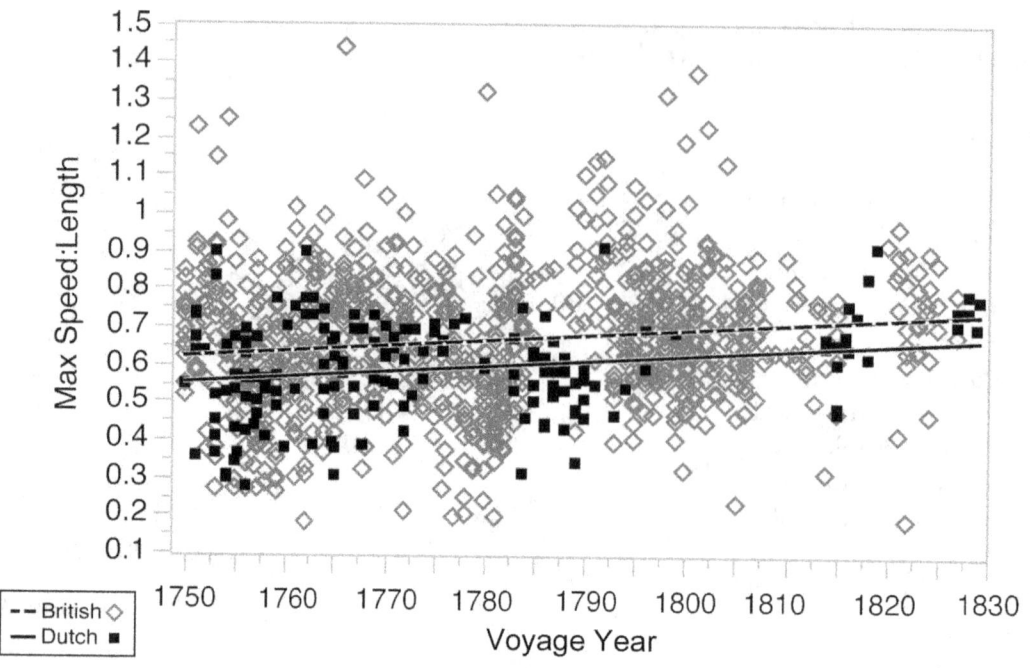

FIGURE 4. MAXIMUM SPEED–LENGTH RATIO OF DUTCH AND BRITISH SHIPS 1750-1830 (N=1090). THE DIFFERENCE BETWEEN DUTCH AND BRITISH SHIPS IS SIGNIFICANT WITH P <.0001.

Maximum speed–length ratios increased by 0.12 from 1750 to 1830, which means a ship 100 feet long could be expected to have a best day's run of 28.8 nm more in 1830 than in 1750. British ships were faster than Dutch ships (p <.0001), achieving maximum speed–length ratios 0.07 higher on average, indicating that their best day's run could be expected to be 16.8 nm higher than those of Dutch ships of the same length. As with the average speed–length ratios, excluding Dutch merchant and unknown ships makes the effect of nationality less clear (p <.08).

Discussion

Mounting evidence supports an increase in ship speed during the period from 1750 to 1830. Not only did the absolute ship speed increase, in agreement with Kelly and Ó Gráda (2014), but the speed–length ratio also increased significantly, indicating that this gain was in fact due to improvements in ship design. As described in Kelly's analysis, copper plating appears to account for a significant part of improvement in the average speeds of ships. The maximum speed–length ratio of ships also increases significantly, but the introduction of copper plating does not appear to have had a noticeable effect.

Nationality also had a significant influence on the data, with British ships travelling faster than Dutch ships.

This was caused by the slow speed of Dutch merchant ships, which agrees with the poor reputation they held at this time. The sharp jump in speed of Dutch merchant ships after 1800 (Figure 3a) and the lack of difference between Dutch and British naval ships suggests that this difference in speed was caused by the management of the Dutch merchant companies. However, it is not clear whether this was due to ship design, which was closely regulated by the VOC (Bruijn, et al. 1987:37–55), or to traditionalist navigators, excessively tight regulations, poorly equipped ships, underfed sailors, or any of a number of other factors on which contemporaries blamed the slow speed of the Dutch ships (Boxer 1982).

Further Research

The CLIWOC database is a rich source of data for historians and nautical archaeologists alike. In the hopes of facilitating interdisciplinary research, the international research team who compiled it included information on ship type, company, guns, tonnage, crew size, ports of call, and even notable events such as deaths or punishments on board, in addition to the meteorological data they were seeking. Although the database is freely available online (CLIWOC [2003]), in the twelve years since the project was completed, it has drawn limited attention outside of climate studies, an oversight that this paper hopes to begin to remedy.

References

Bingeman, John M., John P. Bethell, Peter Goodwin, and Arthur T. Mack
    2000   Copper and Other Sheathing in the Royal Navy. *The International Journal of Nautical Archaeology* 29(2):218-229

Boxer, C. R.
    1982   The Maritime Twilight of the Voc, 1780–1795: Some Sources and Problems. *Tidschrift voor Zeegeschiedenis* 1(2):114–123.

Bruijn, J. R.
    1980   *Between Batavia and the Cape: Shipping Patterns of the Dutch East India Company.* Cambridge University Press, Cambridge.

Bruijn, J.R., F.S. Gaastra and I. Schöffer
    1987   *Dutch-Asiatic Shipping in the 17th and 18th Centuries: Introductory Volume.* Martinus Nijhoff, The Hague.

Bruyns, W. F. J. Mörzer
    1992   Navigation on Dutch East India Company Ships around the 1740s. *Mariner's Mirror* 78(2):143–154.

Carpenter, Kenneth J.
    1988   *The History of Scurvy and Vitamin C.* Cambridge University Press, Cambridge.

Carrington, Robert C.
    1864   *Foreign Measures and Their English Values.* Walter Spiers, London.

Chapelle, Howard I.
    1967   *The Search for Speed under Sail, 1700–1855.* Norton, New York..

CLIWOC
    [2003]   Climatological Database for the World's Oceans 1750–1850. http://pendientedemigracion.ucm.es/info/cliwoc/. Accessed 3/2/2015.

Colledge, James Joseph
    2010   *Ships of the Royal Navy.* Casemate, Newbury. Degroot, Dagomar and Richard Hoffmann

    1987   The Weather Gage. *Climatic Change* 10: 46.

Hickey, William
    1919   *Memoirs of William Hickey.* London.

Hogendorp, Dirk van
    [1783]   *Correspondentie Dirk Van Hogendorp.*

Kelly, Morgan and Cormac Ó Gráda
    2014   Speed under Sail, 1750–1850. http://hdl.handle.net/10197/5617

Klein, Herbert S.
    1978   *The Middle Passage: Comparative Studies in the Atlantic Slave Trade.* Princeton University Press, Princeton.

Können, G. P. and F. B. Koek
    2005   Description of the Cliwoc Database. *Climatic Change* 73(1–2):117–130.

Morgan, Kenneth
    2004   *Bristol and the Atlantic Trade in the Eighteenth Century.* Cambridge University Press, Cambridge.

North, Douglass C.
    1968   Sources of Productivity Change in Ocean Shipping, 1600–1850. *The Journal of Political Economy* 76(5):953–970.

Nowacki, Horst
    2006   Developments in Fluid Mechanics Theory and Ship Design before Trafalgar. *Proceedings of an International Congress held at the Escuela Técnica Superior de Ingenieros Navales, Madrid, and the Diputación Provincal, Cádiz, 3-5 November 2005.* Escuela Técnica Superior de Ingenieros Navales, Matrid.

Rönnbäck, Klas
    2012   The Speed of Ships and Shipping Productivity in the Age of Sail. *European Review of Economic History* 16(4):469–489.

Tröhler, U
    2005   Lind and Scurvy: 1747 to 1795. *Journal of the Royal Society of Medicine* 98(11):519–522.

Unger, Richard W.
    1997   Design and Construction of European Warships in the Seventeenth and Eighteenth Centuries. In *Ships and Shipping in the North Sea and Atlantic*, R. Unger (editor), pp. 21–34. Ashgate Variorum, Aldershot.

Ville, Simon
    1986   Total Factor Productivity in the English Shipping Industry: The North-East Coal Trade, 1700–1850. *The Economic History Review* 39(3):355–370. http://www.jstor.org/stable/2596345

Walton, Gary M.
    1966   A Quantitative Study of American Colonial Shipping: A Summary. *The Journal of Economic History* 26(4):595–598.

• • • • • • • • • • • • • •

Patricia Schwindinger
Department of Anthropology
Texas A&M University
MS 4352 TAMU
College Station, TX 77843-4352

Into the Blue: Underwater Archaeology in California State Parks

Tricia Dodds
Denise Jaffke

The California Department of Parks and Recreation's underwater parks program was established in 1968 to preserve the best and most unique representative examples of the state's natural underwater ecosystems found in coastal and inland waters. Since that time, Parks has established 19 underwater parks with over 60 proposals for new parks under consideration. An overview of this important program will be given, followed by a review of the current knowledge of submerged cultural resources at California State Parks. Lastly, the goals for future underwater archaeological projects will be outlined.

"California is blessed with many natural splendors. Of the contiguous states, it has the highest peak, the lowest valley, the largest fault system, the oldest and largest trees, and the greatest number of plant and animal species in North America. Its historical superlatives are no less dramatic. Aboriginal California was home to more than 300,000 people, a greater number than any comparable area north of Mesoamerica. It also has a very rich and varied maritime history. What connects California to the World Ocean more than its history? California, a land of legend and mystery, was explored, colonized and described by sea. Thus it's only fitting that we take active steps to understand and manage these maritime heritage sites as part of our legacy from the past" [Foster 2002].

California's cultural resources do not end at the water's edge. With California's vast coastline and rich maritime history, the potential for submerged cultural resources is high, and our focus on the underwater environment can greatly increase our understanding of California's past. Currently, there are over 300,000 recorded cultural resources in California with over 12,000 in the State Parks system alone. However, there are only ten recorded cultural resources in our underwater parks, although there is certainly potential for additional underwater cultural resources to be discovered if we are willing to search for them (CHRIS 2013).

Invaluable information can be learned of California's prehistoric and historic past from the underwater resources. The rise in sea level at the end of the Pleistocene and the beginning of the Holocene caused vast amounts of coastal land to be inundated. Broad coastal terraces now submerged, but exposed during the Terminal Pleistocene and Early Holocene, would have provided ideal locations for human settlement and potentially even a corridor for migration. For example, in Southern California, sea level was 120 meters lower during the last glacial maximum 20,000 years ago, and

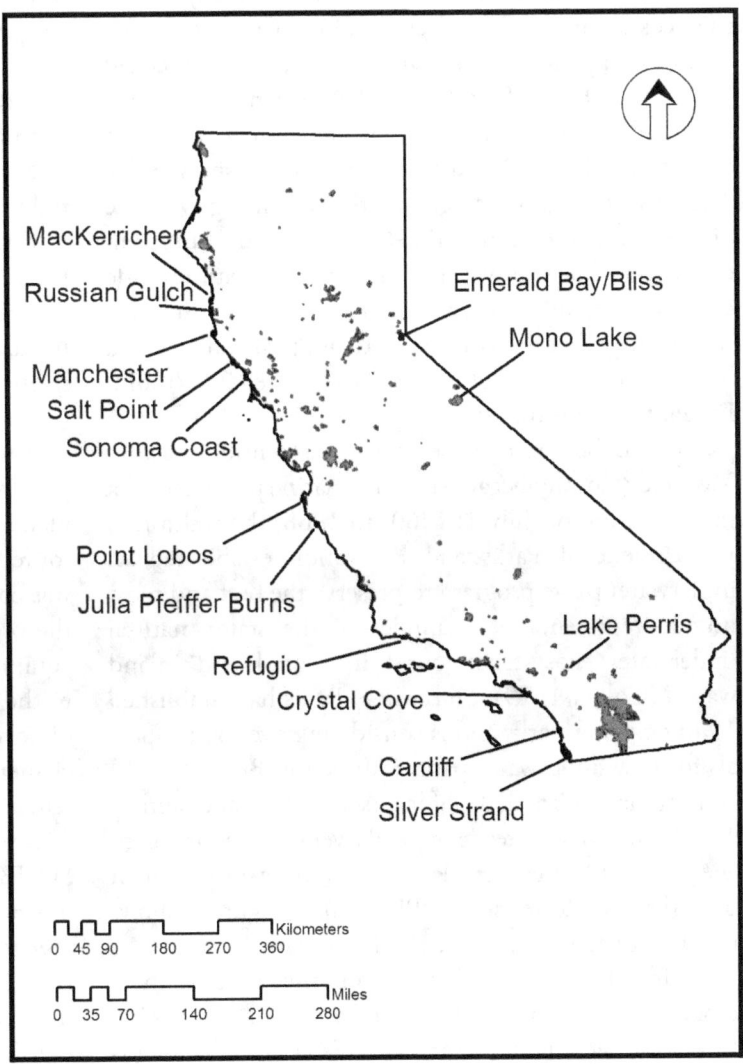

FIGURE 1. CALIFORNIA STATE PARKS' UNDERWATER PARKS (JAFFKE 2015).

the sea level was 55 m lower 12,000 years ago (Jones and Klar 2007). With these prehistoric coastlines that stretched far out onto the continental shelf, the remains of some of California's earliest settlements were most likely inundated following the rise in sea level at the end of the last Ice Age. Archaeological study of these submerged coastal sites may provide new insight into California's earliest inhabitants.

With California's rich history along the coast and inland waters, we can learn a great deal about our past by examining the many shipwrecks in California's waters. The state's nearly 1,100 miles of coastline have challenged seafarers with its treacherous coast for centuries. Beginning in the 16th century, European exploration sparked a magnitude of vessels to sail the Pacific Ocean, including along the Californian coast. Until the 20th century, charts were incomplete and often misleading, and navigational aids such as lighthouses and buoys were nonexistent until the 1850s, which caused many vessels to wreck along the coast (Terrell 2007). California's first recorded shipwreck is the *San Augustin*, which wrecked in 1595 at Drake's Bay (Collier 1984). Since that time, thousands of vessels have sunk in our waters. There are an estimated 15,000 known Californian shipwrecks. These ships and their cargos are the remaining evidence of California's rich maritime legacy. From European exploration and westward expansion to maritime trade to the fishing industry, California has a prominent maritime history that can connect us to our past and give us a better understanding of our heritage (Terrell 2007; John Foster, pers. comm. 2015).

Point Lobos State Reserve on the central coast in Monterey County became the first marine protected area in the Nation on July 1, 1960. In 1968, the California Department of Parks and Recreation established its underwater parks program to preserve the best and most unique representative examples of the state's natural underwater ecosystems found in coastal and inland waters (Collier 1979). Since then, Parks has established 19 underwater parks and is considering over 60 proposals for new underwater parks (Smith and Breece 2002). Almost one third of California's coastline and almost 1,000 miles of lake, reservoir, and river frontage are managed by California State Parks (California Department of Parks and Recreation [DPR] 2002). Figure 1 shows the underwater parks throughout the state.

California State Parks has accomplished much archaeological work in its underwater parks. The following three examples highlight some of Park's accomplishments and the potential for underwater archaeology in the State Parks' system.

Fort Ross State Historic Park and the S.S. *Pomona*

Located along the northern coast of California, Fort Ross is rich in archaeology. The South Cove contains the remains of early shipping industries associated with Fort Ross. Following Fort Ross' occupation, the Call family purchased the land and shipped lumber until the 1920s (Carlson 1975). The top of the North Cove and face contain the remnants of iron pins in the rocks where the lumber chute and wharf were secured for the lumber trade. The wreck of the steamship *Pomona* is located at the North Cove and is marked by a historic shipwreck buoy. The site is listed in the National Register of Historic Places. In addition to the S.S. *Pomona*, there are 10 other wrecks recorded in the State Lands Commission's "Reported Vessel Losses in California" database for this area, but only the *Pomona* has been identified as of yet (Smith and Breece 2002).

In 1908, S.S. *Pomona* was traveling from San Francisco to Eureka when the vessel struck an uncharted rock two miles from Fort Ross reef. The rock punched a hole in the steel hull, and Captain Swanson decided to beach the vessel in the cove. The ship rode up over the top of a large rock that impaled the ship's hull. As water began to rush into the steamship, all 147 passengers and crew safely escaped to shore with help from a nearby vessel (Beeker 2005).

An initial salvage effort was attempted the following year by the Coast Wrecking Company. The salvage team planned to refloat the vessel and tow it to San Francisco for repairs, but the effort was quickly abandoned when it was considered too dangerous. Eventually, they salvaged the propeller, triple expansion steam engine, and other equipment before the S.S. *Pomona* split in two and sank to the bottom in Fort Ross' waters. In 1959, skin divers discovered the wreck and soon stole many of the other elements as trophies. State Parks conducted its first systematic underwater survey in 1981 on the *Pomona* site. This project included magnetometer survey followed by SCUBA reconnaissance of identified "anomalies," resulting in the discovery and initial documentation of the *Pomona* wreck (Foster 2001). In 1988, James Delgado, maritime historian from the National Park Service at the time, led a team that produced a preliminary site plan of the shipwreck. Under the direction of John Foster and Charles Beeker a decade later, students from Indiana

University, University of Southern California, Cal State University Northridge, San Jose State University, and Sonoma State, further analyzed the wreck and drafted a more detailed site plan. Archaeological features identified on the wreck include the rudder and stern post, steering assembly, drive shaft, boilers, engine pistons, and steam driven electric generator (Beeker and Foster 2007).

Crystal Cove State Park and the F4U Corsair

Located off the Pacific Coast Highway between Newport and Laguna Beach, Crystal Cove State Park remains one of Orange County's largest examples of open space and natural seashore. Archaeological evidence suggests that the earliest human presence occurred 7,500 years ago within the area. Sporadic European contact occurred as early as the mid-1500s, but extended contact did not occur until 1776 when the Spanish established the Mission of San Juan Capistrano. After the migration of people with the California Gold Rush and statehood, the area was used as a ranch by the Irvine family and then later developed into a coastal community (Smith and Breece 2002). Today, the historic cottages are one of the few remaining examples of early Californian beach life and are on the National Register of Historic Places (Byrnes 1978). California State Parks acquired the property at Crystal Cove in 1980. In 1982, Parks designated the offshore area out to the 120-foot contour a Marine Managed Area. Six historic vessels have been reported lost within the underwater park (Smith and Breece 2002).

Navy reserve pilot William Anderson was assigned to Los Alamitos Naval Air Station to serve training duty. On July 5, 1949, he left for San Diego in the Corsair on a routine training flight. On the return trip to the naval air station, his engine failed, and Anderson readied the plane for a water landing about a half mile off Crystal Cove. The plane began to sink after it hit the water, but Anderson was able to escape the Corsair and was quickly rescued and taken to shore. The plane was rediscovered in 1961, and Navy divers investigated the discovery and confirmed that the plane was a Corsair. The Navy's diving unit salvaged the engine with a cable and salvage tug, and they positively identified the plane using the plates attached to the salvaged engine. A 1977 issue of *Skin Diver* magazine described the Corsair as largely intact, with some damage to the tail section. A subsequent article in 1981 observed that the wreck had greatly deteriorated. Unfortunately, the plane rests in popular fishing grounds today and is frequently hooked by anchors, causing further damage to the site (DPR 2005; Beeker and Smith 2005).

In 2005, Sheli Smith and Annalies Corbin of the Partnering Anthropology with Science and Technology (PAST) Foundation along with Charles Beeker of Indiana University conducted a research mission to study and map the site of the crash. They observed that the wings were still largely intact, and the study identified the instrument panel outlets, rudder controls, and cockpit wiring of the Corsair (Beeker and Smith 2005).

In the fall of 2014, the State Parks Dive Team returned to the Corsair as part of their training to complete a condition survey of the site. The divers conducted site maintenance, took measurements, and recorded its current condition to update the Corsair site to determine a management plan in the future. Observation of the wreck indicates that the plane is rapidly deteriorating from saltwater corrosion and underwater currents that continually move remnants of the wreckage across the ocean floor (Figures 2 and 3).

Lake Tahoe and Emerald Bay

Submerged stumps in Lake Tahoe indicate Mid-Holocene drying trends. These inundated stumps caused from prolonged drought suggest that Lake Tahoe's waters

FIGURE 2. STATE PARKS DIVERS RECORDING THE ENGINE COMPARTMENT FRAMEWORK OF THE FRONT OF THE CORSAIR (DODDS 2014).

FIGURE 3. STATE PARK DIVERS RECORDING THE REMAINS OF THE FRONT PORTION OF THE CORSAIR (DODDS 2014).

may have remained below its current rim for at least a period of 1,500 years, between about 6300 and 4800 years B.CE. with the water rising at a fairly constant rate after that (Lindstrom 1990). Emerald Bay is located on the western shore of Lake Tahoe. Prehistorically, the surrounding area is the territory of the Washoe people. Bedrock mortar evidence above and below the current water levels reveal that the lakeshore was inhabited as early as 7500 B.C. Soon after immigrants entered the Lake Tahoe region, they began to visit Emerald Bay. Surveyor John Fremont is said to have discovered Emerald Bay in 1844, and people began to develop the area by the late 1860s. By the 1880s, Emerald Bay was billed as "one of the natural wonders of the world," and weekly boat excursions attracted tourists to the bay for sightseeing (Scott 1957).

Beginning in the 1990s, extensive underwater archaeology has occurred at Emerald Bay led by John Foster, Sheli Smith, and Charles Beeker. They have documented two barges scuttled on the south side of the bay. The barges were built locally on the lake and were most likely used for car ferrying and the transportation of construction material and general goods. The barges are marked with an underwater monument and now serve as a popular dive spot (Smith 1991).

Offshore of boat camp, the historic site of the Emerald Bay Resort, rests the remains of what is known as "the miniature fleet," which includes nine small recreational boats that sank at their moorings. These boats were scuttled when the resort was demolished after the State Park was created. Included among the miniature fleet are a hard-chine skiff, a metal hourglass stern rowboat, a kayak, and a wooden rowboat (Smith 2005). The sunken vessels tell us a more complete story of early tourism at Emerald Bay and of Lake Tahoe, in general.

In 2014, the dive team discovered a previously unidentified boat. Since we had limited bottom time, we quickly captured a few still images and video, but we plan to finish recording the vessel next season. After reviewing photographs of historic boat types common to Lake Tahoe, our new boat appears most similar to a launch boat called the *Shanghai* found about 10 miles north of Emerald Bay. This brings our Mini-fleet count to 10 submerged boats, although there are likely more yet to be discovered. When the bay was surveyed in 2004 using sonar, Panamerican Consultants, Inc. identified a total of 45 targets, and this boat represents one of those highlighted in the report as having a "distinctive boat outline" (Figure 4).

California State Parks is making future plans to return to the S.S. *Pomona*, Corsair, and Emerald Bay as well as other underwater sites to further research, conduct site assessments, and update site records for ongoing

FIGURE 4. NEW BOAT DISCOVERED AT EMERALD BAY (JAFFKE 2014).

stewardship and public outreach. In addition, we plan to keep developing the underwater archaeology at State Parks to continue the legacy from John Foster and others. We are currently discussing with other government agencies, universities, and non- profit organizations to collaborate on underwater projects. Specifically, we are creating a Memorandum of Understanding (MOU) with NOAA to collaborate on a maritime landscape study of California that includes NOAA's National Marine Sanctuaries and State Park-managed coastline (Tricia Dodds, personal communication 2015). In closing, California's Underwater Parks preserve the offshore environment, its reef and cultural history. "Our mission in California's state parks is to preserve and interpret history. That mission does not stop at the water's edge, it extends offshore as well." (Ken Kramer).

References

BEEKER, CHARLES
2005   S.S. Pomona Shipwreck Project, Fort Ross State Historic Park, California. Report prepared for California State Parks, Sacramento.

BEEKER, CHARLES AND SHELI SMITH
2005   Crystal Cove F-4U Corsair Airplane Wreck, Scuba Maintenance and Survey Dive, Summer 2005, Close of Field Work Interim Report. Report prepared by Indiana University Underwater Science Program and submitted to California State Parks, Sacramento.

BEEKER, CHARLES AND JOHN FOSTER
2007   Site Plan, S.S. Pomona Shipwreck Project, Fort Ross State Historic Park, California. Prepared by Indiana University Underwater Science Program in cooperation with California State Parks.

BYRNES, ILSE M.
1978   National Register of Historic Places Inventory-Nomination Form for Crystal Cove Historic District.

CALIFORNIA DEPARTMENT OF PARKS AND RECREATION
2002   News Release, June 24, 2002. Electronic document, http://ohp.parks.ca.gov/pages/712/files/062402.pdf, accessed June 25, 2014.

2005   Navy Corsair Fighter at Crystal Cove. Electronic document, http://www.parks.ca.gov/?page_id=23871, accessed June 29, 2014.

(CHRIS) CALIFORNIA HISTORICAL RESOURCES INFORMATION SYSTEM
2013   Maintenance and Operations Action Plan for Phases One and Two of the Modernization and Sustainability Plan. Prepared for California State Parks, Office of Historic Preservation.

CARLSON, EARL V., FRED MEYER, NORMAN L. WILSON
1975   Fort Ross State Historic Park Resource Management Plan and General Development Plan. Prepared by California Department of Parks and Recreation. Sacramento.

COLLIER, KENNETH
1979   Underwater Parks Master Plan. Prepared for California Department of Parks and Recreation. Sacramento.

1984   Underwater Parks Master Plan. Prepared for California Department of Parks and Recreation. Sacramento.

FOSTER, JOHN
2001   Watching Cows and Fighting Devil-Fish: An Overview of History and Archaeology at the Site of the S.S. Pomona, Fort Ross State Historic Park. Paper presented to California Council for the Promotion of History Conference, Long Beach, California.

2002   Archaeology and History Beneath the Sea: The Preservation, Management, and Interpretation of California's Heritage Resources. Report prepared for California Department of Parks and Recreation, Sacramento. Paper presented at California and the World Ocean Conference, Santa Barbara. Electronic document, http://www.parks.ca.gov/?page_id=23514, accessed June 25, 2014.

JONES, TERRY L. AND KATHRYN A. KLAR, EDITORS
2007   California Prehistory: Colonization, Culture, and Complexity. Alta Mira Press, Plymouth, United Kingdom.

LINDSTROM, SUSAN
1990   Submerged Tree Stumps as Indicators of Mid-Holocene Aridity in the Lake Tahoe Basin. Journal of California and Great Basin Anthropology 12(2):146-157.

SCOTT, EDWARD B.
1957   The Saga of Lake Tahoe: A Complete Documentation of Lake Tahoe's Development Over the Last One Hundred Years, Volume 1. Sierra-Tahoe Publishing Company, Tahoe.

SMITH, SHELI O.
1991   Emerald Bay Barges. Report prepared by Los Angeles Maritime Museum and submitted to California State Parks, Sacramento.

2005   Emerald Bay Mini-Fleet DPR 523 Site Record. Prepared by PAST Foundation, Columbus, Ohio and submitted to California State Parks, Sacramento.

SMITH, SHELI O. AND LAUREL H. BREECE
2002   California State Marine Managed Areas: Cultural Resource Survey 2001/2002. Report submitted by Long Beach City College Maritime Archaeology Certificate Program.

TERRELL, BRUCE, EDITOR
2007 Fathoming Our Past: Historical Contexts of the National Marine Sanctuaries. Prepared by NOAA/National Marine Sanctuary Program, Silver Spring, Maryland.

· · · · · · · · · · · · · · · · ·

Tricia Dodds
California State Parks
 Ocotillo Wells District,
5172 Highway 78, #10,
Borrego Springs, CA 92004

Denise Jaffke
California State Parks
Sierra District
P.O. Box 266
Tahoma, CA 96142

A Job Market and Benchmarking Survey of Maritime Archaeology

Lynn B. Harris
Jennifer F. McKinnon

In 2014 the Advisory Council on Underwater Archaeology supported a job market and benchmarking survey to investigate the skills and qualifications maritime archaeology employees within the US desire of recent graduates. The survey polled a variety of employers including State and Federal agencies, private companies, non-profits, museums, and academia with a success rate of nearly 27 percent. The results of this survey are expected to improve teaching and learning experiences and address expectations of students, recent graduates and employers. The results are presented along with future directions for research.

Introduction and Methodology

One of the major challenges for teaching and learning in maritime archaeology are perceived and real deficiencies in professional qualifications of students. A disconnect between what skills and qualifications employers, academics and students feel newly graduated students should possess can create unrealistic expectations. There has been little opportunity as of yet for the field of maritime archaeology to discuss university education, employer needs and student expectations. As a result, members of the Advisory Council on Underwater Archaeology (ACUA) presented an idea to conduct a survey of the profession within the US during 2014. The survey aimed to collect information about the skills and professional qualifications that are desirable within the field of maritime archaeology. It was designed as a "benchmark" for enhancing teaching and learning outcomes for employers, students and academics. Benchmarking can be helpful in shedding light on current and ongoing issues affecting the discipline, providing a basis for improving academic teaching and learning, and addressing expectations of students and employers (The Nautical Archaeology Society 2009; Beck and Balme 2005). This survey proposed to identify and provide a common set of statements about the professional qualifications and skills expected of recent maritime archaeology graduates.

The survey targeted those organizations that specifically hire or have hired maritime or underwater archaeologists. A list of State and Federal agencies, private companies, non-profits, museums, and other organizations were compiled using an existing survey list which was modified (Catsambis 2012). A total of 108 employers who represent their organizations were targeted via email, and in some instances multiple employers from a single organization were sent the email so as to ensure a good response. The email included an introduction to the survey and a deadline for completion. It also requested that if the person was not involved in hiring, that they pass the survey along to those responsible for hires within their organization. If the hire was a team effort, the individuals were asked to collaborate with their colleagues. Finally, the email stated that the responses could and would be used in various forum and publications, but that no personally identifiable information would be collected or associated with the response and the results would only be presented in aggregate form.

The survey platform utilized was SurveyMonkey.com™ as this procedure is familiar to most and inexpensive. This allowed participants to easily access the survey and eliminated issues with completing paper questionnaires. The survey was open for a total of 18 days, from April 14 to May 1, with invitees receiving a reminder note on April 25. A total of 29 responses were received for a response rate of nearly 27 percent. Though the response rate may allow for certain trends to be inferred, it is important to note that sectors of the field may not have been adequately represented in the respondent pool, such as maritime archaeologists affiliated with academia and museums.

Results

The following is a description of the results in numerical order and a discussion of what the results may indicate with regard to the job market and benchmarking.

Q1. Please select the type of organization you most closely represent? (29 responses)
34.38% (10) reported as Private Sector Cultural Resource Management Companies, 17.24% (5) as Federal Agencies and 17.24 % (5) as State Agencies. No museums participated. 3.45 % (1) reported as a research institution and 3.45% (1) as a university.

Q2: Has your organization been actively involved in the hire of maritime archaeology employees? (29 responses)

79.31% (23) reported YES to hiring underwater archaeologists actively, while 20.69% (6) reported NO.

Q3: If yes, when is the last time you hired a recent graduate from an academic program focusing in whole or in part on maritime archaeology? (24 responses)

Most respondents reported hiring underwater archaeologists within the last 1-3 years (2010-2013).

Q4: If yes, how much field experience did the recent hire have? (22 responses)

36.36% (8) reported 5 years or more experience. 22.73 (5) reported 1-2 years of field experience, while 22.73% (5) reported 1 year or less field experience.

Q5: If yes, what is the highest degree or academic credential level held by the recent hire? (23 responses)

75.86% (22) reported that recent hires had an MA or MS degree, 10.34% had a BA or BS degree, 3.45% (1) had a Ph.D. and 3.45% (1) had a graduate diploma.

Q6: Please note the minimum academic credentials required for an entry level maritime archaeology position in your organization. (29 responses)

75.86% (22) required an MA, 10.34% (3) required a BA or BS, 6.90% (3) required a high school diploma, and 3.45% (1) required a graduate diploma. None accepted a graduate certificate or diploma as a minimum qualification.

Q7: Please rate the following in terms of importance in assessing a potential new hire. (29 responses)

75.86% (22) rated the candidate's ability to meet the advertised criteria as very important, 69.97 % (20) rated the interview as very important, 41.32% (12)

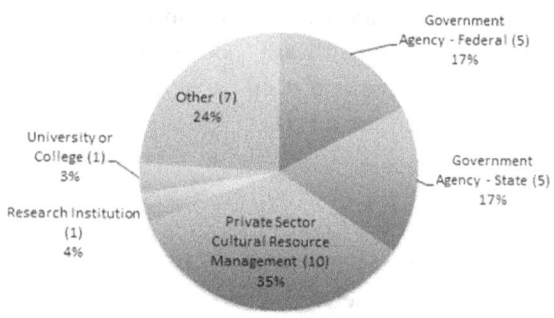

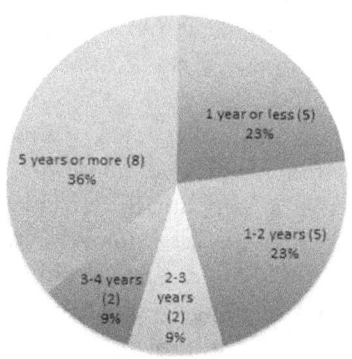

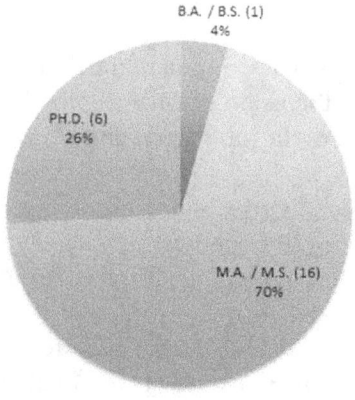

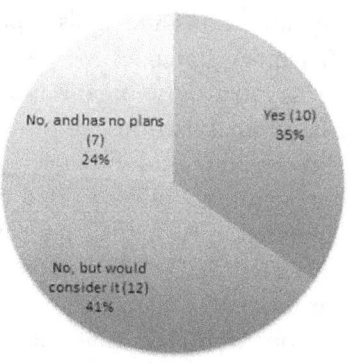

FIGURE 1. GRAPHICAL REPRESENTATIONS OF Q1, 4, 5 AND 9.

rated references as very important. 39.93% (11) rated feedback from colleagues as very important, 24.14 % (7) rated the job application (CV, Cover letter) as very important while 58% considered this important.

Q8: Has or would your organization be willing to hire a current student working toward a graduate degree whose requirements are not yet complete? (29 responses)

69.97% (20) reported YES and 31.3% (9) reported NO.

Q9: Does or would your organization participate in an academic internship program? (29 responses)

41.38% (12) reported that they did not participate, 34.48 % (10) reported that they did participate, 24.14% (7) did not participate and had no plans to do so in the future (Figure 1).

Q10: Please rate the following professional organization memberships in importance to your organization. (29 responses)

20.69% (6) of respondents reported the Register of Professional Archaeologists was very important while the same amount, 20.69% (6), found Society for Historical Archaeology very important and 31.03% (9) found it important. Interestingly, 51.72% (15) found Archaeological Institute of America as not relevant and 41.38% (12) found North American Society for Oceanic History as not relevant.

Q11: General Knowledge and Experience. Please rate in importance to your organization the skills and knowledge necessary for a new hire graduating from an academic program. (28 responses)

60.71% (17) of respondents reported historic preservation laws as very important, followed by understanding and application of scientific methods at 50.00% (14), maritime heritage ethics and policy issues at 46.43% (13), shipwreck sites at 46.43% (13), and submerged cultural resource management at 42.86% (12). Looking at the ranking of important the following both ranked at 50% (14): theory and development of underwater archaeology and project management. Interestingly, 17.86% (5) found dive supervision and logistics as not relevant.

Q12: Specific Knowledge and Experience. Please rate in importance to your organization the skills and knowledge necessary for a new hire graduating from an academic program. (28 responses)

Public speaking had the highest rank as very important at 42.86% (12). It was followed by historical/archival research at 35.51% (10), maritime history at 31.14% (9) and field record management at 28.57% (8). When looking at what ranked important, maritime history ranked 46.43% (13) and in situ conservation ranked 42.86% (12). Notably, the following were all ranked at or above 50% as not relevant: foreign language skills, ethnographic skills, museum studies and curating and display of artifacts (Figure 2).

Q13: Technical Skills. Please rate in importance to your organization the skills and knowledge necessary for a new hire graduating from an academic program. (28 responses)

An overwhelming response to report writing at 75% (21) was considered very important, followed by basic underwater archaeological survey at 60.71% (17) and geo-referencing and positioning at 42.86% (12). Respondents reported as important ship construction survey and reconstruction at 39.29% (11) and illustration at 35.71% (10). Underwater photography at 39.29% (11) and boat handling or training at 35.71% were found not important.

Q14: Software and Hardware Skills. Please rate in importance to your organization the skills and knowledge necessary for a new hire graduating from an academic program. (28 responses)

Remote sensing and GIS ranked very important as follows: side scan use and post-processing 53.57% (15), overall remote sensing data collection and post-processing 46.43% (13), magnetometer use and post-processing 46.43% (13) and geographic information systems 46.43% (13). Illustrative computer software capabilities rank important at 42.86% (12). Not relevant ranking was as follows: autonomous underwater vehicle use 42.86% (12), total station use 42.86% (12), three-dimensional modeling 35.71% (10), remotely operated vehicle use 32.14% (9) (Figure 3).

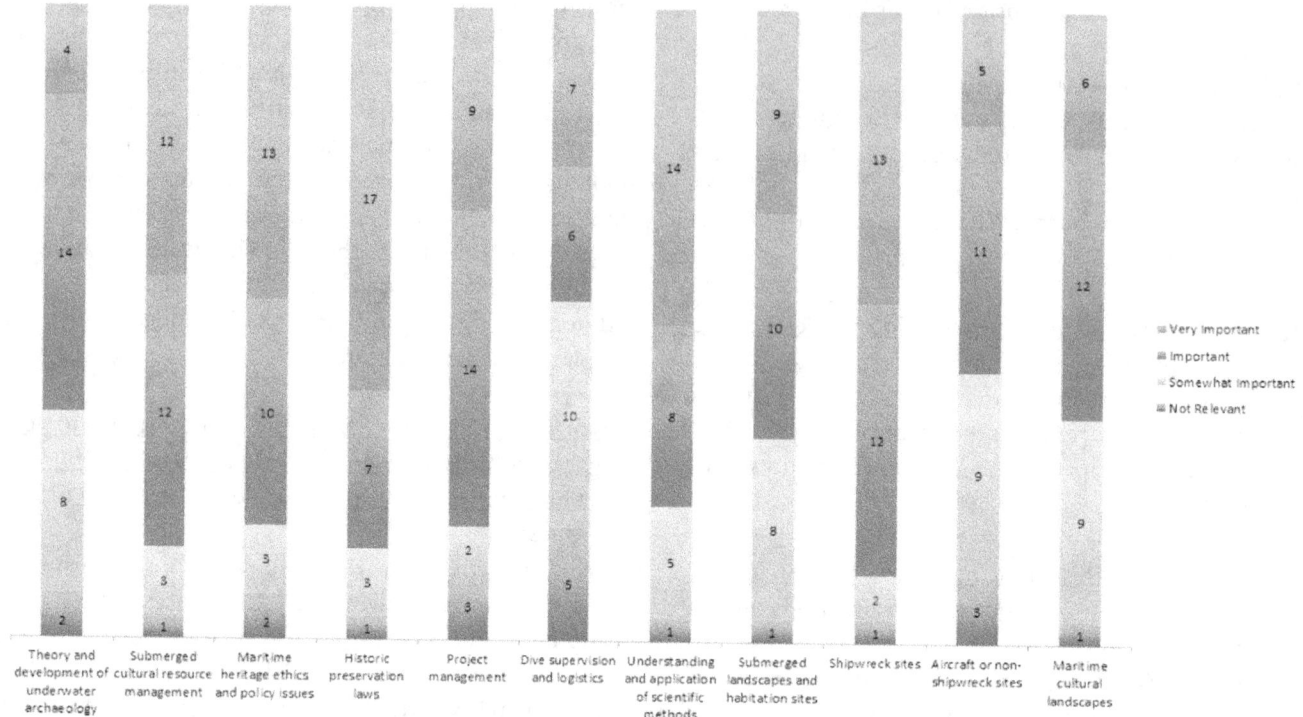

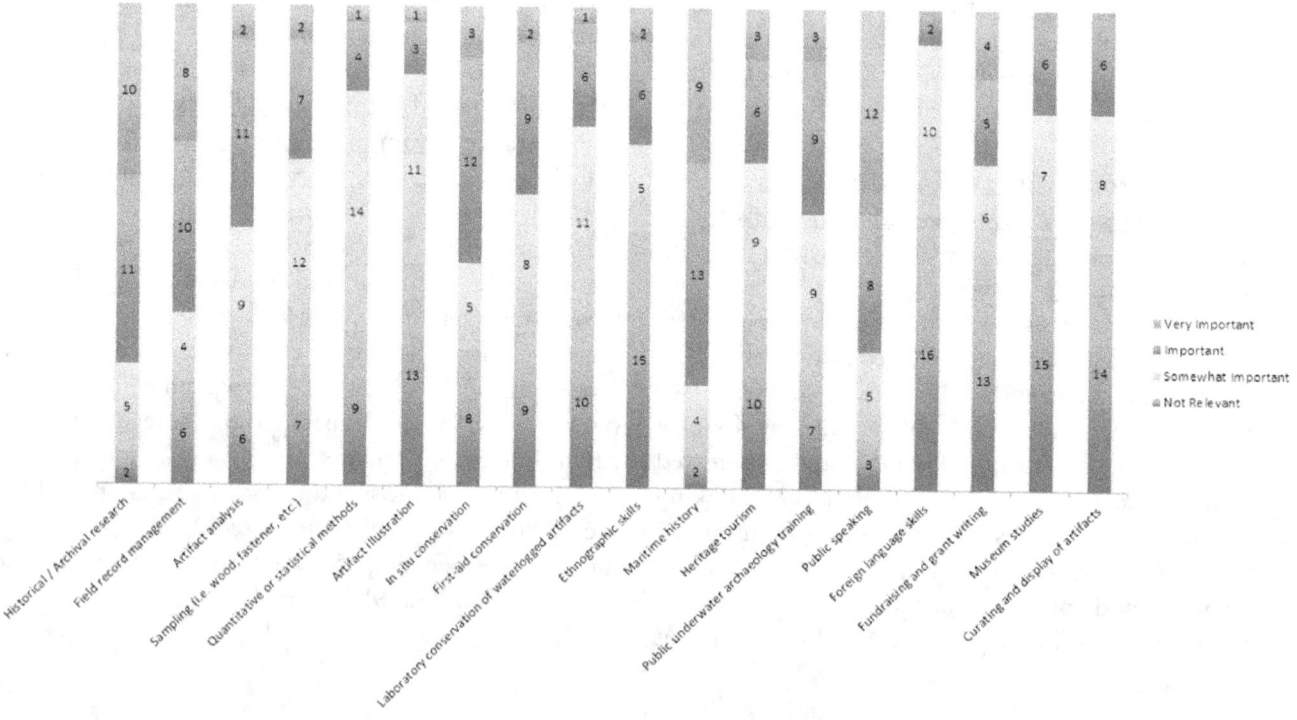

FIGURE 2. GRAPHICAL REPRESENTATIONS OF Q11 AND 12.

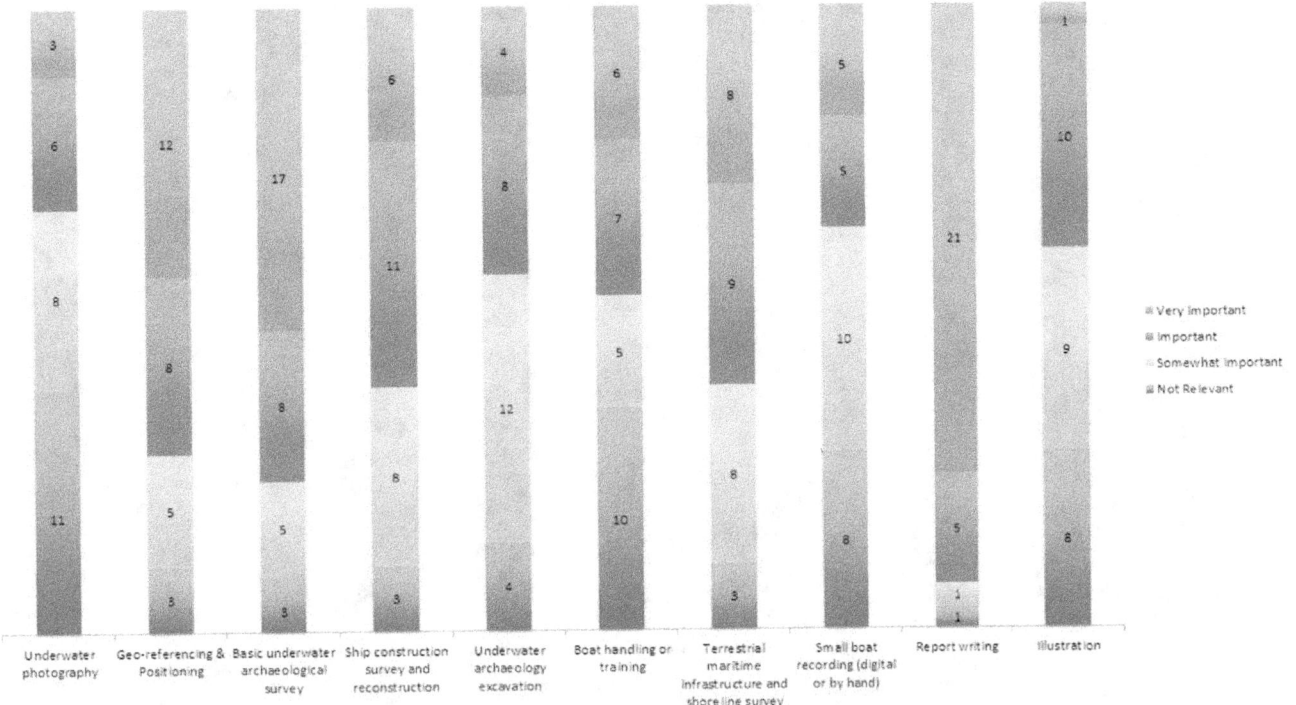

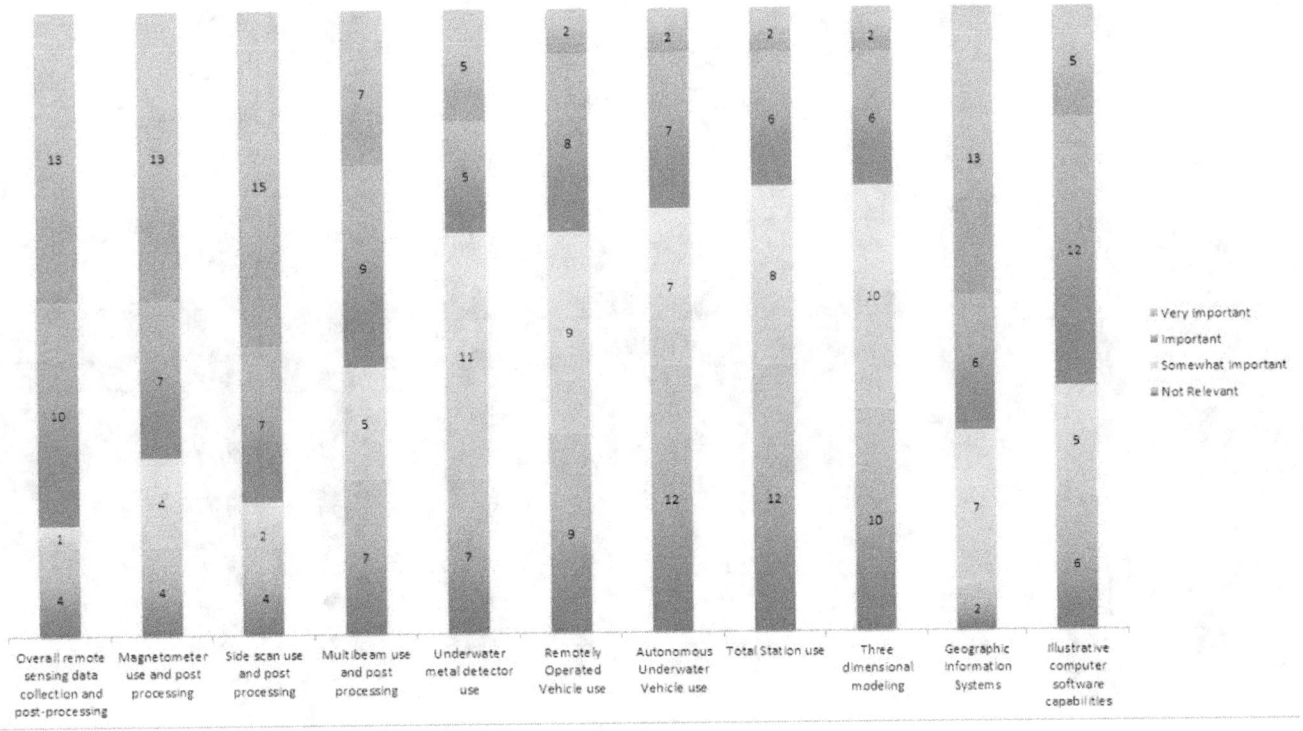

FIGURE 3. GRAPHICAL REPRESENTATIONS OF Q13 AND 14.

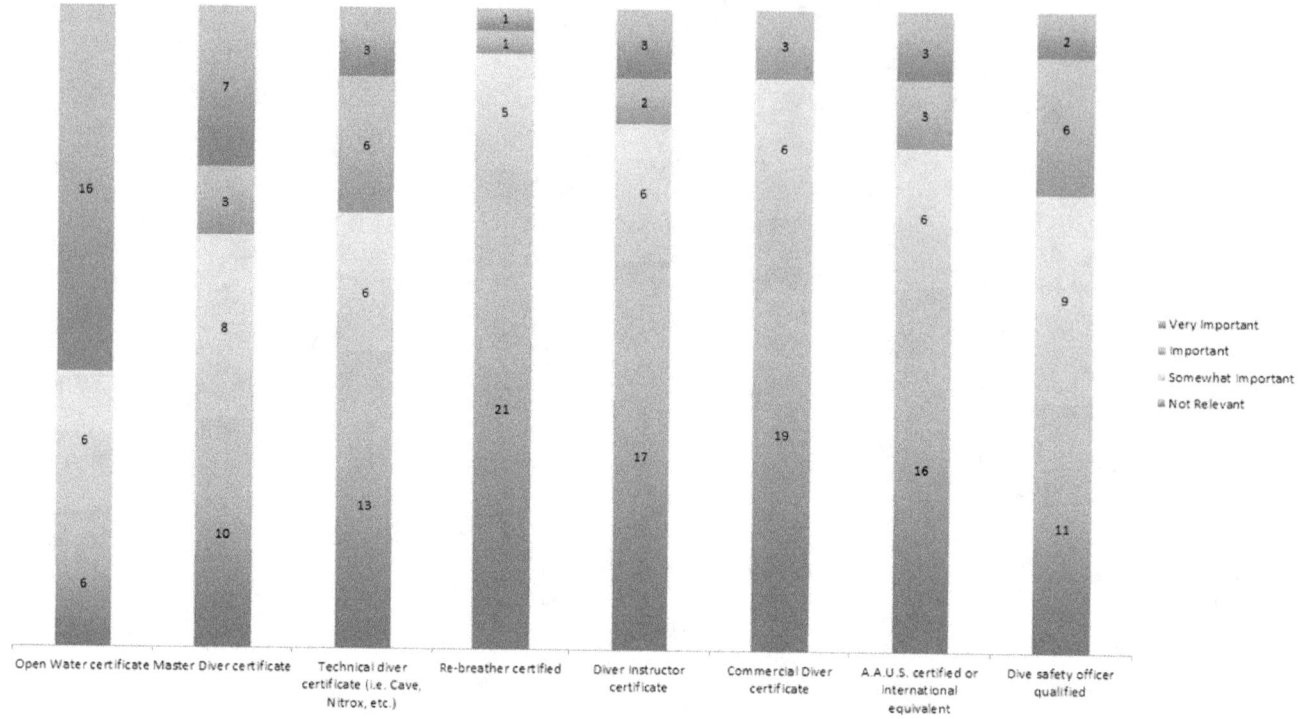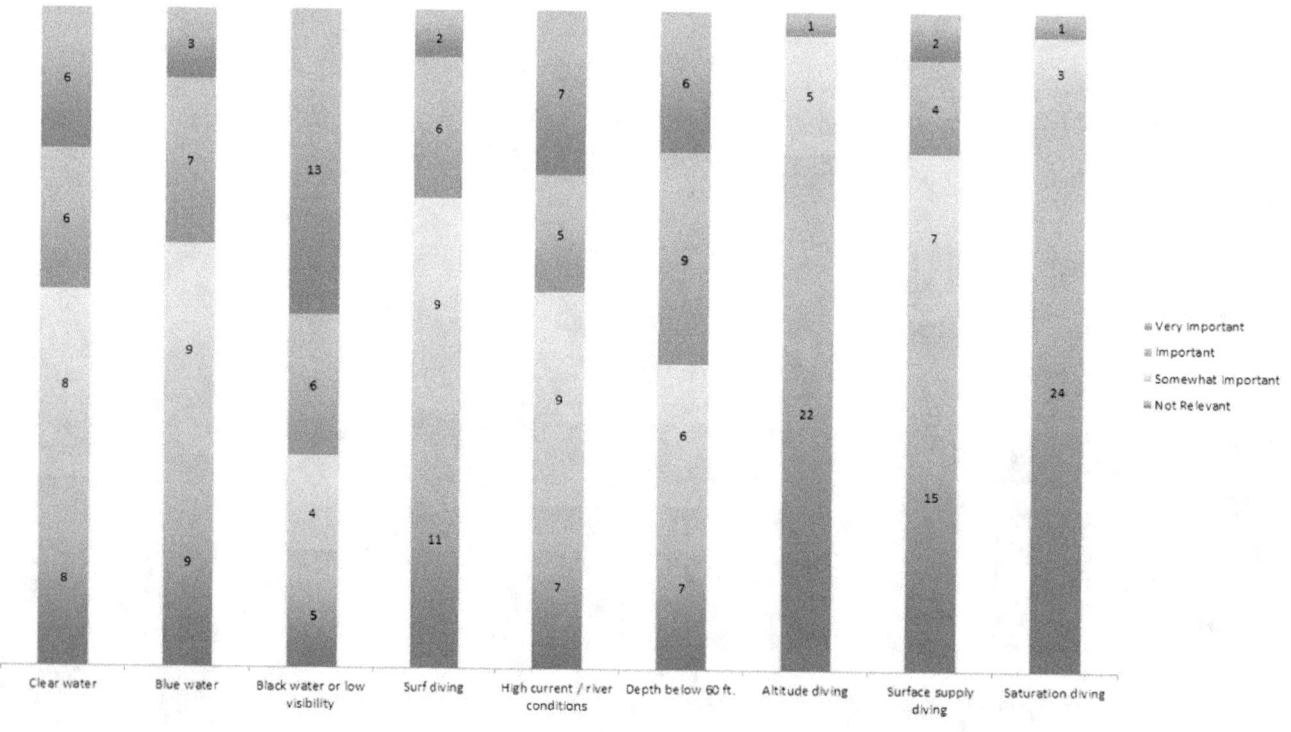

FIGURE 4. GRAPHICAL REPRESENTATIONS OF Q15 AND 16.

Q15: Diving Qualifications. Please rate in importance to your organization the credentials necessary for a new hire graduating from an academic program. (28 responses)

Open water certificate ranked as very important at 57.14% (16) and master diver certificate ranked at 25% (7). Interestingly, both re-breather certified at 75% (21) and commercial diver certificate at 67.86% (19) were ranked as not relevant.

Q16: Diving Experience. Please rate in importance to your organization the variety of diving experience necessary for a new hire graduating from an academic program. (28 responses)

Blackwater or low visibility ranked very important at 46.43% (13) followed by clear water at 21.43% (6) and depth below 60ft at 21.43% (6). In the not relevant rank saturation diving at 85.71% (24) and altitude diving at 78.57% (22) ranked high (Figure 4).

Q17 Publications Record. Please rate in importance to your organization the types of publications necessary for a new hire graduating from an academic program. (28 responses)

Technical report ranked highest in very important with 50% (14) of respondents and in important with 28.57% (8). In the not relevant category journal editor, book author and book editor all ranked the same at 53.57% (15) respondents.

Discussion

The results of the survey provide some insight into the expectations of employers in regard to the skills they desire in applicants. Respondents reported that the most frequent hiring criteria for an entry level position was an MA or MS degree plus the candidate's ability to meet the job criteria. Most (69.97%) were willing to hire the candidate of choice prior to completion of the degree. None had accepted a certificate or graduate diploma as a minimum requirement, but a small percentage offered employment for candidates with BA/BS degrees and high school diplomas. Field experience criteria was important for hiring with respondents favoring candidates with 5 years (36.36%) or more and 22.73 (5) reported requiring 1-2 years of field experience. A little over half of the respondents offered internships to students. Many that did not offer internships had no plans to do so in the future.

Unfortunately one sector of the industry was not represented – museums – while other respondents, such as research institutions and universities were underrepresented. The numerical breakdown of organizations targeted for the survey was as follows: Federal Agencies (18) with a response rate at 27.77%, State Agencies (16) with a response rate at 31.25%, Universities (16) with a response rate at 6.25%, Museums and research institutions (27) with a response rate at 3.70%, and Private Sector Cultural Resource Management Companies (22) with the highest response rate at 45.45%. Despite being invited to participate, no museums completed the survey. This deficiency likely skewed the results slightly, which was particularly noticeable in Q12 where ethnographic skills, museum studies and curating, and display of artifacts all ranked as not relevant by 50% or more of the respondents.

In regard to coursework and relevance to the job market, respondents reported historic preservation laws as very important, followed by understanding and application of scientific methods, maritime heritage ethics and policy issues, shipwreck sites, and submerged cultural resource management. Courses considered important were maritime history and in situ conservation. Not relevant were foreign language skills, ethnographic skills, museum studies and curating and display of artifacts.

Field technical skills considered most important were basic underwater archaeological survey processing and geo-referencing and positioning. Boat handling and training were unimportant. In regard to technology, the survey identified that skills operating highly technical pieces of equipment such as remote and autonomous vehicles are not as relevant as the basic toolkit of an underwater archaeologist – the side scan sonar and magnetometer. This is most likely the result of a large number of respondents who were affiliated with the cultural resource management field where the majority of jobs are available. Furthermore, the diving certifications required of new hires are also minimal, with open water or master diver certifications ranking high, and more technical diving certifications, such as commercial and re-breather ranked as not relevant.

A promising response in regard to maritime and underwater archaeology's engagement with the public was demonstrated in Q12, which ranked public speaking as the highest in specific knowledge and experience skills. This demonstrates that employers value potential employees who can engage with the public, though the same skill is vital when engaging with clients and often makes the difference between clients willingly or grudgingly protecting a resource.

Some unsurprising and somewhat expected responses were confirmed with technical report writing ranking high for publications, as well as report writing ranking high in the technical skills area most likely associated with cultural resource employment sector in maritime archaeology. In the not relevant category were journal editor, book author and book editor, all priorities for the underrepresented academic community of maritime archaeologists.

Finally, it appears that maritime archaeologists do not exclusively have the luxury of working in crystal clear or deep waters. Respondents noted that black water, low visibility and depths below 60 feet were ranked as highly relevant within the diving experience category.

Future Directions

There are several options for expanding the survey to address respondent bias and the global job market. Maritime archaeology scholars in museums and academia could be engaged for gathering more substantive empirical and qualitative data sets. Another consideration is a survey of the maritime archaeology student body to gauge perceptions and misperceptions as they begin to navigate the job market after graduation. This survey could address entry level employment versus higher level positions for senior maritime archaeologists. Finally, comparison between countries and regions might yield significant global variations in the needs of employers in skills sets and education.

Acknowledgments

This survey was prepared by an ACUA sub-committee comprising Lynn Harris, Jennifer McKinnon, Alexis Catsambis, Amy Mitchell-Cook and Kimberly Faulk. We thank all the respondents who took the time to complete the survey.

References

Catsambis, Alexis
    2012   Preserving the Submerged and Coastal Maritime Heritage of the United States. Doctoral dissertation, Department of Anthropology, Texas A&M University, College Station, TX.

Beck, Wendy and Jane Balme
    2005   Benchmarking for archaeology honours degree in Australian universities. Australian Archaeology 61:32—40.

The Society for Nautical Archaeology
    2009   Benchmarking Competence Requirements and Training Opportunities related to Maritime Archaeology. Report to English Heritage, London, from The Society for Nautical Archaeology, Portsmouth, UK

....

Lynn B. Harris
Program in Maritime Studies
East Carolina University
Admiral Eller House
Greenville, NC 27858-4353

Jennifer F. McKinnon
Program in Maritime Studies
East Carolina University
Admiral Eller House
Greenville, NC 27858-4353

www.ingramcontent.com/pod-product-compliance
Lightning Source LLC
Chambersburg PA
CBHW081450070526
44586CB00019B/2286